PUBLICATIONS OF THE
MODERN HUMANITIES RESEARCH ASSOCIATION
VOLUME 19

SPRING SHOOTS: YOUNG BELARUSIAN POETS IN THE EARLY TWENTY-FIRST CENTURY

ARNOLD MCMILLIN

SPRING SHOOTS: YOUNG BELARUSIAN POETS IN THE EARLY TWENTY-FIRST CENTURY

by
ARNOLD MCMILLIN

Modern Humanities Research Association

2015

Published by

The Modern Humanities Research Association
Salisbury House
Station Road
Cambridge CB1 2LA
United Kingdom

© The Modern Humanities Research Association, 2015

First published 2015

ISBN 978-1-78188-227-6
ISSN 0581-0280

CONTENTS

PREFACE

When my previous book, *Writing in a Cold Climate* (2010), was about half-written, the greatest of Belarusian prose writers, Vasiĺ Bykaŭ died (2003), and when the present attempt to describe and discuss contemporary poetry was also half-written, the leading Belarusian poet Ryhor Baradulin also died (2014). Though both had lived long and fulfilled lives, they leave a great gap in the beleaguered literature to which they contributed so much. They have, of course, successors among their younger contemporaries, but the youngest generation of poets discussed in the present monograph represent, in a sense, the future of Belarusian poetry. In many cases it is a very promising future.

The original idea of writing only about poets' first books was not merely quixotic, as has been suggested to me by sympathetic Belarusian critics, but also impractical in several ways, and the temptation of commenting on prose too has been great. One of the attractions of writing about this group of poets, however, has been that the majority of them have at the present time received little attention in Belarusian critical literature.

As with all my previous attempts to assess the writing of this country, a hindrance has been not only plain ignorance, but also the inadequacy of Belarusian dictionaries, and, even worse, the difficulty of obtaining primary texts. I have, however, been greatly helped and encouraged by the number of young poets (too many to mention individually) who have generously presented me with their books; I also owe a great debt of gratitude to all those who have given me support and practical help. They include Valia Aksak, Uladzimier Arloŭ, Aksana Biaźliepkina, Uilleam Blacker, Alla Bradzichina, Viera Burlak, Ben Chatterley, Jan Čykvin, Jim Dingley, David Gillespie, Ihar Ivanoŭ, Wojciech Janik, Voĺha Kaliackaja, Siarhiej Kavalioŭ, Hanna Kiślicyna, Sierž Minskievič, the late Alexander Nadson, Uladzimir Niakliajeŭ, Inna Panova, Aleś Paškievič, Iryna Šaŭliakova, Aleksandryna Zubiec, Viktar Žybuĺ and, as always, my loyally supportive wife Svetlana.

INTRODUCTION

The aim of this monograph is to introduce two score of the youngest generation of Belarusian poets, mostly represented by their debut collections. The latter appeared at or near the beginning of the twenty-first century, and their authors began writing during the present regime. All were born in or after 1980, an arbitrary but convenient date, albeit not without inconsistencies. For instance, a few of the poets considered at the end of my last book (under the heading 'Four Poets of the Future') were also born in this period: Valžyna Mort (b. 1981), Volha Hapiejeva (b. 1982), Vika Trenas (b. 1984) and Valieryja Kustava (1984).[1]

The book is divided, hardly less arbitrarily, into eight thematically titled chapters, the aim being to bring a modicum of order into the presentation of a large number of diverse and highly individual poets. Assignment to a particular group implies that the poet's themes and concerns are at the very least represented there. Within each group will be between three and seven discrete sections, almost all devoted to a single writer. For the majority, the subject of their group is only a part of their thematic range; indeed there are very few monothematic poets here. The groups are introduced by a few words relating to general aspects of the particular theme or topic. These poets are all, to a greater or lesser extent, finding their poetic voices at the start of their careers; some are more sophisticated, others still at an early stage. Together they afford great hope for the future of Belarusian literature.

It must be said, however, that these young writers have not, for the most part, received a particularly warm welcome in their native country: Žmicier Višnioŭ (b. 1973), a very active poet of the previous, Bum-Bam-Lit, generation has written fairly scathingly about his successors,[2] despite doing sterling work in bringing a considerable number of them to the light of day in his publishing house, Halijafy; an older writer, Aliaksandr Lukašuk (b. 1955) in 2014, during an interview for Radio Liberty, compared young Belarusian poets to cats and dogs who understood everything but could express nothing; finally, at a conference in the same year, the present writer, at the end of a paper about politics and criticism in the work of these poets, was asked by a questioner, himself obsessed by originality, why their expression of discontent was not more original, like that of an earlier poet Slavamir Adamovič (b. 1962) who in 1997

---

[1] Arnold McMillin, *Writing in a Cold Climate: Belarusian Literature from the 1970s to the Present Day* (London: Maney Publishing for the Modern Humanities Research Association, 2010) (hereafter McMillin, *Writing*).

[2] Žmicier Višnioŭ, 'Halasy hubliajucca ŭ šorhacie liesu', *Maladość*, 2014, 2, pp. 25–26.

famously sewed up his lips as a sign of protest; a form of demonstration unknown in Belarus before or since.

In some cases the decision to write only about poetry has been limiting, but the idea that these young poets could say nothing interesting is far from the truth; moreover the view that originality and talent are intrinsically connected is decidedly limited; one only has to think of Mozart, whose genius made questions of originality redundant. Nearly half the poets here, consciously or not, follow e.e. cummings in his pioneering rejection of the rules of capitalization and punctuation, but their conventionality or otherwise does not appear to have any bearing on the themes or, indeed, quality of their poems.

Another way in which these poets may be divided is by place of birth: about half of them were born and brought up in Miensk, and the others in various provinces of Belarus or, in two cases, outside the country itself. Particularly worthy of mention is the Homiel-based school of young writers led by the distinguished poet Nina Škliarava (b. 1947) who had valiantly championed the status of the ever-threatened Belarusian language in the 1960s. About half of the 'provincial' poets here are from Homiel and its surrounding region.[3] As almost all the poets were born within a dozen years of each other, the brief list of biographical data that follows gives, where known, their dates and place of birth, studies, any prizes and, if appropriate, place of work as well as the titles and dates of their first publications.

Naturally, *Spring Shoots* is a book without an end, in the sense that all its subjects are still very much alive and in many cases promising fruitful development. It is to be hoped that it may introduce to new readers some exciting young talents, and give an overall picture of the present enthusiasm for poetic expression in Belarus. To these poets belongs the future.

---

[3] A useful recent anthology is: Anatoĺ Baroŭski (ed.), *Palac. Litaraturny aĺmanach. Homiel.2013* (Minsk: Knihazbor, 2014). Almost simultaneously appeared a comparable anthology of writing from Harodnia: Ju. Holub (ed.), *Novy zamak. Litaraturny aĺmanach. Hrodna, 1 MMXIII* (Minsk: Knihazbor, 2013).

BIOGRAPHICAL DATA

Anochin, Kiryla. Born in Miensk in 1987. Graduated in history at the Belarusian State University (hereafter BDU). A prize winner in the Festival of One Poem (2011). First publication, *Aściarožna, drevy začyniajucca* (2013).

Aŭčyńnikava, Hanna. Born in Harodnia in 1986. Studied at Harodnia State University, going on in 2010 to postgraduate work in historical and comparative philology. She was already teaching in the university at the time of her first publication, *Ad začynienaj bramy* (2011).

Baradzina, Maryja. Born in Miensk in 1981. First publication, *Vyšej za paŭnočny viecier* (2006).

Baranoŭski, Aleś. Born in the village of Cierucha, Homiel region in 1989. Studied at Homiel State University 2006–11, and from 2012 began work at the Academy of Sciences in Miensk. First publications: *Čujnaje акно* (2008), *Viaśliar* (2010), and *Dyjamientavy nimb dlia aniola* (2012).

Bryĺ, Anton. Born in Miensk in 1982. Defended a doctorate at the University of Trento, Italy in 2008. Currently lives and works in London. First verse publication: *Nie ŭpaŭ žolud* (2011).

Čajkoŭskaja, Volia. Born in Viciebsk in 1987. First publication: *Lupy* (2007).

Čumakova, Hanna. Born in Rahačoŭ, Homiel region in 1984. In 2006 began teaching Belarusian language and literature at Homiel State University, but now lives and works in Miensk. First publication: *Moj aniol pryśniŭ mianie* (2012).

Filon, Nadzieja. Born in Homiel in 1988. First publication: *Kropli śviatla* (2012).

Hluchoŭskaja, Kaciaryna. Born in Miensk in 1995. Studied philology at BDU. First publication: *Kali drevy rastuć z halavy* (2013).

Ivaščanka, Anatoĺ. Born in Miensk in 1981. Studied at BDU and then the Academy of Sciences where he wrote a thesis on Aleś Razanaŭ. From 2003 worked for the Union of Belarusian Writers, and in 2006–12 taught Belarusian at the National Technical University, later working for the independent journal *Dziejasloŭ*. A finalist in the PEN Centre's competition in memory of Natallia Arsieńnieva in 2003, and a finalist in the 'Zalataja lira' contest in 2005. First publications: *Vieršnick* (2006) and *Chaj tak* (2013).

Jemialianaŭ-Šylovič, Aleś. Born in Kryčaŭ, Mahilioŭ region in 1987; now lives in Miensk. Studied biology at BDU. A finalist in several competitions. First publication: *Parasoniečnaść* (2013).

Kaciurhina, Anastasija. Born in Homiel in 1992. First publications: *Pad vietraziem ranku* (2011) and *Parason* (2011).

Koŭhan, Siarhiej. Born in Russia in 1984. Lives in Miensk. First publication: *Pieršyja kroki* (2002).

Kucharevič, Śviatlana. Lives in Miensk. First publication: *Ščyra* (2009).

Kudasava, Nasta. Born in Rahačoŭ, Homiel region in 1984. Studied philology at BDU. First publications: *Liście maich ruk* (2006) and *Ryby* (2013).

Kulikoŭ, Ihar. Born in 1988. Winner of the Belarusian Pen Club prize in 2009 and the 'Debut' Maksim Bahdanovič prize in 2011. First publications: *Pavarot da mora* (2011) and *Svamova* (2013).

Kuźmienka, Žmitrok. Born Miensk in 1980. First publication: *Pakuĺ žyvu, spadziajusia …* (2012).

Lienski, Juraś. Lives in Miensk. First publication: verses in *Jana-Try-Jon* (2010).

Makarevič, Kaciaryna. Born in Miensk in 1988. A finalist in the Larysa Hienijuš competition of the Belarusian PEN centre in 2010. First publication: *Soĺ i niespakoj* (2012).

Malachoŭski, Rahnied. Born in Magadan region, Siberia in 1984. Has lived in Miensk since 1987. First publications: *Bieražnica* (2005) and *U dzionnaj mituśni* (2012).

Mancevič, Nasta. Born in Viliejka, Miensk region in 1983. First publication: *Ptuški* (2012).

Martysievič, Maryja. Born in Miensk in 1982. First publications: *Cmoki liatuć na nierast* (2008) and *Ambasada* (2011).

Niatbaj, Taćciana. Born in Polacak in 1982, and now lives and works in Warsaw teaching at the Marie Curie University. First publication: 'Žyćcio praciahvajecca', *Termapily*, 16 (2012).

Nilava, Taćciana. Born in Homiel in 1984. Winner of the Kiryl of Turaŭ literary prize. First publication: *Hotyka tonkich padmanaŭ* (2008).

Novik, Hanna. Born in Homiel in 1990. First publication: *Sumioty ahniu* (2010).

Novik, Julija. Born in Salihorsk in 1985. Studied inter-cultural communication at Miensk State Technical University. First publication: *Sonca za terykonami* (2007).

Pačkoŭskaja, Vijalieta. Born in Miensk in 1985. First publication: *Arechapadzieńnie* (2012).

Papoŭ, Aleś. Lives in Miensk. First publication: *Nia ščyra* (2009).

Plian, Žmicier (real name Ladzies). Born in Miensk in 1984. First publication: *Taksydermičny praktykum* (2004).

Prylucki, Siarhiej. Born in Biareście in 1980. Finalist in several competitions. First publication: *Dzievianostyja forever* (2008).

Rahavaja, Voĺha. Born in Miensk in 1982. Studied music, which she now teaches at the Achremčyk College of Art. First publication: verses in *Jana-Try-Jon* (2010).

Ryžkoŭ, Vitaĺ. Born in Mahilioŭ in 1986 and now lives in Miensk. First publication: *Dźviery zamknionyja na kliučy* (2010).

Siamaška, Viktar. Born in Miensk in 1980. First publications: *Maryja S.* (2006), *ReRa* (2011) and *Habitacyja* (2013).

Sidorka, Naścia. Born in Biareście in 1997, but now lives in Žabinka, a town in the same region. First publication: *Pialiostki* (2013).

Siviec, Taćciana. Born in Miensk in 1982. Studied at the Maksim Tank Pedagogical Institute. First publication: *Lipieńskaja navaĺnica* (2003).

Ścieburaka, Usievalad. Born in Žlobin in 1981. Studied at Vialiejka and Miensk. Winner of the 'Zalaty apostraf' prize in 2004. Teaches Belarusian history and politics at the State Technical University. First publications: *Krušnia* (2007) and *Bieh pa samaadčuvańni* (2013).

Šostak, Adam. Born in Baranavičy in 1982. Studied at the local music school and then took courses in art and music at the University of Culture in Miensk. In 2006–10 he was employed in various galleries, but now mainly works with computers. First publications: *Spatkańnie. Nie* (2006) and *4.33* (2012).

Upala, Anka. Born in Mahilioŭ in 1981. Winner of several prizes for prose. First publication: *Dreva Entalipt* (2012).

Vieliet, Ciemryk. Born in Miensk in 1988. First publication: *Most* (2007).

Yvanoŭ, Viktar (real name Lupasin). Born in Miensk in 1982. Studied mechanics and later philology at BDU. First publication: *Asarci* (2009).

CHAPTER 1

~

The Historical Heritage

History is an important element in Belarusian culture, and many young poets touch on historical themes, ranging from the Garden of Eden and the mythology of classical times, through imaginary and real occurrences from the period of the Grand Duchy of Lithuania (to which Belarus is one of the main successor states), to significant events and personages of the 18th and the 19th centuries, and even to the most recent history of the 1990s. A few poets also write about the Second World War, a favourite topic in Soviet Belarusian literature, despite the fact that they were all born long after those events; Stalin, virtually unmentionable in Soviet poetry, also finds a place. Some of these themes are treated by the three poets in this section, others elsewhere. The potent image of *mankurtstva*, the phenomenon by which people are taken into captivity and deprived of their memory, central to questions of the Belarusian past, is invoked more than once. Memory, like history, is a vital component of national consciousness.

Bryĺ

Anton Bryĺ, grandson of the distinguished prose writer, Janka Bryĺ (1917–2006), has earned a high reputation both as an original poet and also as talented translator from English-language literature including Yeats, Tolkien, Susanna Clarke, Irish folk tales and Old English poetry; in 2013 he published a splendid Belarusian translation of *Beowulf*. A particular inspiration has been Catullus, whose work is very relevant to Bryĺ's first book, *Nie ŭpaŭ žolud* (There fell no acorn, 2011), published in an edition of only 200 copies.

The work of Bryĺ is unlike that of any other of the young generation of poets discussed in this book. He evinces a keen interest in rhyme and versification, and has a strong feeling for the past, seeing both classical times and the Grand Duchy of Lithuania (referred to as Litva in the poems) as his heritage. The latter is expressed through the inclusion of semi-mythical historical figures and a powerful sense of closeness to the earth. *Nie upal žolud* is rich in fantasy and imagination, with many legends and fantastic monsters; his strong feeling for nature is most evident when he describes forests and marshes that are, for the most part, far from benevolent. Several poems are set in shadowy evenings and night time, and there is an unmistakeable religious element evident at the end of his longer poems, which unfortunately cannot be quoted satisfactorily, even in part.

Bryĺ's lines, ranging in length from tetrameters to those of sixteen and seventeen syllables, employ a variety of rhyme schemes. Most of the words he uses are plain enough, but the overall sense of some poems may be elusive, and. clearly realizing this problem, the poet supplies explanations in extensive Commentaries.[1] As a whole the book is intended to mirror the construction of the sole surviving book by Catullus, and it is introduced by a poem to the latter's friend, Helvius Cinna: 'Pryśviačeńnie Hieĺviju Cynie' (A dedication to Helvius Cinna, 2008), written in 11-syllable lines, expresses his wish to send to Cinna, on a boat down the river Nioman, his enquiries about the mysteries of life inscribed on oak bark. The book proper starts with a poem that is formally a stylization of an English ballad, but, as Bryĺ tells us, always a blues.[2] The title, 'Koramni-dell' (2004) has no obvious meaning, and serves as a refrain, albeit with only one 'l'. The otherwise simple words reflect a gloomy obsession that he will never see Koramni-del. Also a kind of ballad with musical repetition, 'Braciec son i siastra śmierć' (Brother dream and sister death, 2010) shows the eponymous siblings emerging at night-time to fulfil their roles:

Брацец сон і сястра смерць

Згасла неба, ўзышоў маладзік і сусвет у ценях заціх,
І брацец сон і сястрыца смерць ідуць ад жытлаў сваіх,
І брацец сон шукае таго, каму спакою няма,
А сястрыца смерць шукае таго, каго абярэ сама,
І брацец сон суцяшае таго, хто з пачаткам працы сядзеў,
А сястрыца смерць суцішае таго, каму заставаўся дзень,
І брацец сон юнаку пяе і згадкі вядзе ўваччу,
А сястрыца смерць замыкае ключом вусны яго дзяўчу,
І брацец сон аблятае свет паводле волі сваёй,
А сястрыца смерць абнаўляе свет паводле волі сваёй,
Але неба святлее, радзее цень і дзесьці певень пяе,
І брацец сон і сястрыца смерць ідуць у жытлы свае. (Nuž, 6)[3]

---

[1] The commentaries begin with the title itself, which is said to derive from an English folksong.
In his desire to explain, Bryĺ resembles another fairly young, but very different writer, Alhierd Bacharevič (b. 1975) whose explanations of contemporary Germany have nothing to do with antiquity.
[2] This view, not repeated in the book, was given in 2004 by Bryĺ in the online Live Journal.
[3] 'The sky darkened, the new moon rose and the world fell silent in shadows, / and brother dream and sister death left their homes, / And brother dream looks for someone who has no peace, / But sister death looks for someone she will choose herself, / And brother dream consoles someone who was sitting at the beginning of his work, / But sister death will calm someone who has only one day left. / And brother dream sings to a youth and brings

'Prostaje vosieńskaje rando' (A simple autumn rondo, 2007) also treats mortality, with the simple message that life and death should be accepted alike. 'Ziamlia' (Earth, 2011) is an unusual love poem in which the poet's embracing an oak tree is compared to embracing his beloved; the tone is conversational, but the feeling seems serious. 'Važaniatki' (Hedgehogs, 2005) is folksy in tone, as the eponymous animals look for food from the snakes, frogs and so on which are hiding to avoid being fried and eaten. Comparable in tone is 'Vidymin' (2011), which combines history with folk elements, and 'Balotny ahieńčyk' (The little fire of the marshes, 2006), which vividly describes wandering in the forest at night and finding amidst the undergrowth a mythical figure (*malieńki pačvarčyk*) that leads the poet astray before succumbing to remorse.

'Kastryčnik' (October, 2008) is the first of Bryĺ's historical poems that require some explanation. It features two 'grey-haired' (*sivy*) Radzivils leaning over a table, clearly referring to 'Mikalaj the Red' and 'Mikalaj the Black' but, as Bryĺ acknowledges, the latter only lived to the age of fifty and was therefore unlikely to be grey (Nŭž, 41). The word *sivy* is used widely in this poem, but hardly by accident. Incidentally, 'Mikalaj the Red' also figures in 'Cieni' (Shadows, 2010), a quasi-historical poem in which the leader rides towards Ašmiany, only to discover that there has been a fierce battle to take the town. Most of Bryĺ's historical poems are too long to quote, but 'Kastryčnik' serves as a not untypical example:

Кастрыьнік

Па нябёсах ветах сівы брыдзе,
Ды яшчэ адзін — па ільдзяной вадзе,
А вятрыска лісце з галін ірве
Па сівых лясох на сівой Літве.

А ў вакне ў палацы, у сівым святле —
Разгарнутая кніга на старым стале,
І над ёю схілёны дзве галавы —
Радзівіл Сівы ды Радзівіл Сівы.[4]

Bryĺ has a strong interest in versification, as is evinced in 'Vihintuna' (2012) in which he attempts to create a new form with three stanzas of seven lines each and a rhyme scheme aBaBcBc. The latter point, although clear from the text itself, is spelt out in the author's Commentary. There is also a loose reference to

reminiscence to his eyes, / But sister death locks the lips of his girlfriend, / And brother dream flies around the world at random, / But the sky is growing brighter, the shadows thinning and somewhere a cock is crowing, / And brother dream and sister death return to their homes' Numerical references preceded by Nŭž are to *Nie ŭraj žolud*.

[4] 'October // Through the skies wanders a grey waning moon, / And there is another across the frozen water, / And a lively wind tears the leaves from their branches/ In the grey forests in grey Lietuva. // and in a window of the palace, in grey light / A book is opened on an old table, / /and over it are bent two heads — / Radzivil the Grey and Radzivil the Grey' (Nŭž, 10).

'Wieczór sobotni' (Saturday evening, 1832), a poem collected by the nineteenth-century Polish lexicographer and folklorist Jan Karłowicz.[5] Bryĺ's verse is set at night time when the poet's disquiet is calmed by imagining someone weaving his (considerable) hair as a thread. As in much of Bryĺ's work there is a convincing feeling of country life and its sounds. In 'Navaĺnica' (Thunderstorm, 2004), for instance, the poet's national heritage in old Litva (now better known as Lietuva) is specific, namely the Nalibocki forest and the walls of Harodnia, albeit quite without romanticism, as may be seen from the last line of the second stanza and the concluding line: Я народжаны гэтаю чорнаю злою зямлёю [...] Мае ногі пускаюць карэнне ў няплодную глебу'[6]

Gothic elements abound in Bryĺ's poems, such as 'Stupieni' (Steps, 2003), 'Raka' (The river, 2007), 'Identité' (Identity, 2008), for example. Several of the poems containing dialogues between father and child look back to Goethe's ballad 'Der Erlkönig', made famous by Schubert's song of the same name. In another poem of dialogue, 'Hinvil' (2011), a stranger approaches a homestead that is not locked; a boy tells his father, and the latter plans to repel him (Nuž. 15). 'Śnieżań' (December, 2010) resembles Goethe's poem even more closely, as a father is insensitive and unresponsive to the appeals of his son only repeating, 'А мне і справы няма' (It has nothing to do with me, Nuž, 17). 'Survila' (2010) concerns a fifteenth-century noble about whom little is known so that the poet has free rein: the eponymous hero rides magnificently, repeating as a refrain: 'А ты ж мая дзетачка, засні, засні / Ох, дзетачка, дзетачка, хутчэй засні';[7] in the last stanza, however, the rein goes limp in his translucent hand. Also quasi-Gothic are 'Vierasień' (September, 2005) and 'Čaroŭny narod' (Magical people, 2004). In the former, mist is personified as a transparent girl; when a sycamore comes to life, falling down as an iron serpent, the girl climbs on its back and with a cry plunges to her death in a bog (Nŭž, 22).[8] In the latter poem the lyrical hero feels himself besieged by a magical feeling that his people want something from him, although he does not know what; he barricades himself into his house, declaring again that he understands nothing: 'Цішэй, цішэй, чароўны народ, / Ну нашто вам ізноў патрэбны я?'[9]

Some poems have a strong moral sense. In 'Pieśnia śviatoha Marcina' (Song about Saint Martin, 2010), for instance, a frozen beggar receives charity from Marcin, alone of three guards. The beggar is later revealed as having been Jesus

---

[5] The poem was first published in: *Podania i bajki zebrane na Litwie staraniem Jana Karlowicza*, Cracow, 1887, p. 101.

[6] 'I was born by this black, evil soil [...] My feet lower roots into the unfertile earth' (Nŭž, 12).

[7] 'And you, my child, sleep, sleep / Oh child, fall asleep more quickly' (Nŭž, 23).

[8] There are many snakes and serpents in Bryĺ's first book, other examples being 'Smuha' (Mist, 2009). 'Hiedrus' (2010) and 'Hoĺša' (2009).

[9] 'Quiet, quiet, magical people, / Well what do you need me again for?' (Nŭž, 21).

in disguise, so that Saint Martin lives as an eternal symbol of charity and kindness. In 'Žaludy' (Acorns, 2010) these small objects are to become the nation when they mature. People are invited to make a pledge and throw a paper with the acorns into the river. Facing this poem in the book is a declaration in Old Church Slavonic letters with a stylized medieval picture of an armed horseman.

The last two poems are rather longer than the others, both written in pentameters. 'Holša' (2009) receives over three pages of explanation in the Commentary: its three sources are a desire to follow the already mentioned Roman pattern, an attempt to resurrect part of the Lithuanian (Lietuvan) chronicle, and to contest the use of the word 'myth' by the philosopher Valiancin Akudovič (b. 1950). The connection with Belarusian history is not entirely clear and the poet admits some anachronisms. The eponymous Holša is one of Raman's five sons who, after a misspent youth, is told to find a wild beast to kill that will show him where to build a town; a huge aurochs is not enough, but he eventually defeats a fierce serpent and achieves his ambition. Curiously, the poem ends with 'Amen', not in the Belarusian or Russian spelling of the word. In 'Hiedrus' the hero builds a wonderful castle where there had previously been only marshes and reeds. A bear is set to guard it, but twice it burns down. When the bear hides, three serpents come out of the forest, and one of them is persuaded to cast off its skin and become Hiedrus's wife. At the end we are told that a good wife is a castle without grief, smoke is a support for the heavens and so on. Again the ending is a seemingly pious 'Amen'.

Anton Bryĺ in his first book shows himself to be a poet of vivid imagination and considerable learning, as well as poetic skill. It may be hoped that his intellectual curiosity will continue not only in scholarly research and translations, but also in poetry where he has made a truly auspicious start.[10]

Baradzina

Maryja Baradzina is a broadly educated poet who often writes about the past, from mythology to the Garden of Eden, the Roman Empire, the crusades, days of chivalry and other periods. She has also published translations from various foreign authors, including Federico Garcia Lorca and Seamus Heaney. Baradzina shows a particular taste for cycles, ballads and other short narrative (sometimes dramatized) poems, often with surrealist elements, and always with inventive, sometimes challenging imagery. She uses free verse skilfully to paint scenes and describe events concisely but vividly, with a tendency to use long words, although not the long lines characteristic of some other poets writing about the past such as Anton Bryĺ, for instance. She is certainly a poet who promises much for the future.

---

[10] In 2014 he published a short historical story, *Jan Jalmužna*.

Baradzina begins her first book, *Vyšej za paŭnočny viecier* (Higher than the north wind, 2006), with a bleak poem, 'Ničoha niama. Dzień adychodzić …' (There is nothing. The day is departing …), which at the end of the second stanza refers to 'var'jaty-paety' (madmen-poets, Vpv, 3);[11] and in the last verse of the final part of the poetic sketch 'Alie' (But), beginning 'z rudnikoŭ vieršavanych …' (from the versified pits …) she writes:

з руднікоў вершаваных
ніхто проста так не вяртаўся.[12]

Other poems relating to writing include 'Paet' (The poet) and 'Bardy' (Bards), both somewhat enigmatic verses: in the former, the solution for the poet seems to be friendship with the wizard Merlin, and, in the latter, bards are singing in a refuge from barking dogs. Also rather bizarre is 'Balieryna-zima nie stalieje, nia sudzić …' (Winter, the ballerina, does not mature, does not judge …) where the eponymous dancer makes a present of salty fish to dead poets who, 'like us' (present-day poets?) are inconsolable (Vpv, 72). On the whole, however, Baradzina does not dwell on writing or her personal role as a poet.

Turning to works about the past, the cycle 'Imperatar Trajan' (The Emperor Trajan) begins with a poem of the same title in which the great leader finds that, for all his fame, he has nobody to whom he can complain; in the next poem, 'X Fretensis', the Commander of a prominent Roman sea legion of that name, engages in dialogue with an ambitious Iberian soldier about their dreams. In 'Zdahadka' (Riddle) we see the legion returning from battle but without receiving an official triumph: the riddle is that there is no satisfactory way of returning home after fighting, as the last line spells out: 'шчаслівы той, хто не вярнуўся з ловаў' (happy is he who did not return from hunting, Vpv, 9). A comparable theme is found in 'Rasstajny Rycar' (The distant knight), where spiritual resistance proves enough to repel the cavalry of a conquering army. Another interesting poem is 'Preč z Rymu' (Be gone from Rome) addressed to Marcus Trajan; after much description of the man and his fate, the poet asks to be allowed to accompany him: 'Марк, / віхурай ці кропляй — вазьмі з сабой …' (Marcus, / take me with you, as a snowstorm or a drop of water, Vpv, 10). The above short verses are followed by 'Gaia', a rather complex semi-rhymed dramatic poem about the earth goddess and Marcus Ulpius Trajan.

History in the work of Baradzina is not only imagined but sometimes fantastic, as, for instance, in 'Ptaliamej' (Ptolemy) where the eponymous hero is represented

---

[11] Numerical references preceded by Vpv are to *Vyšej za paŭnočny viecier*.

[12] 'from the versified pits / nobody at all has returned' (Vpv, 106).

There appears to be a reference, not apparent in translation, in the word *rudnikoŭ*, since the word *rudy* (meaning reddish-brown) occurs not infrequently in Baradzina's work, including the last two poems before 'z rudnikoŭ vieršavanych …'.

by his younger brother in a poem that includes a variety of mythical and historical characters. The first six lines give something of the poem's flavour:

Мой брат старэйшы, Пталямэй
лавіў нявольнікаў-міцараў
пятлёю аксамітнай цёмных валасоў

складаў у пазалочаныя труны …
а ўдзень ён спаў у бацькоўскай скрыпцы
і калыханку сам сабе сьпяваў[13]

A cycle of poems entitled 'Čaroŭnaja liampa: Erotyka' (A magic lamp: Erotica), places an epigraph from Luis de Góngora between the two parts of the title. The subjects of this cycle include Delphinius, an unfrocked priest, a Minotaur, Innana (the goddess of fertility and warfare), knees, bards, the drinking of Madeira, memory and Albino doves. 'Maharadža' (Maharajah), the last of the cycle, has an epigraph from the fourteenth-century Persian poet Hafez; it describes a once all-powerful ruler waiting humbly for his Little Prince, with veins that may have been swollen by opium or the hot wind (Vpv, 64). Other quasi-historical verses include 'Hruby dyjamant' (The rough diamond), 'Indziejski prync' (The Indian prince) and 'Prync karčmy' (The prince of the inn); in the latter poem dancing, merrymaking and sex raise the question: who will the Prince smell of afterwards?[14] Ballads, often but not always linked with history, are exemplified in interesting form twice in this book: 'Balada pra aniolaŭ' (Ballad of angels) is an imaginative and fantastic poem with angels variously described as 'with cunning eyes', 'eyes like whips' and 'with falcon's blood'; they are hunted and murdered, as well as being magically produced by a clown from behind his collar:

зь ніаватай усьмешкай паяц
бледнатвары заходзіць, сядае насупраць
дастае з-за каўнера жывога анёла.[15]

Another interesting ballad, 'Da kanca suśvietu (baliadabiezpačatku)' [sic] (To the end of the universe [aballadwithoutbeginning]), starts with a little dialogue

---

[13] 'My elder brother, Ptolemy /caught mizars prisoner / with a velvet loop of dark hair // He put them into gilded coffins … / and by day slept in his parents' violin / and sang a lullaby to himself' (Vpv, 71). Perhaps he was sleeping not in a violin but in a box (*skrynka*) of which *skrypka* is either a dialectal variant or a misprint.

[14] Interestingly, a Polish critic sees this poem as reflecting universal religious ideas: Katarzyna Bortnowska, *Białoruski postmodernizm: "pokolenie Bum-Bam-Litu"*, Warsaw, 2009 (hereafter Bortnowska), p. 147. Noting that the generation she is discussing wrote few conventionally religious poems, she mentions as an exception Baradzina's 'Sanet pra daloni' (Ibid., p. 140).

[15] 'with a guilty smile a pale-faced / clown begins to walk around, then sits opposite / getting from behind his collar a living angel' (Vpv, 46).

between a child and his parent, with the latter promising, hardly enticingly, to return like a mouldy crust. Comparable dialogues conclude each of the first three of the ballad's four parts (mysteriously entitled 'Pierad imi' [Before them], 'Za imi' [After them] and 'Nad imi' [Above them]), as the child, though exhausted by the journey, is gradually consoled (Vpv, 30–31). 'Zimovaja balada' (Winter ballad) is set in the middle ages, with much lively imagery; towards the end of the poem a generous widow enjoys sex, whilst in the last stanza there is a discussion of illumination of sins; at the end a red devil in the epilogue seems satisfied with everything (Vpv, 41). Finally may be mentioned 'Bielyja i zalatyja perlinki' (White and gold pearls), a ballad in three parts set in royal times.

The crusades are described, with not a trace of romanticism, in a number of poems such as 'Padnosiačy kielich' (Bearing a cup) where the poet enters fully into the horror and squalor of this period. Comparable is 'Kryžy liapiŭ sa śliny i pylu …' (He moulded the crosses from spit and dust …). A third poem, 'Nie plač, tut skladzieny ŭsie śpisy …' (Don't weep, all the lists are collected here …), gives a vivid picture of the situation after the crusaders' initial success. Here is the second stanza:

> прыступкамі на дол сыходзяць людзі —
> паход крыжовы супраць мора
> паход крыжовы ўкрыжаваных —
> зьліпаюцца ў камяк у горле[16]

Amongst Baradzina's best occasional poems is 'Čorny chlieb' (Black bread), written to mark the death of Vasiĺ Bykaŭ in 2003. The first stanza immediately introduces an entirely appropriate mood of disaster:

> І заплачуць народныя людзі, і скажуць:
> — Збажына не ўрадзіла, як нехта закляў …
> Закацілася хлебная зорка, і Стражнік
> рэшткі літасьці Божай за пояс схаваў …[17]

Bykaŭ was, of course, well known for the honesty of his realism, and in the second part of one of Baradzina's narrative poems, 'Bielyja i zalatyja perlinki' (White and gold pearls), she produces a picture of urban desolation almost worthy of the black realism of Jury Stankievič (b. 1945). After a grim picture of a church and its parishioners, she turns to the town itself:

---

[16] 'people go down the steps — / a crusade against the sea / a crusade of the crucified — / and stick together like a lump in the throat' (Vpv, 21).
[17] 'And country people will weep, and say / The corn did not bear fruit, as if someone had put on a curse on it … / The star of grain had gone down, and the Guard / hid behind his belt the remains of God's grace' (Vpv, 79).

Горад, няварты таго, каб узьняць яго з друзу,
ціха марнее пад сонцам гумовым, зацятым.
Ты не пазнаў яго тут! Вераб'іны
віск (ці праклён?) хіліць долу цьвярозыя дрэвы.

Колер асеў на падногцях, адно толькі колер
сьветлай тваёй, алебастравай, пеннай шыі.
Мрояцца-марацца лебедзі, і мімаволі
з даху ляціць мой у тройцы палаючы голад.

Горад мой, куфар бязь люстраў, стары ды спарахнелы
з бляклым узорам, якому штоночы
сотні вачэй цацучыных у скоках шалёных
ўсё прыглядаюцца зь пільнасьцю п'янай і енчаць.[18]

With experience, or even imagination, of such a place, it is perhaps not entirely surprising that Baradzina sometimes imagines herself in prison, as we see, for instance, in a powerful poem 'Ahonii bialiava-kisly smak …' (The whitish-bitter taste of agony …). After a bleak introduction about waiting for death, she turns to the prison itself. Here is the second stanza:

мне цесна, душна ў гэтых абцугах
у вязьніцы, аплеценай дрымотным
распусным вінаградам, ад якога
ў набухлых шнарах загусае стогн[19]

A torture chamber also figures in 'Biez abličču' (Without features). In this poem a couple, falling asleep, start casting off their masks, and their dream becomes increasingly fantastic, as the lovers experience a number of horrors before the surrealist ending, in which they build a boat to sail to the window of a red tower where the last princess hung herself, and, when the masks are finally removed, flowers grow out of their hair. The first three stanzas are distinctly nightmarish:

Пакідаючы маскі, як брудныя боты
ля ўваходу ў сон
мы хінемся
тонкай-тонкай хрыбцінкай крыві
да адзінага ў сьвеце пляча —
там, дзе падаюць зоры

---

[18] 'The town, unworthy of being raised from rubble, / quietly fades under a merciless rubbery sun. / You would not have recognized it here! The squawk (or curse?) / of sparrows bend the sober trees downwards. // Colour has settled on nails, just the colour / of your bright, alabaster, foaming neck. / Swans dream exhaustedly, and involuntarily / from the roof flies in a troika my burning hunger. // My town, a chest without mirrors, old and rotten / with a faded pattern, towards which every night / hundreds of rats' eyes, jumping crazily, / gaze at everything with drunken attentiveness and groan' (Vpv, 44).

[19] 'I feel tight, stuffy in these pincers / in the prison, which is entwined by a sleepy vine / that has run to seed, from which / in swollen scars the groan grows thicker' (Vpv, 24).

забалелі разам ўсе шнары
запалалі ўсе вогнішчы
гэта там
нас палілі калісьці, нам ляпалі
чорнай смалою па шчоках
хімэры прычын і высноваў

на дзьвярах катавальні
нехта гушкаўся …
ты штоночы выходзіў
са сьценаў сырых, прасякнутым стогнам
і ў сьцены вяртаўся
а сьцены зрываліся ў рогат[20]

This is far from the only poem which links love with torments. In 'Pliacie vuzly chalodnaja smuha …' (Cold mist ties knots …), for instance, she depicts the daily secret torments of a light blue blade dancing during sleep. The lyrical heroine's thoughts, however, are conflicted between rejection and its impossibility, as may be seen from the last two lines:

дазволь забыць дарогу да цябе
як забываюць свой уласны голас[21]

Life seems better when waking up, to judge by another imaginative poem, 'Piaro druhoje. Son' (Second pen. Sleep). In part 4 of 'Pieśni bury' (Songs of the storm) contact seems, to put it mildly, difficult between lovers. Here as an illustration are the first three and last two lines:

Я напішу табе
ў край
куды лісты не прыходзяць

[…]

і ўспыхнула стосам папераў мая інквізыцыя,
дружа[22]

Baradzina's poems about love are decidedly unusual: for instance, 'Ja i ty' (You and I), in which she describes herself as only a conversation with her lover, whilst

---

[20] 'Casting off our masks, like dirty boots / at the entrance to a dream / we bend over / with an ever so thin spinal cord of blood / to the only shoulder in the world — there where stars fall // all our scars have started to hurt at once / all the fires have started to burn / it is there / that once set us alight, that covered / our cheeks with black tar / chimeras of reasons and conclusions // on the doors of the torture chamber / someone was swinging … / every night you would go out / from the damp walls, saturated with groaning / and would return to the walls / and the walls would burst into a guffaw' (Vpv, 73).

[21] 'let me forget the road to you / as people forget their own voice' (Vpv, 5).

[22] 'I shall write to you / in a country / where letters do not arrive // […] // and my inquisition flared up in a pile of papers, friend' (Vpv. 37).

he keeps looking into his prayer book; in 'Imhnieńnie' (Moment) the lover spreads his bright green feathers, whilst in 'Trupiarnia i viančaĺnaja śviečka' (A morgue and wedding candle) the move from death to happiness has at least a happy, though slightly mysterious ending:

<Я гляджу празь вішнёвыя плечы,
я прашу цябе, будзь …>[23]

'Šept' (A whisper), dedicated 'to him who does not reproach', is another bizarre poem referring to the lover's 'surrealism', and with a pen slipping to the floor (during love making?). It does, however, seem considerably more sensuous than any of the poems collectively described as 'Erotica'. Curiously, the most 'normal' of Baradzina's poems in this genre is 'Pirat' (The pirate), with its historico-fantastic setting. Here is a short excerpt from the middle of the poem, as the pirate foresees his end:

За каўнер заліваюцца рукі твае
блаславёныя рукі
і патрэскваюць полымем крышталёва-чырвоным мае пазванкі,
не дазнацца, адкуль ты прыходзіш
і ня вымаліць голас твой ў час майго скону.[24]

Baradzina's taste for exoticism finds pure expression in an elegant little poem, 'Arabeska' (Arabesque):

Арабэска

Надоечы вярнуліся бэрбэры.
дзе хмель палаў у зрэнках леапарда —
там вырасла сандалавае дрэва.

І сябра мой у сьне закаркаваным
успыхнуў іншаземна белым іклам
ва ўсьмешлівым паўмесяцы заранным.[25]

The poem from which the book's title derives, 'Adnojčy ja pasivieju …' (One day I shall go grey …) seems at first to concern ageing, although the elegiac notes found in some young Belarusian poets are not evident here. No less important to the poet is the eternity of the natural world into which she hopes to be reborn:

---

[23] "'I look at you through cherry shoulders, / I ask you, be there …'" (Vpv, 99).
[24] 'Behind my collar slip your hands / blessed hands / and my backbone crackles with a crystal red flame. / there is no discovering where you have come from / and no begging for your voice at the time of my end' (Vpv, 53).
[25] 'Arabesque // The Berbers returned recently. / where the intoxication of passions in the leopard's pupils / is where a sandalwood tree grew. // And my friend deep in sleep / flashed a white fang exotically / in the smiling crescent of early morning' (Vpv, 55).

Аднойчы я пасівею.
Мой дом па цаглінцы расьцягнуць
жабракі бяз броваў
падобных да крылаў сьмерці

Над морам
вышэй за паўночны вецер

Мяккія крокі туману
спалохаюць сьпеў скамянелы
ноч, цяжарная галасамі
нарэшце захоча памерці

Над морам
вышэй за паўночны вецер
сьветлы тапелец

Позна …
Ціша зноў набрыняла пагоняй
мой кляштар за мяне
ўсе імёны запомніць
я сыйду, каб нарэшце прачнуцца
Над морам,
Вышэй за паўночны вецер²⁶

To conclude this review of a fascinating, demanding and at times enigmatic poet, here is a last verse, which is in some ways related to the previous one in its concern with life, death and memory: 'Vosień' (Autumn), is dedicated to the poet's mother:

Восень

Штосьці ўспомніць, каб жыць —
і балотны агеньчык
памяць няздатную зьліжа. Пустыя дамы.
Хопіць, панове. Сабраныя лёгкія строі
і чаравічкі мільгаюць у дрогкіх адбітках жывых.

Зьвесіла косы ўніз
з каляровае вежы
восень. Радзімыя знакі сабрала ў кулак
іх рассыпае па дахах, балюе, гарэзіць
як куртызанка, у чырвань шнуруе свой стан.

---

²⁶ 'One day I shall go grey. / My house will be dragged apart into bricks / by beggars without eyebrows / like the wings of death // Over the sea / higher than the north wind // The soft steps of the mist / alarm the petrified melody / the night pregnant with voices / will at last wish to die // Over the sea / higher than the north wind / is a light drowned corpse // It is late … / The quiet is again saturated with the chase / my monastery will remember / for me all the names / I shall depart, in order to awaken at last // Over the sea. Higher than the north wind' (Vpv, 19).

Вочкамі, поўнымі сьлёз
пазірае з-за кратаў драўляных
цмочак маленькі, страсае духмяны пылок
з крыльцаў карункавых, і залатыстыя ніткі зьбірае
каб асьвяціць неспакойны, нястрыжаны змрок.[27]

The ambitious and thematically diverse texts in this book are unusual, challengingly imaginative and linguistically rich. They predominantly concern the historical past, but also respond to Belarus's heritage and, indeed, daily life. Maryja Baradzina is undoubtedly an original and stimulating voice in young Belarusian literature of today.

Jemial'janaŭ-Šylovič

The poet and bard Aleś Jemial'janaŭ-Šylovič writes in both prose and verse. His debut collection of poetry, *Parasoniečnaść* (the untranslatable title is a mixture of 'umbrella' and 'sunny') was published in 2013. It is divided into four sections: 'Polis' (Polity), 'Miesca' (Place), 'U pošukach piaščoty' (In search of bliss) and 'Eŭryka' (Eureka). They are preceded by the title poem, dedicated to Liudmila Rublieŭskaja (b. 1965), in which an umbrella wants to be not only opened against rain, but to clear away the invisible ink in which the disobedient wind writes verse; the image is continued to the end, when the umbrella sits on the floor to make corrections:

выпраўляць памылкі
дапушчаныя нябачным аўтарам
рабіць найнатуральнейшую рэдактуру (Р, 3)[28]

The subject matter of his verse is extremely varied, and it contains an abundance of cultural and classical allusions, successfully making many unforced links between knowledge and imagination. The opening of 'Polis' is a poetic triptych, 'Armienija' (Armenia), with an epigraph from the Russian poet Osip Mandel'shtam, repeated in Belarusian as the closing lines of an imaginative tribute to Armenia's religious and cultural history, especially its literary traditions

---

[27] 'Autumn // To recall something, in order to live — / and the swamp light / licks the inadequate memory. Empty houses. / Enough, ladies and gentlemen. The light lines are assembled / and the slippers wink in the trembling reflections of the living. // Autumn has hung its locks down / from the coloured tower. / It has collected birth marks in its fist / and scatters them over the roofs, it feasts, minces / like a courtesan tying her figure into a scarlet dress. // With eyes full of tears / gazes from behind the wooden bars / a little serpent that shakes fragrant dust / from little lace wings, and collects golden threads / in order to illuminate the unquiet, shaggy darkness' (Vpv, 17).

[28] 'To correct the mistakes / made by the unseen author / to perform the most natural of editing work' Numerical references preceded by P in this section are to *Parasoniečnaść*.

(P, 4–5). 'Hierastracijada' (Herostratiada), described as an un-poetic triptych, includes an interesting debate between Alexander the Great and the historian Theopompus on the impermanence of worldly glory and, with light humour, the dangers of fire (P, 14–15). Other Greek figures, by implication, include Archimedes, but nearer to our times is the Renaissance Swiss-German medical pioneer Paracelsus; to celebrate him, the poet describes the state of medicine at the time. Closer to home is 'Daŭmont' (a ruler of Pskov), a highly patriotic poem, which also introduces an episode from the hero's love life, making use of a characteristic device of this poet — the use of repeated words. A poem devoted to the origins of Marc Chagall gives his name in Hebrew letters.[29] The poet's cultural interests, as reflected in his first book, include an epigraph from Joseph Brodsky and a small adaptation of Lorca. Particularly interesting, however, is a poem about old films, 'Čorna-biela-tumannaja kinastužka z hadoŭ tryccatych …' (A black and white misty film clip from the thirties …). Here the lyrical hero imagines himself a participant in a silent thriller such as *Nosferatu* (1922), while he wanders around an anonymous Miensk suburb, feeling no connection to the blocks of flats, which he is sure are deaf to language.

In 'Parasoniečnaść' the wind was a poet, and in another poem, 'Viecier', it is described as the first contemporary poet:

Вецер

колер нябёсаў брудна-ліловы
Вецер
сняжынкі вуснамі ловіць
Вецер
нервам ірае голым
напружваючы пабялянае горла —
стогне хрыпіць захлынаецца слінай
вые крычыць рагоча ўсхліпвае
словы глытае й выкідае ў сусвет
Вецер —
найпершы сучасны паэт[30]

In 'Krok' (A step), the poet describes a long search, at the end of which a successful line is considered divine; here is the conclusion:

---

[29] The title poem of the section 'Eŭryka' is given in Greek letters. Such elaborations seem curiously old-fashioned in the modern world,

[30] 'the colour of the skies is a dirty lilac / the Wind / catches snowflakes in its mouth / the Wind / plays like an exposed nerve / straining the faded throat — / it groans wheezes chokes on saliva / howls cries guffaws sobs / it swallows words and throws them out into the universe / the Wind is / the very first contemporary poet' (P, 27).

Ма —
       ю слоў
Сколь
       кі слоў
Толь —
       кі ёсць
Ёсць адно
Гэта клёк
Толькі крок
Дзе радок
Там і Бог[31]

In 'Parohi' (Thresholds), an extremely enthusiastic triptych about Prague and the Czech language, it is suggested at the end of the first part that, by contrast, in Belarus poets are not allowed citizenship even posthumously:

Дружа, хіба не чуў ты пра
тое, што ў роднай краіне
паэтам на'ат пасля смерці
не даюць грамадзянства![32]

In a comic poem 'Piatnica Milaš i Ty' (Friday Miłosz and You) he asks forgiveness for his bold *vers libre* (P, 35), and in the second stanza of 'Pieraprašeńnie' (Apologies) he explains light heartedly a particularly artificial rhyme:

ды занурана маўчаць — не лепей выйсце, —
б'е на скронях цішыня ў сто дваццаць герцаў,
даравання папрашу не для карысці …
засталося толькі ўжыць тут рыфму <сэрца> …[33]

In 'sustreŭšy na svaim šliachu …' (meeting on my way …) a poem of telephonic frustration with the hero's lover ends with a telling comparison:

цішыня
няскончаная паэма ў сшытку
паэма маўчання кветак[34]

The topic of love evokes a number of other interesting verses ranging from the bold to the timid, from the relatively conventional to the very imaginative or even bizarre. In 'Adzinota' (Loneliness) a dialogue between the lyrical hero and his

---

[31] 'I have some words /So many words / Only there is / One more thing / That is good sense / Only a step / Where there is a line / There also is God' (P, 24).

[32] 'Friend, maybe you have not heard / that in my native country / even after their death / poets are not allowed citizenship' (P, 12).

[33] 'and to be miserably silent is not the best solution, / the silence beats against my temples at a rate of 120 Hz, / I ask you to forgive me not for seeking profit … / all I had left was to use the rhyme "heart" …' (P, 50).

[34] 'silence / is an unfinished poem in a folder / a poem of the silence of flowers' (P, 47).

lover about the subjective nature of dignity compared with the undoubted existence of baking heat ends with her agreeing, albeit in a strange way:

> Ты не спрачаешся й мякка шапочаш на вуха: <Я
> у тваім існаванні толькі часовы госць.
> Прыходжу часцей надакучліваю задухаю,
> калі мяне клічаш, зажураны ягамосць>.[35]

In 'Hadavanaja žnivieńskaj nočč

u …' (Brought up by the August night…) the poet describes love at first sight and being bowled over by the woman's eyes. In another poem, 'Ruki Tvaje' (Your Hands), the eponymous hands smell of Antonov apples, and he is at first tempted to bite his lover's finger. In 'noč zazirnuŭšy ŭ tvaje vočy …' (the night having gazed into your eyes …) the night itself is blinded and driven crazy by their light, leading the lyrical hero to imagine himself blind:

> ноч зазірнуўшы ў твае вочы
> ад святла іх аслепла і звар'яцела
> і я нібы невідушчы шрыфт Брайля
> разбіраю на выгінах твайго цела[36]

He is more timid in 'ad maŭčańnia tvajho niamieju …' (I am struck dumb by your silence …), where his silent lover is nonetheless dear to him:

> ад маўчання твайго нямею
> напэўна таму што не ўмею
> пачуцці хаваць у кішэню
> мяне без цябе ўсё меней[37]

Comparable ideas are raised in 'Patajemnaje' (Secret), a poem rich in inventive imagery:

> Патаемнае
>
> недасмажанаю яечняй
> сонца з талеркі аблокаў
> распаўзаецца па заснежаных дахах
> у грудзях маіх тваё сэрца
> звонам калядным заб'ецца
> ты са мною і не са мною
> маўчыш

---

[35] 'You do not argue and quietly whisper in my ear "I / am only a temporary guest in your existence. / I mostly come as tiresome stuffiness / when you call me, your sad excellency"' (P, 6).
[36] ' the night having gazed into your eyes / was blinded and driven crazy by their light / and I am apparently unable to see / I write in the blind Braille script on the curves of your body' (P, 63).
[37] 'I am struck dumb by your silence / probably because I cannot / hide feelings in my pocket / without you there is ever less of me' (P, 53).

вочы ўтаропіўшы долу
пачую капытны пошчак —
паляванне сучаснага Стаха
абвастрае чуццё
хутка паеду дахам
як назваць пачуццё
што па жылах пульсуе
кіпячай смалы гарачэй
для цябе я не болей чым сябра
ты побач яшчэ?
вартаю сэрца[38]

A final example of this poet's love lyrics is 'Dziaŭčyna' (Girl), which describes
graphically his passionate love for a girl of indeterminate age who attracts him
with her youthful body, whatever her national or other background. He seems
fated, however, as we see from the last lines:

я ведаю
ты прыйдзеш апоўначы
каб зноў зацягнуць мяне
ў багну шалу і жарсці
а я кахаю цябе і ненадвіджу
кахаю і ненадвіджу
Дзяўчыну
якая ніколі не стане жанчынай[39]

Aleś Jemial'janaŭ-Šylovič's promising first book displays a genuine and varied
talent, including the ability to make readers empathize with his lyrical hero's self-
doubts and emotional problems, as well as drawing them into a world of rich
imagery and extensive cultural and historical references.

---

[38] 'Secret // like an undercooked fried egg / from the plates of clouds the sun / spreads over the
snowy roofs / your heart is in my breast / beating like Christmas bells / you are with me and
not with me / you are silent / you cast your eyes down / I hear the clatter of hooves — the hunt
of a contemporary Stakh / sharpens my ears / soon I shall go crazy / how am I to call the feeling /
that is pulsing through my veins / hotter than boiling pitch / for you I am no more than a
friend / are you still beside me? / I am guarding my heart' (P, 38).
    Stakh is the eponymous hero of one of Uladzimir Karatkievič's most popular quasi-historical
works, *Dzikaje paliavańnie karalia Stakha* (The Wild Hunt of King Stakh, 1964).
[39] 'I know / you will come at midnight / in order to again draw me / into a swamp of madness
and passion / and I love you and hate you / I love and hate / the Girl / who will never become
a woman' (P, 43–44).

CHAPTER 2

~

Religion and Various Forms of Piety

Most Belarusians have for several centuries adhered to the Uniate faith, although their powerful neighbours, Poland and Russia, have sought to impose respectively Catholicism or Orthodoxy. There is a good deal of piety in the work of the young poets, sometimes specifically Catholic, occasionally humorous and familiar with the Deity, whilst Orthodoxy, the officially sponsored religion in present-day Belarus, is for at least one poet a cause of misunderstandings among his friends. Occasionally, hostility is expressed to all religious faiths. Nonetheless, religion as a theme for this generation of poets is almost certainly more important than it is for the majority of their West European counterparts.

Siamaška

Viktar Siamaška is a talented bard and intriguing poet. His debut was on Belarusian radio in 1992, and since then he has made a considerable career as member and organizer of various successful folk and other musical groups. His books of verse include *Marija S.* (2006), *ReRa* (2011), which mainly contains poems from the second half of 2008, and *Habitacyja* (2013) comprising poems from 2006–08. It is on the second two of these chronologically close collections that the following will be based.

Habitacyja consists of three poetic cycles, 'Habitacyja', 'Dafarencyja' and 'Hzyms', whose titles require some explanation: the first is the name of a village near Budslaŭ; Dafarencyja is a village in the Miensk region; and Hzyms means a cornice; ReRa is a dialectal Belarusian word meaning a dishevelled person. None of these unusual names appear to have any relevance to the individual poems.

An almost ubiquitous element in Siamaška's works is his strong Catholic faith. In other respects his thematic range is considerable, though familiar: from nature, particularly wind, to concern for the future of Belarus, including a number of bold political statements. To begin with religion, many of the poems on spiritual themes are far from simple. In 'Patanok' (The float), for instance, after being told by a wise prophet that a goal will ruin him, the believer turns to God:

<Куды далей? Пане Божа,
няўжто я тут яшчэ патрэбны?> —
кленчыць вернік,
адчуваючы сябе патанком
не дапірае, што сьмерць трэба заслужыць (На, 82)[1]

'Na Vialiki post', a mixture of unrhymed verse and prose, ends with the following stern injunction:

<Памятай, ты прах і прахам станеш>[2]

'Aŭtaspyn' (Hitchhiking) is an unexpected title for one of Siamaška's most intimate spiritual poems:

Аўтаспын

Чым больш набліжаесься да Яго,
чым больш намагаесься Яго разумець,
тым больш адчуваеш
уласную нямогласьць,
слабасьць, старасьць,
нетрываласьць,
няздатнасьць

час прыпыніцца

мне не хапае моцы,
каб служыць Табе, Пане

час прыпыніцца

выходжу з касьцёлу,
як апошняя гніда

каб рушыць далей[3]

For this poet intellectual activity is far less important than belief, as we read in 'Hluzdy' (Brains), of which these are the last six lines:

---

[1] '"Whither forward? Lord God / Am I really still needed here?"' / the believer kneels / feeling himself a float / he does not understand that death has to be earned' Numerical references preceded by Ha are to *Habitacyja*.

[2] '"Remember, you are dust and will become dust"' (Ha, 62).

[3] 'Hitchhiking' // The more you approach Him. / the more you strive to comprehend Him, / the more you feel / your own impotence / weakness, age, / instability, / inability // it is time to stop // I do not have enough strength, / to serve You, Lord // it is time to stop // I leave the church, / like the most worthless wretch // in order to go on further' (Ha, 22).

НЕ!
лепей займацца верай
маліцца моўчкі
й бязглузда
малітва — не значыць "кажы"
малітва — гэта, каб слухаць (Re, 61)[4]

A final example of the poet's philosophical attitude, undoubtedly derived from his belief, is the following simple couplet:

калі памру — ня трэба сьлёз,
бо сьмерць — жыцьця апатэоз[5]

Siamaška, best-known as a musical performer, does not have a great deal to say about writing as such, though one simple but effective poem, 'linija niebaschilu za sosnami …' (the line of the horizon behind the pines …) is worth quoting:

лінія небасхілу за соснамі —
празрыстая восень

з птушкай у носе
пералічваю зерне
            зорак
            зерне …

восень
        дорыць
            паэту
                натхненьне[6]

In another poem, 'Na prypynku' (At the stop), he brings humour to the question of creation, and the following four lines may have resonance with other poets striving for originality and coping with repetition:

мала напісаць слоўца
трэба паўтарыць яго колькі разоў запар
пакуль яно ня здолее прывабіць увагу
й канчаткова ня страціць сэнс[7]

---

[4] 'NO! / it is better to devote yourself to prayer / to pray silently / and without using your brain / **a prayer does not mean "say"** / **a prayer is in order to listen**' Numerical references preceded by Re are to *ReRa*.

[5] 'when I die, there is no need for tears, / for death is the apotheosis of life' (Re, 30).

[6] 'the line of the horizon behind the pines — / transparent autumn // with a bird in my nose / I count grain / stars / grain … // *autumn / gives/ the poet / inspiration*' (Re, 57–58).

[7] '*it is not much to write a good word / you must repeat it constantly,/ until it succeeds in attracting attention / and does not finally lose its meaning*' (Re, 68).

In the examples of Siamaška's poems cited hitherto, there has been some alliteration but no rhyme as such. In a more fantastic humorous poem, 'Son u nos' (A dream on the nose), he uses rather facile rhyme, which may serve as a reminder of the musical background to these poems, where rhymes are often accepted without scrutiny:

Сон у нос

увечары хочацца піць,
а з раніцы аніякае смагі
відаць, заместа вады сон

засынаў з моцнай крыўдай,
а прачнуўся — боль мінуў
замяніў памяць сон

так паступова страчваю чалавечы фасон:
　у чэрапе тушыцца патысон
　расьце з хрыбетніка парасон …
і ня трэба нічога піць![8]

Siamaška's far from conventional nature poems are rich in imagery and sensory perceptions, a good example being the rather long 'Sok ziamli' (Juice of the earth). In 'Dzień i noč' (Day and night) he asserts the centrality of nature in human life:

шукай праўду ў зямлі
пад сьмецьцем думак[9]

'Čornaja stronha' (The black trout) combines simple description, extensive personification and effective imagery:

Чорная стронга

Месяц устае
з-за жоўтых бярэзін, малых арабін
займае
　　　звыклае мейсца
над полем
прасунуў у хатку нашу
　　　　　промень
з вакна ў вакно

---

[8] 'A dream on the nose // in the evening I want to drink / but in the morning there is no thirst / *it seems that a dream has replaced water* // I went to sleep with a strong sense of grievance. / but when I awoke the pain had passed / *my dream had replaced my memory* // thus I gradually lose my human style: / custard marrow is stewed in my skull / in my spine there grows an umbrella … / **and you must not drink anything!**' (Re, 46–47).
[9] 'look for truth in the earth / under the garbage of thoughts' (Ha, 72).

яблыні,
          быццам елкі калядныя
ўжо не гараць
толькі звонку так звонка
          цыкадамі
зорка зорку пільнуе
ліхтар за ліхтар

чорнай стронгаю ноч
заглынула абшар
          ахінула сьляпою
          празрыстасьцю[10]

Far from nature, unless one thinks of the ice on a hockey pitch,[11] are several references to the country's leader, a keen amateur of the sport. First, in the last two lines of 'Murašnik' (The ant heap), is an appeal to the Lord to free Belarusians from their epidemic, imprisoned, as they are, by elections:

Пане, пазбаў ад пошасьці
нас, зьняволеных выбарамі[12]

More damning is the reference in a linguistic *jeu d'esprit*, 'Faršasklad' (Layers of stuffing):

Літары — лідэры
лідэры - підары[13]

Finally, the first two unambiguous stanzas from another verse, 'Dyk' (So), that begins with heavy alliteration:

дыктатар —
хакею аматар,
азадкаў лапар

дыктатар-кастрат
дыктуе трактат
пра трактар[14]

---

[10] 'The black trout // The moon rises / from behind the yellow birches, the little rowan-trees / it takes / its usual place / over the field // a beam of light / pushes into our house / from one window to another // the apple trees, like Christmas trees / no longer shine / only the cicadas / from outside ring out / one star looks after another star / light for light / night like a black trout / has swallowed the whole space / has enveloped it in blind / transparency' (Ha, 67).
[11] In Belarus, Russia and some other countries 'hockey' means 'ice hockey', whereas the hockey known in warmer countries is called 'grass hockey'.
[12] 'Lord, save from this epidemic / us who are imprisoned by the elections' (Ha, 43).
[13] 'Letters — leaders . leaders — pederasts' (Re, 73).
[14] ' the dictator is / a lover of ice hockey, a fondler of bottoms // the castrated dictator / dictates a tract / about a tractor' (Ha, 14).

Turning, finally, to Siamaška's romantic poems, we find total devotion in 'Haspadynia' (The lady), of which these are the closing lines:

> я бы голуб
> бы рыба
> бы раб
>   ля ступняў тваіх,
>   гаспадыня[15]

Several poems are about lost and/or unrequited love, for example, 'Boliej' (More), 'stoma i sliota …' (weariness and drizzle …) and 'ad toje da hetaje Paschi …' (from that to this Easter …). The last of these recalls a girl who even two years ago did not return his calls (Ha, 85), and the second says that his relationship is highly ambiguous: 'сузіраць цябе аднолькава салодка й горка' (contemplating you is equally sweet and bitter, Ha, 40). Most touching, however, is 'Boliej':

> Болей
>
> Мае сьлёзы —
>   пялёсткі пад твае крокі
>
> твой пот
> пунсовыя шчокі
> завіткі на скронях —
>   толькі мроі
>
> разумею, таму няма, на што крыўдзіцца
>   няма, на што скардзіцца
>   абурацца
>
> вось і ты
> сьмяесься мне ў твар
>
> мы адзін аднаму — спакуса
> бачыць ці ня бачыць цябе —
> як пакутлівей?[16]

After such agony, even the vulgarity (for instance, the smell of vaginas) in 'Non-stop' comes as a relief, but, to end this survey here is a short but blissfully happy romantic poem, 'tvoj vobraz …' (your image …)

---

[15] 'I would be like a dove, / like a fish / like a slave / at your feet / my lady' (Ha, 10).

[16] 'More // My tears are petals beneath your steps // your sweat / your crimson cheeks / curls on your brow are only day dreams // I understand that there is nothing to be offended by, / nothing to complain of / or be indignant about // here are you / you laugh in my face // we are temptation to each other / to see or not to see you — / which is the greater torment?' (Ha, 34).

твой вобраз
пачынае чытацца —

рухі, абрысы
разам зь імгненнымі фарбамі
й няўлоўнымі пахамі ў такт

ты йдзеш са мной поруч
мы прачынаемся
ў нашым ложку

твая пяшчота перапаўняе сусьвет,
тваё чыстае цёплае зьзяньне[17]

The above review of between three and four years of Siamaška's literary career reveals a man of varied talents in this field, in addition to his other cultural activities. His religious faith, though clearly deep, is far from obscuring other aspects of his life as a poet.

Filon

Nadzieja Filon's first book, *Kropli śviatla* (Drops of light, 2012) shows her to be a poet of strong spiritual conviction, and some of her poems, all in rhyme, take the form of prayers. She has also written many nature lyrics, concentrating on winter snow and the coming of spring. Like several other young poets she seems fond of repeating words and lines. Unlike many, however, her lyrical heroine appears to be consistently happy, as may be seen in the first poem in the book, '"Ščaślivaja", — mnie kažuć liudzi ŭšled …' ('A happy one', people say after me …), which endorses this impression immediately. The first two lines are quite unambiguous:

<Шчаслівая>, — мне кажуць людзі ўслед.
Я цалкам з імі згодна. Так. Шчаслівая. (Kś, 3)[18]

Such happiness is a good advertisement for Filon's religious faith, and a short verse, 'Prastora, iścina i viera …' (Space, truth and belief …) is emblematic in that it names the three pillars of her spiritual world:

Прастора, ісціна і вера —
Тры складнікі душы маёй.
У свет мне адчыняюць дзверы,
Таемнай вабяць чысцінёй.

---

[17] 'your image is beginning to be read / movements, contours / together with momentary colours / and elusive rhythmical smells // you go hand in hand with me / we awaken / in our bed // your caresses fill the whole universe, / your pure warm glow' (Ha, 44).
[18] '"A happy one", people say after me / I agree with them completely. So it is. I am happy' Numerical references preceded by Kś are to *Kropli śviatla*.

Няма ў іх бруднага, благога,
Што выклікае ў сэрцы жах.
Бяруць пачатак свой ад Бога,
Жыццёвы асвятляюць шлях.[19]

Amongst poems that are essentially prayers may be mentioned 'Prysutnaść' (Presence) which begins with a direct address to God, and two others, less immediately direct, that are inspired by sunrise and sunset: 'Kali ŭzychodzić sonca nad ziamlioj …' (When the sun rises above the earth …) and 'Kali schiliajecca na zachad dzień …' (When the day sinks in the west …). The poet's life is entirely governed by her beliefs, as is shown by poems such as 'Uhliadajusia ŭ žyćcio praz pryzmu viečnaha …' (I look at life through the prism of eternity …), and there are at least two direct statements that Christ is her constant support: 'Kali, Chrystos, sustrelasia z Taboju …' (When, Christ, I met You …), and a short verse 'Z Taboj zaŭsiody ŭ sercy radaść maju …' (With You I always have joy in my heart …):

З Табой заўсёды ў сэрцы радасць маю,
Хоць на шляху ёсць цяжкасцей нямала,
Але мяне Ты за руку трымаеш,
Каб я не спатыкнулася, не ўпала.[20]

Even friends are sent by God; here is the first stanza of 'Nie byvaje daremnych siabroŭ …' (There is no such thing as useless friends …):

Не бывае дарэмных сяброў,
Бог нам лішняга не пасылае
На спляценні жыццёвых шляхоў
Выпадковых сяброў не бывае.[21]

The words for way or path (*šliach* and *ściežka*) occur frequently in Filon's poems. In 'Sustreča z niebam' (Meeting with heaven) she points out the multitude of paths leading to a meeting with Christ, and in 'Chviliny dnia nie zatrymaju …' (I do not hold back the minutes of the day …) it is the stars that provide the path; here is the last stanza:

На цёмным небе зорнай сцежкай
Імклівы ранак крочыць зноў.
Вітае сонечнай усмешкай
Бясконцасць зменлівых шляхоў.[22]

---

[19] 'Space, truth and belief / Are the three components of my soul. / They open doors for me into the world, / Enchant me with secret purity. // There is nothing dirty or bad in them / To arouse fear in my heart. / They originate from God, / And illuminate life's path' (Kś, 38).

[20] 'With You I always have joy in my heart, / Although there are many difficulties on my path, / But You hold me by the hand, / So that I do not stumble and fall' (Kś, 53).

[21] 'There is no such thing as useless friends, / God does not send us anything superfluous. / At the intersections of life's paths / There are never any chance friends' (Kś, 18).

[22] 'In the dark sky on a starry way / The morning swiftly comes again. / With a sunny smile it greets / The endless number of changing paths' (Kś, 24).

The Milky Way is the path to the heavens, the poet's constant dream. Here is the last stanza of 'Vabić nieba načnoha prastor …' (The expanse of the night sky enchants me …):

> І маланкамі думкі ляцяць,
> Абрываюць аблокаў тканіну.
> Я люблю на зямлі разважаць …
> Сэрца ж рвецца ў нябёсаў краіну.[23]

Other themes in this book worth mentioning include childhood ('Uspaminy dziacinstva, jak soniečny dzień …' [Memories of childhood, like a sunny day …]), the wide variety of people in the world ('Jak jarka i piaščotna sonca śviecić …' [How brightly and affectionately the sun shines …]), and the nature of sincere and insincere apologies ('Pakryŭdziŭ, asudziŭ i praminuŭ …' [He offended me, judged me and passed by …]). Another verse lacking the poet's characteristic radiance is 'Adrynuty' (Abandoned), the tragic tale of a small child abandoned by his parents. Moreover, her own personal relations, though not so dramatic, seem at times to be less than smooth: 'Ja vieĺmi rada našaje sustreču …' (I am very pleased that we are meeting …) concerns the pain of parting, whilst 'Liažać liliei ścipla na rukach …' (The lilies lie modestly in my arms …) suggests that although their appearance may be a sign of fidelity, their scent is one of jealousy; here is the last stanza, which ends on a characteristically buoyant note:

> Няхай патухне рэўнасці пажар,
> Неразумеласці.
> І шчырасцю напоўніцца душа
> Аб узаемнасці.[24]

Filon's already mentioned attraction to winter and snowflakes are clearly reflected in 'Śniažynki, niby zorački kryštaĺnyja …' (Snowflakes like little crystal stars …) and 'Bielaja śniažynka na daloni …' (A white snowflake on my palm …). In the former, snow's purifying qualities are central, and in the latter the short life of individual snowflakes leads the poet to hope that they will have a redeeming effect. Here is the second stanza:

> Дык няхай жа пры сустрэчы з вамі
> З чалавечых душ знікае лёд.
> Каб нікому не нанесці раны
> Сярод крыўд жыццёвых і нягод.[25]

---

[23] 'And my thoughts fly like flashes of lightning, / Tearing apart the fabric of the clouds. / On earth I like to reflect … / But my heart strives to the land of the heavens' (Kś, 9).
[24] 'Let the fire of jealousy die down, / Also that of misunderstanding. / And my soul will fill with sincere feelings / About reciprocity' (Kś, 41).
[25] 'And so, when meeting you / May the ice disappear from people's souls. / Let no one inflict wounds on others / Amidst life's injuries and misfortunes' (Kś, 31).

In an early poem, 'Majo žyćcio — sukupnaść kropieĺ drobnych ...' (My life is a mass of tiny drops ...), the poet declares herself to be formed from complex Universal rain, and reflects on her future as a poet:

Маё жыццё — сукупнасць кропель дробных
Складанага Сусветнага дажджу.
Мне невядома, калі вусны змоўкнуць
I колькі добрых слоў яшчэ скажу.

Не ведаю, дзе шчасце прыхавана
I колькі напішу яшчэ радкоў,
Сустрэну колькі я натхняльных ранкаў,
На кветках колькі ўбачу матылькоў ...

Перада мной — сцяжынка са шматкроп'ем,
Ды скрыжаванні бачу на шляху ...
Маё жыццё — сукупнасць кропель дробных
Складанага Сусветнага дажджу.[26]

Nadzieja Filon's poetry is deeply spiritual, and the title of the last poem in *Kropli śviatla*, 'Na absiahach viečnaści' (On the spaces of eternity, Kś, 60), seems to sum up well her self-perception as part of a limitless continuum.

Aŭčyńnikava

Hanna Aŭčyńnikava is a romantic, thoughtful young poet whose technically simple rhyming verse goes beyond the experience of love to reflections on philosophical and political themes. Her first book, *Ad začynienaj bramy* (From a closed gate, 2011), is divided into two parts: 'Kielich žyćcia' (The cup of life) and 'Pieśni kachańnia' (Songs of love). Aŭčyńnikava's romantic verse often links nature, especially, autumn, with her personal feelings. In a poem from the second part, 'Pieśnia 3' (Song 3), for instance, she describes herself as a sounding wind, declaring autumn to be when she feels most secure: 'Восень — мой дом' (Autumn is my home, Azb, 40).[27] Many of her poems are about night and dreams, and there are frequent references to God and heaven. On a more earthly level, she also shows some political irony and anger. In his Introduction to the book, mysteriously called 'Kielich nieadekadansu' (The cup of neo-decadence), fellow-poet Anatoĺ Brusievič (b. 1977) describes Aŭčyńnikava's path as developing from

---

[26] 'My life is a mass of tiny drops / Of complex Universal rain. / I do not know when my lips will fall silent / And how many more good words I shall say. // I do not know where happiness is hidden / And how many more lines I shall write, / I shall meet many inspiring mornings, / And see many butterflies on the flowers ... // Before me is a path with ellipses, / And I see crossroads on my way .../ My life is a mass of tiny drops / Of complex Universal rain' (Kś, 4–5).

[27] Numerical references preceded by Azb are to *Ad začynienaj bramy*.

selfish introspection to enquiry into the lofty role of an artist and his Word,[28] a proposition that does not entirely reflect the text of her debut collection.

'Kielich žyćcia' begins with a verse picturing a misty autumn day, but in the second poem, 'Jakaja dziŭnaja patreba …' (What a strange need …), her lyrical heroine appears conflicted in her wish either to bury herself in despair or to seek in the overgrowth of September the signs of colours and words. Here are the last four lines:

Якая дзіўная нягода —
Мой шлях, заганны і святы:
Да адрачэння ад свабоды
І далучэння да бяды.[29]

Most of the early poems, however, are ecstatic in their depictions of nature, often linking it closely with personal feelings, especially love, good examples being 'Palyn' (Wormwood) and 'Paliubila ja vodar travy …' (I loved the scent of grass …). The coming of autumn is important to this poet, and she celebrates the Slav seasonal celebration in a poem with the same name as that of Mickiewicz's great narrative poem, *Dziady* (Forefathers' eve). Although too long to quote *in toto*, a few lines from the middle of Aŭčyńnikava's verse will give the flavour:

— Вечар добры, маладзіца!
Змоўклі цені ля труны …
Замутняецца крыніца,
Высыпаецца кастрыца,
Гасне вечар ільняны.
Лён і попел. Стол засланы.[30]

Even quasi-domestic scenes can have a disturbing side: for instance, 'Noč na Kaliady' (Christmas Eve) may only have an element of fantasy, but 'Jablykam vosień liažyć na stalie …' (Autumn lies on the table as an apple …) describes the poet's memories of childhood, which she dare not even touch.

The image of prison and captivity is not uncommon in Aŭčyńnikava's poetry: in 'Adzinoty viečnaj palanianka …' (A prisoner of eternal loneliness …), for instance, she may only be trapped by loneliness, but in another poem, 'Viartańnie' (Returning) she comes back from thoughts of abroad to 'žadany prypynak —

---

[28] Although the word decadence was largely discredited in Soviet times, it clearly has some significance for Brusievič, the first letters of whose 'Akravierš' (Acrostic poem) reads 'DEKADENT BRUSIEVIČ'. See McMillin, *Writing*, 789–90.

[29] 'What strange bad weather — / My path, faulty and holy: / To renunciation of freedom / And connection with misfortune' (Azb, 9).

[30] '"Good evening, young woman!" / The shadows near the graves have fallen silent … / The spring grows turbid, / The chaff is scattered, / The flaxen evening fades. / Flax and ash. The table is set' (Azb, 15). Another touching poem about loneliness is 'Šukaju ŭ žyćci svaim blizkich i rodnych …' (I seek in my life close and dear people …).

astrożny spakoj' (the wished-for refuge — the peace of prison, Azb, 19). Another poem, 'Toj, chto paet — nazaŭsiody ŭ palonie …' (He who is a poet is always in captivity …), ends with lines that recall the closing words of T.S. Eliot's 'East Coker' ('In my end is my beginning'). It also expresses many of the poet's feelings about the difficulties and even dangers of her calling in present-day Belarus, as may be seen from the opening lines:

> Той, хто паэт — назаўсёды ў палоне,
> Бо незаўважна
> Кожнае слова, што вымавіш сёння,
> Каменем ляжа.
> Дзеляць бясконца цябе між сабою
> Воля і краты.
> А калі песняй слугуеш сваёю —
> Гэта ёсць здрада![31]

Religion plays a considerable but unobtrusive part in Aŭčyńnikava's poetry. In 'Z hlybini' (From the depths), for instance, she describes attempting to reach God by her own efforts alone, whilst in 'Kaloža' (The Kaloža church), set once again in autumn, she anticipates the potential healing properties of the oldest church in Harodnia. In 'Ja Tvajoj dačkoju zastajusia …' (I remain Thy daughter …) she feels herself His daughter, but also reflects on her native country, where even echoes of freedom are not universal:

> Я Тваёй дачкою застаюся
> І наяве бачу дзіўны сон,
> Нібы на прасторах Беларусі
> Заблукала рэха вольных дзён.
> І калі жыцця яно не мае,
> Дык яшчэ нагадвае яго …
> Заціхае на палове Краю,
> і амаль не чуецца ў другой.[32]

Aŭčyńnikava is not at all passive, as another poem also makes clear, 'Aby nie bylo vajny' (Only let there be no war), the title, later repeated, is a commonly heard phrase in Belarus. The work begins mildly but before long changes into a lament about various negative aspects of contemporary life, as may be seen from the second half:

---

[31] 'He who is a poet is always in captivity, / For unnoticed / Every word you pronounce today, / Lies like a stone. / Freedom and prison bars. / They endlessly share you with each other. / And if your song is intended to serve — / That is treachery!' (Azb, 30).

[32] I remain Thy daughter / and while still awake see a wondrous dream, / As if on the broad spaces of Belarus / There wandered the echo of days of freedom. / And when it does not exist in life, / It still comes to mind … / It has grown quiet in one half of the Country, / And can barely be heard at all in the other' (Azb, 26).

Паволі змагацца трэба.
Навошта табе - хутчэй?
Жалезную моц Пагоні
На кветкі і каласкі
Змянілі! Сядзяць на троне
Вар'яты-кіраўнікі,
Нашчадкі стаптанай мовы,
Ганебных часоў сыны!
На вуснах — чужыя словы …
Абы не было вайны!
Мы мірныя, братка, людзі,
Мы любім святло вясны.
А будзе тыран, не будзе —
Абы не было вайны …[33]

Not all Aŭčyńnikava's poems about love come in the second part of her book. In what starts as a seemingly light poem from the first one, for example, 'Pad flejtu vietranaha rańnia …' (Accompanied by the flute of early morning …), the mood changes when a jealous woman mixes poison with the wine, and bitterness enters the Cup of Life (Azb, 20). The second part of the book starts with four numbered songs about love. The first contains memories, in the second the poet seems to find it easy to leave her lover's sphere, whilst in the third there is more (autumnal) affection. The last of the quartet, 'Pieśnia 4 (Vita Nuova)' (Song 4 [New Life]), describes starting a new (love) life. For young Belarusian poets — and Aŭčyńnikava is no exception — the course of true love never seems to run true (to paraphrase Shakespeare). In a rather bleak poem, 'Ty hliadziš na vilhotnuju šybu …' (You look at the damp window pane …) she reveals her difficulty in completely committing herself to her lover, whilst in 'Da ciabie' (To you) she seems frustrated but determined to hang on:

У каханні душа мая будзе з табой,
Хоць падумаеш ты, што заўсёды адзін.[34]

In 'CODA' the poet muses rather soberly on marriage and life afterwards. More fantastically, in 'Sustreča 2 (Elaida)' (Second meeting [Elaida]), the lyrical heroine meets the goddess of love in the streets of Harodnia, and the goddess tells her

---

[33] 'We must struggle slowly. / Why do you need to go quicker? / The iron force of the Pahonia / For little flowers and ears of corn / Has been exchanged! Sitting on the throne / Are crazy leaders, / Descendants of the trampled language, / Sons of ignominious times! / On your tongues are alien words … / Only let there be no war! / We are peaceful people, brother, / We love the brightness of spring, / And whether there is a tyrant or not — / Only let there be no war …' (Azb, 28).
[34] 'In love my soul will be with you, / Although you will think that you are alone for ever' (Azb, 48).

that the little stars will be her children and the wind her lover, to which her response is:

> 'Так і здарыцца …
> ў лепшым Сусвеце.'[35]

In a mildly comic poem, 'Ramonak' (Camomile) the eponymous flower (in this context the English equivalent in the dandelion) is asked whether her lover is thinking about her. And finally, in 'Pieśni tvaje paliaciać da ablokaŭ …' (Your songs will fly to the clouds …), with more warmth than in some other of Aŭčyńnikava's songs of love, there is a great optimism and sense of wellbeing. Here are the last two lines:

> Бог паяднаў нас адною дарогай.
> Свет чалавечы і Боскі — ў табе.[36]

To conclude, here is a poem, already mentioned, that reflects the uncertainty about hope found in several of Aŭčyńnikava's verses:

> Адзіноты вечнай паланянка
> Запляла пралескі ў валасы
> І сядзіць пад ветразямі ранку
> Між блакіту неба і расы
> Ды глядзіць, паглыбленая ў гора,
> Каб багацця рэшты не згубіць.
> А багацце — скрыначка Пандоры,
> Дзе надзея стомленая спіць.[37]

Hanna Aŭčyńnikava's first book, in addition to spirituality and love, ranges over several other subjects, including music and reading. It is a worthwhile debut and further enhances the already distinguished literary profile of her native Harodnia.

Hluchoŭskaja

Kaciaryna Hluchoŭskaja is one of the youngest poets in this study, who was still, at the time of her first book's publication, a student of philology at BDU. In his Introduction to her debut collection, *Kali drevy rastuć z halavy* (When trees grow out of your head, 2013), the poet Viktar Lupasin (aka Viktar Yvanoŭ, b. 1982), welcomes the lack of 'stinking postmodernism' including her refreshingly unfashionable regard for poetic form. All the verses here were written in

---

[35] 'That is what will happen … / In a better Universe' (Azb, 47).

[36] 'God united us on one path. / The human world and the Divine in you' (Azb, 53).

[37] 'A prisoner of eternal loneliness / Wove sunbeams into her hair / And sits under the sails of morning / Between the blue of the sky and the dew / And watches, deep in grief, / In order not to lose the remains of her riches. / But riches are a Pandora's box / Where weary hope sleeps' (Azb, 19).

Hluchoŭskaja's teenage years, and recurrent themes are writing, religion, birds, both alive and dead, trees and flowers, as well as exotic, often imaginary, wild beasts; her relatively few love poems are oblique and apparently contradictory. The formality of Hluchoŭskaja's verse is in part vitiated by excessive use of repetition and some forced rhymes. She does, however, display considerable imagination in the settings of her poems, which range from historical themes such as Stalin's repressions or Napoleon's ignominious retreat from Moscow, to life in distant, exotic lands.

The opening verse, 'Lietucieńnie halavy' (My head's daydream, 2013) goes some way to explain the book's title:

Летуценьне галавы

Ціха, ціха, не зь няўдачы —
Ціха ў вочы дожджык плача,
Ціха дыхае сьвятлом
Над зязюліным гняздом
Гэтак ціха, звар'яцела
Прарастае з глебы цела:
Вочы — кветкі, валасы —
Дзе сцяблінкі, дзе хмызы,
Дзе ці мох, ці мурава —
Вось якая галава.

                    *

З галавы такой ахвоча
Конік думкамі стракоча,
З галавы такой пяю
Жаваронка ды зьмяю.
Адшукаць у ёй — ня меней! —
Трэба шчасьце — голку ў сене;
Бохан сонейка крышыць,
Галавы ўспамінам жыць,
Ці прыдумай, ці ўяўленьнем —
Вось якое летуценьне. (Kdr, 7)[38]

---

[38] 'My head's daydreams // Quietly, quietly, not from failure - / a shower weeps in my eyes,/ quietly there breathes light / over a cuckoo's nest. / just so quietly, crazily / there grows a body from the earth: / eyes are flowers, hair is / where there are stalks, or bushes, / where there is moss or thick young grass — that is what the head is like // * // From such a head / a grasshopper gladly flashes with thoughts, / from such a head I sing / of a nightingale or a snake. / One has to find in it nothing less than / happiness, like a needle in a haystack; / the loaf-like sun crumbles, / to live by the recollection of the head, / or by invention, or by imagination — / that is what a daydream is like' Numerical references preceded by Kdr are to *Kali drevy rastuć z halavy.*

Allowances must be made for this prolific poet's youth, but she is not unaware of who she is now and what she wants to be, as we read in 'Adnojču' (One day, 2012), where she describes herself as one of the romantic poets, declaring: 'Я аднойчы стану сапраўднай паэткай' (One day I shall become a real poetess, Kdr, 94), going on to discuss the effect of drinking on her poems, and concluding that it is a waste of time if nobody becomes intoxicated by them. More fancifully, in 'Hnom' (The gnome, 2011), the eponymous creature leaves some fragrant wine by her window with the following enigmatic words:

> Кажа, вып'еш яго раз —
> Выйдзе казка, а не сказ …[39]

Hluchoŭskaja often links her writing with religious faith and also music. In 'Lieta raschinaje niebaschil …' (Summer opens up the firmament …, 2013), for instance, she concludes with an affirmation of the two mainstays of her life:

> Да якой сьмяшлівасьці маёй
> Можа, дойдзе сумнае вар'яцтва?
> Гэта проста на душы — спакой.
> Валадарства веры ды мастацтва.[40]

In 'Aŭtar' (The author, 2013), writing and religion are similarly linked, as they are also, less categorically, in 'Vieršaplioty, vieršaputy …' (Versifiers and verse fetters …, 2013) where poetry is said to give the writer life: 'Верш — жывільная вада' (Poetry is life-giving water, Kdr, 87). Here is the poem's final stanza:

> Вершаплёты, вершапуты —
> Вершы — мой сьвяты закутак.
> Вершам да жыцьця прыкутай
> Застаюся бачыць смутак.[41]

Religion is ubiquitous in Hluchoŭskaja's verse. It is closely linked in her mind not only to creation but to all beauty, as may be seen in a very short poem, 'Zabiraje nas viečnaje Charastvo …' (We are seized by eternal Beauty …, 2013), in which the word for Beauty is rhymed with that for the birth of Christ:

> Забірае нас вечнае Хараство,
> Адмаўляе ціхая памяць.
> Застаецца адно на зямлі Раство,
> Застаецца ўзьлятаць ці падаць.[42]

---

[39] 'He says, once you drink it — / it will turn out as a fairytale and not a story …' (Kdr, 13).
[40] 'To what my ridiculousness / Will perhaps lead gloomy lunacy? / It is simply peace in my soul. / The ruling forces are of belief and art' (Kdr, 82).
[41] 'Versifiers and verse fetters — / Poetry is my sacred corner. / Chained to life by poetry / I am left to see sadness' (Kdr, 87).
[42] 'We are seized by eternal Beauty, / Quiet memory declines. / The birth of Christ alone remains on the earth, / All that remains is to soar upwards or to fall' (Kdr, 104).

Christ is more than once depicted as a poor beggar struggling through snow, for example, in 'Pryśviatki. Rastvo. Čakajem Boha …' (Christmas Eve. We await God …, 2010). In 'Bielaja pieśnia' (White song, 2012) He is even suspected of casting an evil eye on the naive population (Kdr, 74), whilst in 'Pra Boha' (About God, 2013) the poet also shows how the Deity often remains unrecognized:

Пра Бога
Сустрэнем, калі Ён ёсьць.
Пабачым, якім Ён будзе.
А зараз — навокал людзі.
І кожны ідзе наскрозь.[43]

In Hluchoŭskaja's 'Malitva' (Prayer, 2013) for once the intensive repetition does not automatically seem inappropriate, as it does in many other of her poems especially, for instance, 'Anatomija ŭ pozirku' (Anatomy under inspection, 2013) and 'Šar' (The ball, 2011).

At this stage may be mentioned the poet's four attempts at writing triolets, the best probably being 'Sad' (The garden, 2012) about the Garden of Eden; the others are devoted to the Belarusian poet Ciotka (pen name of Alaiza Paškievič, 1876–1916), to the subject of stinging nettles, and to writing about love or lamenting one's lot.

Unlike some, even most, young Belarusian poets, Hluchoŭskaja writes relatively little about love. In 'S.A.D.' (2011) she notes her friend's general competence and musical prowess, but feels inadequate by comparison:

І мне слоў было мала. Мне слоў — да цябе — не хапіла.
І звалілася зь лесвіцы вершаў, нібы з хмарачоса.[44]

In another poem of the same year and with the same title, however, she writes about growing and leaving him behind, as she rises under the wings of love and Chagall (Kdr, 114). In 'Na žaľ' (Regrettably, 2010) she finds less spirituality than eroticism in her man, whilst in 'P.K.' (2013) different male virtues are enumerated, although the last line is deliberately bathetic: 'Як шкада, што мы не разам …' (What a pity we are not together …, 2013).

Exoticism in Hluchoŭskaja's verse is exemplified in a sea-crocodile, gnome, and a dancing stork; and many distant places are introduced in 'Paŭdniovy son' (A southern dream, 2013), although at the end she returns to earth, so to speak, with religion. In 'Rusalka' (The mermaid, 2011), however, we are more in the realm of folklore, and, indeed, some of the poet's characteristic repetition may be partly associated with folk verse. Here are the last two stanzas in which the mermaid is encouraged not to sing but to go to a most unattractive 'abandoned land':

---

[43] 'About God // We shall meet Him, if He exists. / We shall see what He is like. / But now there are people all around. / And each of them walks straight through Him' (Kdr, 121).
[44] 'And I had too few words. I did not have enough words — for you. / And I fell from the ladder of poems, as if from a skyscraper' (Kdr, 109).

Ты, русалка, не сьпявай, не сьпявай:
Кліча вецер у закінуты край,

Дзе цябе чакае нехта жывы
Паміж зёлак ды атрутнай травы.[45]

Finally, two examples may be mentioned of historical imagination, rather than exoticism. The feeling of fear during the period of the Molotov-Ribbentrop pact, with continuing political repression, and atrocities against the Jews is well represented in 'Vosień tryccać dziaviataha' (Autumn 1939, 2012). In 'Pa darozie …' (On the road …, 2011) she imagines seeing 'Comrade Napoleon' visiting a market during his retreat from Moscow.

It is too early to say what future awaits Kaciaryna Hluchoŭskaja, and whether she will, indeed, become a 'real poetess', but her first book, although rather uneven, displays energy and imagination, and, despite the frequent references to death and madness in her verse, she should have many years ahead.

Čumakova

Religion is clearly important for Hanna Čumakova. Her very imaginative verse is personal and romantic, though her poems about love often introduce elements of frustration and bitterness. Ancestors, parents and childhood as well as nature, especially autumn (often personified) all figure frequently in her verse.. Despite having been in her late twenties when her first book was published, elegiac notes are not infrequent in her poems, most of which are in rhyme and with many repeated lines, like refrains. She responds actively to some earlier Belarusian writers, while wordplay helps to lighten the tone of her work.

Her debut collection, *Moj aniol pryśniŭ mianie …* (My angel dreamed of me …, 2012), is introduced by a rather fanciful piece, 'Ad aŭtara da čytača i naadvarot' (From the author to the reader and vice versa), in which she describes her verse as a kaleidoscope. The first poem, 'Try slovy' (Three words) ends with them: faith, hope and love. The last five lines establish their significance:

Блізкія словы,
Боскія словы —
Шэпча іх сэрца маё зноў і зноў —
Тры ахоўнікі, тры анёлы —
ВЕРА, НАДЗЕЯ, ЛЮБОЎ. (Март, 7)[46]

---

[45] 'Do not sing, mermaid, do not sing: / The wind is calling you to an abandoned land, // Where some living person is waiting for you / Amid the dried-up sods and poisoned grass' (Kdr, 16).
[46] 'Close words. / Divine words — / My heart whispers them again and again — / Three guardians, three angels — / FAITH, HOPE, LOVE' Numerical references preceded by Март are to *Moj aniol pryśniŭ mianie …*

Several poems throw more light on exactly what Čumakova understands by these key words. Religion is reflected in many of them, including the rather whimsical 'Moj Boh znajšoŭ mianie na vulicy …' (My God found me in the street …), in which she longs for living water and finds drips from a gutter far from ideal (Мартр, 8). Also unusual is an untitled verse with an eloquently explanatory first line: 'Ja chvareju na nieba, jak liudzi chvarejuć na hryp …' (I am sick with heaven, like people are sick with the 'flu …). 'Kali navat nie pračynajucca' (When they are not even waking up) is a humorous poem about sleepy angels going to work. The poem that gives the book its title, 'Moj aniol pryśniŭ mianie …' (My angel saw me in a dream …), addresses her angel in a very familiar, intimate manner. Here are the last ten lines:

> Ты прабач мне, анёл, што ад ног тваіх збалелых і стамлёных
> Кроў на камянях,
> Мо лягчэй другім анёлам,
> Але Богам заклінаю — не пакінь мяне
> Ды не памяняй.
> Ты вярні маёй матулі яе ўсмешкі, яе вочы,
> Ночы без трывог.
> Дай руку мне і пакрочым
> Можа, з песняй, можа, моўчкі
> Шмат яшчэ дарог …[47]

Finally may be mentioned her 'VIERš dlia čytańnia' (A poem for reading)[48] in which there is much wordplay on the relationship between the Belarusian words for belief and for poetry (Мартр, 16–17). Most of the poem, however, is about frustrated love, a topic that is treated later.

As in several other poets' work, hope overlaps with religion semantically in Čumakova's verse. As for love, there is a world of difference between divine love (agape) and physical love (eros). Although the former is clearly the one in the poet's 'trinity', nonetheless she has written a number of strong poems about the difficulties and joy of human relations. Before turning to them, however, her fondness for wordplay found in 'VIERš dlia čytańnia' above is also demonstrated in two poems making play with the word 'love' (kachańnie): 'Choraša da boliu …' (Painfully good …) centres on kachaju (I love), whilst an entertainingly ludic poem, 'Latareja kachańnia' (The lottery of love), examines the word 'kachańnie' in many possible variations, ranging from coughing to guffawing, mocking or protesting; it may be public or private, unexpected or a cry for help. At the end

---

[47] 'Forgive me, angel that from your sick and tired legs / there is blood on the stones, / Perhaps it is easier for other angels, / I entreat in the name of God — do not abandon me / And don't change me. / Bring back to me the smile of my mother and her eyes, / Nights without tribulations. / Give me your hand and let us walk on / Perhaps with a song, and perhaps silently / Many more roads lie ahead …' (Мартр, 68).

the poet observes that they are all thrown into the same sack and wonders who
will choose which:

Латарэя кахання

Ёсць КА-Ха-Ка-Ханне,
              як кашаль,
Калі ловіш пачуцці, бы снег
Вуснамі
      Як дзеткі,
Ёсць ка-Ха-Ха-ХАнне
              Шырока-размашнае,
Быццам вясёлы смех,
Ці каХЕ-Ханне —
              смяшок здзеклівы.

Ёсць каханНЕ-НЕ-НЕ — адмова
І каханНЕ! — пратест,
Каханне — прыгожае слова,
...... — прыгожы жэст ...

Ёсць <каханне для ўсех>,
Ёсць — прыватна-элітнае.
кАХ!анне — нечаканасць,
кА-А-А!ханне — заклік аб дапамозе ...

А зараз усё ў адзін мех,
Пераблытваем,
      пераблытваем,
              пераблытваем:
                      Хто якое возьме?!.[49]

Turning from speculation to reality, Čumakova has written several poems about
love as a not always easy experience. In 'Sustreča' (A meeting) she encounters an
attractive stranger on a train, but all he wants is to do is look out of the window
(Март, 13). A different kind of personal insecurity is found in 'Ty dychaješ u
śnie, tak strymana i cicha ...' (You breathe in your sleep so restrainedly and
quietly ...), a poem that starts touchingly, until at the end suspicions arise that
the man's quiet dreams are not about the poet (Март, 14). Eyes are the key to
faithfulness in 'Dziŭny ŭ vačej kara-zialiony ...' (In your eyes there is a marvellous
browny-green ...', whilst 'Užo nie treba tvaich uśmiešak ...' (I don't need your
smiles any more ...) reflects bitter feelings about infidelity. Bitterness at parting
is related to the gloomy weather in 'Šerаść niabiosaŭ ...' (The greyness of the
skies ...), but the poems about the pain of love are the most memorable: in 'Ja
chaču być symbolem tvajho natchnieńnia ...' (I want to be a symbol of your

---

[48] This translation cannot capture the pun of the title,

[49] Март, 12. Most of this inventive poem defies translation.

inspiration …), for instance, after enumerating the ways in which the poet hopes to be a symbol for her lover, she ends by wanting to be pain (Март, 15). As in the already mentioned 'Choraša da boliu …' pleasure and pain seem inseparable, but in another strong poem, 'Z vusnaŭ ŭ vusny …' (From lips to lips …) the vocabulary is unremittingly that of violence and death:

З вуснаў ў вусны —
Прымаю кахання атруту
Першы раз і апошні, напэўна, ў жыцці …

Да цябе як да крыжа свайго я прыкута,
I, не маючы права прасіць <Адпусці!..>,
Бы фанатка, сваёй захапляюся пакутай …[50]

Love for her family and particularly her grandmother is expressed in 'Lia babulinaj chaty' (Near granny's house) and, very touchingly, in 'Pamiaci babuli' (To granny's memory):

Памяці бабулі

Я цябе не забыла яшчэ,
Бо калісь не паспела запомніць
Усе змаршчынкі ля родных вачэй,
Вечарова-стамлёную постаць …

Пах палынны тваіх валасоў
Успамінаю я часам і зараз,
Калі сніцца апоўначы сон:
Ты цішком уваходзіш у залу.

Сядзеш побач …
    — Твой вобраз жыццём
Быццам дыхае ўвесь у сутонні …
I фізічна амаль пачуццё
Да шчакі дакранання далоні.[51]

Like many young Belarusian poets, Čumakova responds especially warmly to autumn, albeit without romanticising it. In the poem 'Vosień, što padobna na miane …' (Autumn that is like me …) she associates herself very closely with this season. Here are the last five lines:

---

[50] 'From lips to lips / I take the poison of love / The first and probably last in my life … // I am fastened to you as I am to my cross, / And not having the right to say "Let me go! …" / Like a fanatic, I rejoice in my torment …' (Март, 26).
[51] 'To granny's memory // I have not forgotten you yet, / For previously I did not manage to remember/ All the wrinkles near your dear eyes, / Your tired, eventide, body … // The smell of sagebrush in your hair / I recall now and from time to time, / When at midnight I have a dream: / You come quietly into the chamber. // You sit down alongside me … — Your face breathes with life, / As if completely at dusk / And an almost physical feeling / Of your palm touches my cheek' (Март, 45).

І калі ў лістотнай мітусне
Гук знаёмых ты пачуеш
                              крокаў,

Не шукай,
            не кліч,
Бо гэта ж толькі
Восень, што падобна на мяне …[52]

Another of Čumakova's poems about autumn, 'Vosień pavieki ŭznosić …' (Autumn raises its eyelids …) has several interesting features, including its association with femininity, humdrum prose, and with the poet's teacher of Belarusian. In this connection may be mentioned, in passing, another verse, 'Vierš pašarely ad daždžoŭ …' (A poem made grey by the rains …): set against a refrain of rain, rain, rain, she converses with her slightly irritable Russian-speaking lover (Марм, 61–62). In her work the Belarusian language is not stressed by the poet, but is mentioned or implied from time to time. Here is one of her most striking verses about autumn:

Восень павекі ўзносіць,
Нібы раскрывае крылы
Шызая ад марозу
Стайка галубіная.

Восень глядзіць у вочы
І не адводзіць позірк,
Стомлены і жаночы,
Поўны будзеннай прозы.

Ветліва ўсміхаецца
Променем каляровым …
Восень — мая настаўніца
па беларускай мове.[53]

Two remarkable responses to great literary figures of the past conclude this review of Čumakova's first book. 'Adkaz Vieraniki' (Vieranika's reply) makes play with two poems by Maksim Bahdanovič (1891–1917), 'Vieranika' (1912) and his popular romance 'Zorka Vieniera ŭzyšla nad ziamlioju …' (The star of Venus has risen over the earth …, 1909–12). A more recent poet, also cut off in his prime, Anatoĺ Sys (1959–2005), is celebrated in a cycle of verses, 'Nizka vieršaŭ pa Anatoliu Sysu' (A cycle of poems on the subject of Anatoĺ Sys). The first of

---

[52] 'And when in the bustle of foliage / You will hear the sound of familiar steps, / Do not search, do not cry out, / For that is only / Autumn that is like me …' (Марм, 64).

[53] 'Autumn raises its eyebrows / Like a flock of pigeons // Spreading their wings / Blue-grey from the frost. // Autumn looks into your eyes / And does not avert its gaze, / Weary and feminine, / Full of humdrum prose. // Smiling politely / In a colourful ray … / Autumn is my teacher / of the Belarusian language' (Марм, 60).

them, 'Kali chočaš ubačyć imhnieńnie ...' (When you want to catch sight of a moment ...) is about various kinds of perception. The second is a dialogue between mother and son as she tries to explain dreams; the third is a triptych about the forest: 'Zamova' (Incantation), 'Malitva' (Prayer) and 'Kalychanka' (Cradle song). The last poem of the cycle is 'Rekviem pa Sysu' (A requiem for Sys):

Рэквіем па Сысу

Сыс — птах дзіўны
Лічыць гадзіны
Сваёй Радзімы.

Сочыць з пагорку:
Шчасця колькі?
—На адно пёрка ...
А колькі мірыцца
З волей чужынца?
—На адно крыльца ...

Сыс — птах белы.
Беднае цела
Скруха з'ела ...
Незразумелы ...
Непажаданы ...
Амэн.[54]

Hanna Čumakova is a stimulating and inventive poet whose rhyming verse avoids any sense of routine, and whose imagery is fresh and often original. She is one of the most interesting young poets to come from the Homiel region.

Baranoŭski

Aleś Baranoŭski is a prolific poet and scholar who apart from his three first verse collections, in 2011 published a remarkably early critical study of poetry by the influential Homiel writer Nina Škliarava.

His first verse collection, *Čujnaje akno* (A sensitive window, 2008), shows youthful talent as well as occasional signs of technical inexperience; some half dozen of the best poems from it, however, were reprinted in his third collection. From the start he appears interested in classical form, and *Čujnaje akno* contains six triolets, not all of them regular, on themes including religion, silent pain, and

---

[54] A requiem for Sys // Sys is a wonderful bird / He counts the hours / Of his Fatherland. // He watches closely from a little hill: / How much happiness is there? / Enough for a little feather ... / And how much reconciliation is possible / With the will of an alien? / Enough for one little wing ... // Sys is a white bird. / His poor body / Was eaten up by grief ... / Not understood. / Undesirable ... / Amen' (Март, 52).

spring; one of his most convincing attempts at this form will be cited later. Although World War II ended over forty years before the poet was born, he none the less seems able to empathize with those who suffered in it, even to the extent of calling one of his later poems on this subject 'Uspamin pra vajnu' (Memory of war). 'Rekvijem' (Requiem) makes play with the oft repeated 'statistic' 'кожны чацвёрты' (each fourth one), referring to the appalling Belarusian casualties of the conflict, and other poems include 'Nieviadomamu saldatu …' (To the unknown soldier …), on the same subject, 'Vitaju' (I salute), 'List u 42-hi' (A letter to 1942), and a particularly vivid evocation of the period: 'Na biezdarožžy, doždž i niedarod …' (On impassable roads, rain and failed crops …), which concludes in tones that recall Biadulia and Kupala writing about the destructive horror of World War I:

> Тут падаў попел на траву з расой
> І чорная ў рацэ вада стаяла,
> Ды белаю сваёю смерць касой
> Жыццё, як жыта буйнае, зразала. (Ča, 29)[55]

One of the poems reprinted later is 'Slovy śviatyja — Radzima i Maci …' (Sacred words — Native land and Mother …) whose opening lines introduce two of the main themes of this collection:

> Словы святыя — Радзіма і Маці,
> Як той агеньчык, што цепліцца ў хаце …[56]

Another patriotic poem, 'Rodnaja akienca …' (Dear little window), begins and ends with the same four lines:

> Роднае акенца,
> Родная зямля …
> Родненькі куточак —
> Беларусь мая.[57]

In another early verse, however, 'Ja viarnusia' (I shall return), he expresses disquiet at his country's lack of true independence:

> За якія зямныя грахі
> Мы не самі свой лёс выбіраем?[58]

---

[55] 'Here ash fell on the grass with the dew / And black water stood in the river, / And death with its white scythe / Cut down life, like ripe corn' Numerical references preceded by Ča are to *Čujnaje akno*.

[56] 'Sacred words — Native land and Mother, / Like that little fire that gives warmth at home …' (Ča, 41).

[57] 'Dear little window / Dear land… / Dear little corner — / My Belarus' (Ča, 42).

[58] 'For what earthly sins / Do we not choose our own destiny?' (Ča, 9).

The poet's mother and family form the subject of several verses, where remembering the past is given considerable emphasis, for example in 'Raściom i zabyvajem pra baćkoŭ …' (We grow up and forget our parents …, Ča, 12) and 'Pryśviačajecca pamerlaj babuli' (Dedicated to my deceased granny, Ča, 13); other poems clearly value the present time, good examples being: 'Maci, maja, maci …' (Mother, my mother …) and 'Ništo ŭ dušy nie pakidaje viečny žar …' (Nothing in my soul leaves eternal heat …), which ends thus:

> Нішто так моцна не пячэ мне сэрца,
> Як матчына сляза.[59]

Near the end of this brief survey of Baranoŭski's first book may be mentioned his natural introspection and desire to understand life, reflected in poems such as 'Nie zhinie viera, žyć nanova …' (Faith will not perish, to live again …) that ends with the following stanza:

> Няхай уяўную сапраўднасць
> Хаваць недзе ў глыбіні.
> Ідзе, як цень, услед рэальнасць,
> Мані сабе, ці не мані.[60]

Baranoŭski seems to associate writing with pain, but this theme does not dominate his first book. Relatively optimistic are 'Chto adkaža, što takoje ščaście?..' (Who can say what happiness is? …) and 'Lietucieńnie' (Daydreaming), reprinted in *Dyjamientavy nimb dlia aniola*, a hymn to spring and love.

The last verse, 'Pieršy pacalunak' (First kiss), also reprinted, is a relatively mature poem that is not only an acknowledgment of youthful inexperience but also an expression of awareness that time passes all too quickly, as may also be seen in the last stanza of 'Adšumiela lahodnaje lieta …' (The noise of sweet summer has passed …):

> Лістота на дол ападае,
> Каб потым пупышкай ажыць.
> Юнацтва заўжды не хапае,
> І час, як шалёны, бяжыць.[61]

*

The lyrics in *Viaśliar* (The oarsman 2010), like those in *Čujnaje akno*, are in seemingly easy rhyme and with relatively simple lexicon, although, as before, the

---

[59] 'Nothing warms my heart so strongly / As my mother's tear' (Ča, 38).
[60] 'Let us keep imaginary genuineness / Somewhere deep down. / Behind us reality follows like a shadow, / Whether we lie to ourselves or don't lie' (Ča, 23).
[61] 'Leaves fall to the ground, / In order to come to life again as buds. / Youth is never long enough, / And time runs on, like a madman' (Ča, 51).

influence of Russian is occasionally felt in the language. Many poems express straightforward philosophical ideas, frequently but not always, by means of contrasts. An example of Baranoŭski's poetic ambition is a short poem that travels from knowledge to belief, using only words that begin with 'v': 'Viedać, vahacca, vandravać vakol vohnišča …' (To know, to ponder, to stroll around the bonfire …). As will be seen, nature is important to this poet who unfailingly associates himself with it, but his creative life seems painful or at least boring, judging by two lines from the second stanza of 'Ja sydu, nikudy nie padziecca …' (I shall go away, there is nothing to be done …):

> Хтось назваў мой лёс няйначай казкай …
> Толькі казка гэта цераз боль. (V, 4)[62]

In one of the first poems he appears to travel boldly, 'Ja plyvu ŭsio daliej … biez ahliadki …' (I sail ever further … without looking back …), but another description of searching for freedom over bloody snow is a quest in which he seems to have little confidence: 'Šliach na plyni stračanaj sensaŭ …' (A path on the current of lost feelings …) shows some of Baranoŭski's early philosophy, with the characteristic juxtaposition of opposites (for example, benefactors and playboys). In the second stanza the poet considers, by contrasts again, ways of making decisions; death and memory are chains. In the last stanza, which begins with a striking phrase, he calls on the Almighty to grant salvation. Here is the grim first stanza and the last one:

> Шлях на плыні страчаных сэнсаў,
> Часам размыты і зрокам нябачны.
> Сярод дабрадзецеляў і павесаў
> Прорвай глыбокаю — неабсяжнасць.
>
> [...]
>
> Ілжывы хаос … Не адчуць разумення …
> Рука пераксціцца ў трохперсці адвечным …
> Нябесны Ўладар, ты пашлі нам збавенне,
> Не дай пад нагамі травою палегчы.[63]

Not all binary elements in Baranoŭski's first book are contrasted. For instance, the first poem expresses his deeply held conviction: 'Pačatak pačynaejcca z kanca …' (The beginning begins from the end …).[64] A simpler example is the

---

[62] 'Somebody called my fate a real fairy story... / Only this fairy story is through pain' Numerical references preceded by V are to *Viasliar*.

[63] 'A path on the current of lost feelings, / Sometimes washed away and invisible to the eye. / Between benefactors and scoundrels / There is a deep abyss — a boundlessness. // [...] // Perfidious chaos … There is no understanding to be found … / I cross myself with three fingers in the age-old manner … / Heavenly Lord, send us salvation, / Do not allow it to lie like grass under our feet' (V, 6–7).

[64] This idea was also expressed in Aŭčyńnikava's *Ad začynienaj bramy*, p. 30.

already mentioned: 'Slovy śviatyja — Radzima i maci …' (Sacred words — My native land and mother …).

In 'I ŭpadzie apošni list pad nohi …' (And when the last leaf falls under my feet …), a particularly melodious verse, the poet, ever close to nature, comes to dream of himself as a wind:

> І, можа быць, аднойчы мне прысніцца,
> Як я бязвольна гушкаю арэлі,
> Па нечай волі стаўшы цёплым ветрам,
> А раніцай знікаю туманамі.
> Даруйце мне, мядзвяныя пакосы,
> Бо не на вас я ўпаду расою.
> І гіне ліст апошні пад абцасам,
> Што ўчора гушкаў
> Разам з ветрам неба.[65]

The last two lines in *Viaśliar*, from a short poem, 'Nie adtajala noč ad zimy …' (The night had not thawed from the winter …), show a certain optimistic resolution:

> Чым мацней нас сціскаюць трывогі,
> Тым мацнейшымі робімся мы.[66]

*

Interesting as *Viaśliar* undoubtedly is, Baranoŭski's third book is more ambitious in scope and poetic technique, especially imagery. *Dyjamientavy nimb dlia aniola* (A diamond nimbus for an angel, 2012) also shows the poet's quest to discover his place in the universe and more persistent attempts to understand the world. Heaven and God play a larger role, as does, in its various aspects, nature (often personified and in a close relationship with the poet). He frequently seems to be opening doors and windows to nature, and there are many natural images, especially of water, not least in his tortured love poems.

The eponymous angel appears in the opening verse, 'Čorny volas, byccam voran …' (A black hair like a raven …), in which a hair pulled out of his head leads the lyric hero to thoughts of inescapable fate:

> Як бальшак узімку голы
> Сцялася душа (Dna, 3).[67]

---

[65] 'And perhaps one day I shall dream, / How I involuntarily cause swings to sway, / Having by someone's will become a warm wind, / But in the morning I disappear in mists. / Forgive me, copper coloured meadows, / For I do not fall as dew for you. / And under some heel perishes the last leaf, / That yesterday had swayed in the sky / Together with the wind' (V, 10).
[66] 'The more strongly we are burdened by anxieties, / The stronger we become' (V, 11).
[67] 'Like a bare winter road / My soul has a covering of ice' Numerical references preceded by Dna are to *Dyjamientavy nimb dlia aniola*.

He realises the futility of cursing fate, and at the end the angel receives a halo from God. In the next poem, 'Ty ratuješ mianie i katuješ …' (You save me and torture me …) his guardian angel plays a dual role, and the lyrical hero's feelings seem very conflicted:

> Толькі думкі глыбока хаваю
> Што вядуць безупынна вайну …[68]

Loneliness, elegiac moods and the difficulties of personal relations are topoi in the work of many young Belarusian poets, including Baranoŭski; indeed love in its various aspects forms the subject of the second half of *Dyjamientavy nimb dlia aniola*. A poem addressed directly to the first of these themes, 'Adzinota' (Loneliness), personifies this feeling and towards the end introduces, characteristically for this poet, a contrast; here are the last six lines:

> То лагодай ахінаеш, то гаркотай,
> Я з табою быць магу самім сабой.
>
> Ды калі палын-травою каля плота
> Парасце мая сцяжынка на вятрах,
> Я кляну цябе, маркота-адзінота …
> Ты — чужая мне і родная сястра.[69]

Amongst poems concerned with the swift passing of time are 'Minula lahodnaja lieta …' (Sweet summer has passed …),[70] 'Pryvykli ž usio asprečvać …' (We have got used to arguing about everything …), forgetting what happened yesterday in the heat of disputes (Dna, 19), 'Adzichaciać ramonki luhavyja …' (The meadow camomile are fading …), where care for nature is related to its relevance for humans (Dna, 9), and finally the already mentioned 'Raściom i zabyvajem pra baćkoŭ …' (We grow up and forget about our parents …), of which this is the last stanza:

> А час не йдзе, а подбегам бяжыць,
> Не робіць перапынкаў, не чакае,
> Мы доўга разважаем, як нам быць.
> Замест таго каб жыць, мы разважаем …[71]

Another theme popular with young poets, to which Baranoŭski brings an individual approach, is that of inspiration and language. He believes autumn to

---

[68] 'I am only keeping deep down my thoughts / Which are conducting an endless war …' (Dna, 4).

[69] 'Now you envelop me with kindness, now with bitterness, / With you I can be myself. // For when my path in the winds / Grows over with wormwood grass near the fence, / I swear to you, sad loneliness … / You are alien to me and also my dear sister' (Dna, 6).

[70] This poem appeared in *Čujnaje akno* with a slightly different opening line.

[71] 'Time does not walk, but runs quickly, / It does not stop, does not wait, / We debate at length about what we should do. / Instead of living, we debate …' (Dna, 43).

be the best time for poets,[72] and in 'Bialiejuć liliei — apovieść' (The white lilies are a novella), about summer on the water resembling a sheet of paper, Baranoŭski clearly links his writing with nature, describing it as a confession. Here is the last of the four stanzas:

Бялеюць лілеі, як словы
На аркушы сінім вады.
Выводзіць іх тут адмыслова
Нябесны прамень залаты.[73]

A strong early poem is 'Rodnaja mova' (The native language) which, after a gloomy opening about a land overgrown with weeds and with a history that is constantly re-written, proclaims the Belarusian language as the all-important constant, and ends with three very optimistic lines:

Будзе неўміручым тваё слова.
Хай любоў мацнее з году ў год
Да пяшчотных спеваў тваіх, мова![74]

'Tryjaliet' (Triolet), a less than strict example of this classical form, calls for boldness in the use of unspoken words:

Трыялет

Баімся мы нявыказаных слоў ...
На тонкім аркушы паперы белай
Кладуцца думкі рыскаю нясмелай —
Баімся мы нявыказаных слоў ...
Расчыненыя ў сад вясновы дзверы.
Душы ты ўмела струны падбярэш —
На тонкім аркушы паперы белай
Як сведка нарадзіўся новы верш.[75]

Religion, implied in the book's title, is found in various forms, as in his earlier work. Two short examples show how he implores the Deity for help in dealing with his fate and fortune. First is a quatrain, 'Ja ramantyk u viek naš biazbožny ...' (I am a romantic in our godless age ...):

---

[72] In 'Pad kupaj adzieńnia, nie mienš ...' (Under the billowing of your clothes, no less ..., Dna, 31).

[73] 'The lilies are white, like words / On a sheet of blue water. / A heavenly golden beam / Deliberately leads them out here' (Dna, 41).

[74] 'Let your word be immortal. / May love grow stronger year by year / For your blissful melodies, language!' (Dna, 34).

[75] 'Triolet // We fear unexpressed words ... / On a thin sheet of white paper / Thoughts are put down in a timid line — / We fear unexpressed words ... / The doors are opened into a spring garden. / You skilfully pluck the strings of my soul — / On a thin sheet of white paper / As a witness, a new poem has been born' (Dna, 22).

Я рамантык у век наш бязбожны
Можа, я нарадзіўся не ў час?..
Дзякуй Богу, што ёсць спадарожны,
Ён на правым плячы у нас.[76]

In the second example, 'A ja ŭ tuman, znoŭ u tuman …' (But I am entering a fog, again into a fog …) the young lyrical hero feels himself in a mist of indecision, facing a harsh fate, and appeals for divine help. Here are the last three lines:

Дапамажы мне Бог!
Каб свет нябёс я ў сэрцы нёс
I да канца збярог.[77]

Nature is everywhere in Baranoŭski's work and this may be seen in his poems about love, which form the last section of the book, entitled, tellingly, 'Kachańnia ciarnovy vianok' (Love's crown of thorns). The first poem, 'Spliaci mne son z tryśniohu …' (Weave me a dream from cane …), is decidedly unromantic, particularly in the last stanza:

I поўню, не капейку,
Змагу я падарыць.
Не трэба толькі, дзеўка,
Мне галаву дурыць![78]

Conditions for happy love are not easy, but the lyrical hero still reveals hope in the following verse, 'Nie byvaje adnaho spatkańnia …' (There is never just one meeting …), of which this is the last stanza:

Будуць прагнуць бітвы нашы сэрцы,
Патухаць і нараджацца дні.
У жывой душы маёй — цяпельца.
Ты яго ад ветру барані.[79]

In 'Nibyta pryvid, ja biez ciabie tuliajusia …' (Without you, I wander like a ghost …) describes his feelings at having lost his beloved, a theme that is continued, embellished by much nature imagery, in 'Kupliajecca roŭnia u lužynie …' (The full moon bathes in a puddle …):

---

[76] 'I am a romantic in our godless age / Perhaps I was born at the wrong time? … / Thank God that there is a companion, / He is at our right shoulder' (Dna, 20).

[77] 'Help me, God! / That I should bear in my heart the world of the heavens / And preserve them to the end' (Dna, 48).

[78] 'And a full moon, not a copeck, / I can give you. / Only, wench, don't / Pull the wool over my eyes!' (Dna, 49).

[79] 'Our hearts will long for a battle, / Days fade and are born. / In my living soul there is a little flame. / Shelter it from the wind' (Dna, 51).

Купляецца поўня у лужыне.
Зямля ледзь не ўсыпана золатам.
Не я для цябе буду суджаным,
Ты сёння павенчана з холадам.

Альтанка ўспамінамі цешыцца
Пад лівень асенняе музыкі.
Што мы не ўдваіх — не верыцца,
А ноч расшпіліла гузікі …[80]

Love rarely seems comfortable and without regrets, as may seen in another, more regular, attempt at a popular established form, 'Tryjaliet' (Triolet), which begins 'Раскінь Таро і прадкажы мяне …' (Set out the Tarot cards and tell my fortune …, Dna, 50), or in the last two lines of 'Šum žaŭruka liacić balesna …' (The sound of the lark flies painfully …):

Чаму я зноўку спазнаю,
Што для кахання свет твой цесны?..[81]

Other poems of the same kind are 'Vy lios nie moj, ciapier Vy mnie čužaja …' (You are not my fate, now you are alien to me …) and 'Nie śni aier, jaho račulka snić …' (Do not dream of sweet flags, a little river is dreaming of them …), the latter ending thus:

Як мы свае пачуцці не хавалі,
Яны з вадой сцюдзёнаю сплылі.[82]

The last poem in the book, 'Pačućcioŭ vadzica studziona …' (The freezing water of feelings …), ends with the words of the section heading, 'Kachańnia — ciarnovy vianok', confirming the rather deperate impression of most of the poems about love.

Aleś Baranoŭski is clearly a man of varied talents and, one hopes, a happier life than the love poems imply. His verse, clearly developing, is imaginative, apparently sincere and certainly closely centred on warm feelings for Belarus and the beauty of its natural world.

Kudasava

Nasta Kudasava is a poet with a distinctly individual voice. Her first publication, *Liście maich ruk* (Leaves of my hands, 2006), was followed by *Ryby* (Fishes, 2013),

---

[80] 'The full moon bathes in a puddle. / The earth is almost covered with gold. / I shall not be judged for you, / You are today betrothed to cold. // The summer house consoles itself with memories / Under a downpour of autumn music. / That we are not a pair cannot be believed / And night has undone the buttons …' (Dna, 52).

[81] 'Why do I again realize / That for love your world is too cramped? …' (Dna, 57).

[82] 'How did we not preserve our feelings, / They floated away with the freezing water' (Dna, 58).

the latter including a selection of poems from the first book with the addition of verses written in the years 2006–2010. In addition to the themes of writing, poetry and love are elements of religion, reflections on death, and references to many exotic animals, especially wolves and whales; the seasons are important, as is her alienation from big city life. These themes are not discrete, and some poems include several of them. Kudasava's verse is partially rhymed, but assonance and alliteration play a greater part; also widespread is punning and other wordplay. The poet's emotional range seems considerable, and she is capable of drawing the reader into her own world.

Kudasava brings many varied images to describe poetry and the process of writing, as well as acknowledging directly or *en passant* other writers and Belarusian cultural figures of the past. Some of her poems are light-hearted and humorous, for example, those about her contemporaries, whilst other poems treat the creative process seriously. In the first poem of *Liście maich ruk*, 'Vyšyvala arkušy vieršami …' (I used to sew sheets of paper with poems …), one of several verses referring to handiwork, we read:

> Вышывала аркушы вершамі,
> Пакалола словамі пальцы. (Lmr, 3)[83]

The poet appears to own an intellectual cat that is fond of music and art as well as being a literary inspiration, to judge by 'Liubiš sanetnyja formy i formy biassonnych …' (You like the sonnet forms and the forms of insomniacs …). The last two lines give a strong image of their life together:

> Хай жа ясьнее душы несьмяротная форма,
> Ноч аздабляючы вершам, кагорам и хлебам![84]

In 'Moj aniol, šmatmil'jonyja my ŭ haradach …' (My angel, there are many millions of us in cities …) there seems to be no peace for the righteous, whilst the rapacious are herded to safety; poets on the other hand are compared to penguins, presumably suggesting conformity: 'Так сьпяшаюцца ў вырай паэты-пінгвіны' (The poet-penguins so hurry into migration, Lmn, 26). In another untitled poem from her second book the first two lines appear to refer to all contemporary poets, although they are hardly appropriate to Kudasava herself:

> Застаёмся нязграбнымі глупствамі мовы,
> Не зважаючы ўпарта на знакі прыпынку. (Ry, 30)[85]

---

[83] 'I used to sew sheets of paper with poems, / I pricked my fingers with words' Numerical references preceded by Lmr are to *Liście maich ruk*.

[84] 'Let the immortal form be more lucid than my soul / adorning the night with a poem, port wine and bread!' (Lmr, 24).

[85] 'We remain with the graceless stupidities of language, / Stubbornly not paying attention to punctuation marks' Numerical reference preceded by Ry are to *Ryby*.

Even more critical is the description in 'Pryŭzniatyja brovy dubrovaŭ ...' (The raised eyebrows of the groves ...) of poets as being 'built from words' and as 'troublemakers and fools' (Ry, 59). In other poems, however, including the one that gave her first book its title, 'Vierasień — vieršy ...' (September is poems ...), she describes the process of creation as far from easy.

> Верасень — вершы.
> Кастрычнік — казкі.
> Лістапад — лісты
> зь вершамі,
> казкамі,
> лісьцем маіх рук ...[86]

Amongst the beneficial results of being elsewhere, in 'Na tym baku' (On the other side), having hidden all the filth in the river Lethe, she nods to Kolas in describing her new state:

> На тым баку я спаткаю Слова,
> Жывое Слова — мой родны кут.[87]

A grim picture of the poet's lot is given in 'Paet' (The Poet), of which these are the first two lines:

> Стосы лёсаў на Вашых плячох,
> Непраходных вякоў лёхі ...[88]

In 'Lieta' (Summer) Kudasava describes her familiar sadness and pity, hoping not to succumb to the attractions of the familiar in writing verse (Ry, 49).[89] Of this there seems little danger, to judge by another poem, 'Holiemy nam zaviaščali zniamielaje ...' (The golems had bequeathed us dumbness ...), where she produces an extremely striking image: 'вершастваральным акордам залеваў' (of downpours like a verse-creating chord, Ry, 47).

Also imaginative are Kudasava's tributes and references to creative figures of the past: among them are Verlaine, who is linked to autumn, mulled wine and absinthe (Lmr, 60); Salamieja, the celebrated eighteenth-century traveller, writer and lover, described with much word play (Lmr, 36);[90] and Bahdanovič who is acknowledged through his poem 'Stracim-liebiedź (The doomed swan, 1916) in a verse addressed to her beloved river Dnieper, 'Da Dniapra' (To the Dnieper, Ry, 33). Finally may be mentioned a pun on the name of one of her favourite Russian poets, Marina Tsvetaeva:

---

[86] 'September is poems. / October is fairy tales. / November is letters / with poems, / with fairy tales, / with leaves of my hands ...' (Lmr, 49).

[87] 'On the other side I shall find the Word, / the Living Word — my native nook' (Lrm, 59).

[88] 'Bundles of fates on your shoulders, / Underground passages of impenetrable ages ...' (Lmr, 65).

[89] See also, infra, 'Da jasnaha Styksu' (To the bright Styx, Lmr, 31), for play on the word *lieta*.

[90] Another poem rich in word play is 'Lies' (The forest, Lmr, 56).

ЗаМАРЫНАваная Вашымі вершамі,
мая першая[91]

Kudasava's poems about love give only a fleeting impression of her feelings: many of the earlier poems reflect apparently untroubled intimate relations, although several later verses express vividly the potential pain of love. This is prominent in a poem rich in assonance, 'Bol' (Pain), of which these are the last ten lines:

Боль
прасочваецца
праз падушку,
праз душу.
Пішу
рознае
ў запозьненых вершах ...
Навошта
ты
лепшы?[92]

In great formal contrast is an impassioned yet somewhat sad poem written in uncharacteristically long lines, 'Jak hareli daloni, jak vusny chapali pavietra, kab chapila ...' (How my palms burned, how my lips grasped for air, seeking a sufficiency ...):

Як гарэлі далоні, як вусны хапалі паветра, каб хапіла,
каб выпіць да дна гэты роспачны крок,
як стаяла пад небам твая прагнарукая Федра
і спазняўся з адказам пакрыўджаны стомлены Бог,
як у трызненне белых ваўкоў закрадаліся жніўні,
як пад вокнамі гучна здзіўляўся збянтэжаны люд —
я пра ўсё раскажу табе, мілы, а ты раскажы мне,
як бурштынавым ранкам зямлю абуджае <люблю>,
як штовечар ты слухаеш зорак маўкліва сола
і вышукваеш спадчыну поўні ў чырвоным віне,
як дагэтуль ёсць толькі надзея, прыгоства і голас,
і сусвет па-ранейшаму — цуд, але ўжо без мяне ...[93]

---

[91] 'MARINAted by your poems, / my first one' (Lmr, 35).

    Also worth mentioning here is 'Marku Šahalu. Ad "Adzinoty"' (To Marc Chagall. From 'Loneliness', Lmr, 55).

[92] 'Pain / seeps / through my pillow / through my soul / I write / various things / in belated poems ... / Why / are you / better?' (Lmr, 29).

[93] 'How my palms burned, how my lips grasped for air, seeing a sufficiency, / to drink to the bottom this step of despair, / as stood beneath the sky your Phaedra with eager arm / and offended, weary God was late with a reply, / as, like a delirium of white wolves, Augusts crept up / as under the windows the greatly disturbed people expressed loud surprise — / I shall tell it all to you, my dearest, and you tell me, / how the word "I love you" / will awake the earth on an amber morning, / how every evening you listen to the silent solo of the stars / and you seek

Far more reassuring, despite its use of the formal version of 'you', is a poem about the happy exclusiveness of love described with a charming image, 'Sonca ŭzychodzić nad Vašym pliačom …' (The sun rises over your shoulder …). Here are the last three lines:

> Выспаліся.
> І на пару згрызаем
> Ранішні яблык, каханнем памыты …[94]

The reference to the 'delirium of white wolves' above is far from unique in Kudasava's poetry, and there is a sympathetic picture of a female wolf in 'Toĺki tuliajecca i nie prytulicca …' (It only runs around without finding a refuge …), describing the animal's wild beauty in the first two lines of the last stanza:

> Згрэбная … срэбная — выклік і голад.
> Вочы растуць ад вясёлкавых кропляў …[95]

In 'mroiva noču …' (dreaming at night …, Lmr, 58) both the poet's dreams and her voice are described as vulpine, whilst in 'Navahodniaje' (A new year poem) that discusses Plautus's tag, 'homo homini lupus est', she refers to herself as wailing like a wolf from grief. Another poem, '… i pasypliucca radki …' (and lines will scatter …, Ry, 36), features a wolf, hares and a whale, and 'Raźvitańnie z Radzimaj' (Farewell to the Native Land) describes elephants flying from India into migration. A final element in this menagerie is in '… Kab naš razmach nie pieraboĺšaŭ …' (… May our wing-span not exceed …, Ry, 60), where fish in the Dnieper are said to swim in *vers libre*.

Elegiac moods, as has been already noted, are far from uncommon in the work of young Belarusian poets, but Kudasava brings a generally light touch to poems about death, which is not to say that there are no gloomy notes in her work. In 'Dadomu' (Homeward) and 'Horad usich čužych…' (The city of all the alienated …) it appears to be urban life that is the main problem. In the former, the poet seems very uncomfortable with where she lives, as is clear from the opening seven lines:

> Дваццаць шэрых гадоў праплылі
> непрытомна.
> На агромністай гэтай зямлі
> мне бяздомна.

---

for the heritage of the full moon in red wine, / as up to now there is only hope, beauty and voice, / and the universe as it always was is a wonder, but now without me …' (Ry, 14).
[94] 'We have had a good sleep. /And both together bite into / a morning apple that has been washed by love' (Ry, 16).
[95] 'Elegant … silver — a challenge and hunger. / Its eyes grow from drops of a rainbow …' (Lmr, 44).

Мне бязладна, бязмэтна, бязь месца, бязь зьместу.
На бязьмежнай зямлі не жыве
маё места.[96]

'Horad usich čužych ...' (A town of all alien people ...) is not as grim as the opening line might suggest, but at the end she asks, in a phrase reminiscent of Maiakovskii's 'Vo ves' golos' (At the top of my voice, 1929–30),[97] why her gift has stood on her throat:

Дар мой, скажы. Чаму
Ты мне стаў на горла?[98]

In 'Zahartuj i vyratuj ...' (Harden and save ...) she appears to anticipate death by cremation, calmly anticipating that flowers will grow from her ashes (Ry, 15). The adjective applied to the river of death is unusual in 'Da jasnaha Styksu ...' (To the bright river Styx ...), and the poet enjoys punning on the river's other name, Lethe, which in Belarusian is homonymous with the word for summer *lieta*. At the beginning of the second stanza she refers to her sadness (*sum*) and pity (*žaĺ*); the first of these words is also used in its Latin form for punning in the following minimalist poem:

Sum —
Сум[99]

Finally in this review of Kudasava's references to mortality is 'Bielaja' (White), a strongly assonantal poem that ends with the following line, rejecting or postponing the idea of death: 'бялела балела але не памерла я' (I whitened sickened but did not die, Lmr, 69).

Kudasava's religious faith is unobtrusive but ubiquitous in her work. A poem 'Malitva' (A prayer) ends on a negative note, but her generally positive views are more common, and are expressed concisely in the title of 'U biaźvier'i — jak u trunie!' (Lack of faith is like being in a coffin!, Lmr, 13). Her responses to the seasons of nature are richly worded and far from conventional, one good example being an unusual poem on the difficulties of receiving spring, 'Spatkańnie z viasnoj' (A meeting with spring), which ends by acclaiming autumn:

Восень —
вось
мая панацэя![100]

---

[96] 'Twenty grey years have floated by / unconsciously. / On this huge earth / I am homeless. / I am confused, aimless, without a city, without content. / On the boundless earth there is / no place for me' (Lmr, 60).

[97] Vladimir Maiakovskii, *Polnoe sobranie sochinenii v tridtsati tomakh*, Moscow, 1958–61, vol. 10 (1958), pp. 280–81.

[98] 'Tell me, my gift, why / have you stood on my throat?' (Ry, 57).

[99] 'I am — / Sadness' (Lmr, 14).

[100] 'Autumn — / that is / my panacea!' (Lmr, 45–47 [47]).

Kudasava has a truly feminine poetic sensibility, often choosing women as her heroes, including Lilith and Eve, as well as paying homage to prominent female literary figures. Her two books, rich in imagery, word play and a wide range of themes, show considerable promise.

CHAPTER 3

~

Protest at Repression
and Alienation

A substantial number of young poets express open dismay or anger at various contemporary phenomena, ranging from the crushing of political demonstrations and the stream of disinformation from state television to the continuing detention of political prisoners, as well as a wide range of other perceived and real grievances. Those relating to the parlous state of the language will be discussed in the next chapter. The most critically outspoken poets are mainly, but not exclusively, men and from the capital. The last poet here, Nasta Mancevič, is included not so much for her own protest as for the virulent reaction her open declaration of lesbianism aroused in conservative Belarus.

Koŭhan

Siarhiej Koŭhan's early life was truly dramatic. Born in Russia in 1984, he was brought up in a children's home, but when he came of age and left it, he discovered that the flat that had been bequeathed to him was in the hands of Russian criminals, who beat him up (to discourage any future attempts to claim the property), and then deposited him by the roadside near Minsk. He was rescued by a good-hearted Belarusian family, who took him in until he could find his feet in what had become his new country. By the time he was 29 Koŭhan had become leader of a group called 'Anioly' (Angels) whose aim was, and is, to rescue lost and abused persons. In 2002 he published an interesting book, *Pieršyja kroki: Zryfmavanyja dumki pra minulaje i sučasnaje* (First steps: Rhymed thoughts about the past and the present). This slim book of verse is preceded by an exhortation to use and defend the Belarusian language at every opportunity, since language and knowledge of national history are key to its readers' true citizenship and pride in their country.

Koŭhan's poems are short loosely rhymed reflections on the themes of patriotism, national pride, freedom, heritage, folk customs, nature, family and children. His verse is sincere rather than strikingly original, except perhaps in its political boldness. The first poem, 'Dačcie' (To my daughter, Pk, 5)[1] is very personal and rather charming in its hope that with his warmth she will turn from a bud into a flower. 'Budziem žyć' (We shall live, PK, 6–7) is an impassioned cry of belief in Belarus, its history, language and heritage, despite its detractors. It is for parents to teach their children not to feel inferior to citizens of Moscow, Warsaw or London. In 'U. Karatkieviču' (To U. Karatkievič, Pk, 8) Koŭhan acknowledges the lasting inspiration of this writer to believe in the heroic history of Belarus, and hopes that one day Belarusians will become people 'of the world' and pay due homage to him.

Praise for beleaguered Belarus, which has always given itself away to alien people, is to be found in 'Dobry ty i pracavity...' (You are good and hard working ..., Pk, 11–12). These alien people include the present regime, to judge by the bold fourth stanza:

> Вось і зараз чорт вусаты —
> Ці то цыган ці то грэк —
> Беларусаў гоніць гуртам
> У мінулы "светлы век".[2]

The clear implication is that things are no better than under Stalin and Hitler.

Another powerful poem is 'U Kurapatach' (At Kurapaty, Pk, 14–15), the scene of one of Stalin's major crimes, not recognized by the present regime, where the poet writes in the last two lines of the third stanza:

> А нас як ворагаў злых, агідных,
> Пазабівалі свае ж салдаты.[3]

In 'Nie lajdak ty, i nie chlus. Ty — svabodny bielarus...' (You are neither an idler nor a liar. You are a free Belarusian ...) we find another outspoken lament on the state of the country, as may be seen from the opening stanza with its pointedly amusing last line:

> Не лайдак ты, і не хлус, Ты свабодны беларус.
> Каб далей жылось нам лепей, наматай сабе на вус:
> Не растуць грыбы на плоце, хлеб не сеюць на балоце,
> А дзяржавай кіраваць — не даярак прыціскаць.[4]

What is more, Belarusians' famous toleration has been abused:

---

[1] Numerical references preceded by Pk are to *Pieršyja kroki*.

[2] 'And now too the moustached devil — / Either a gypsy or a Greek — / Drives the Belarusians like a herd / Into a past "golden age"' (Pk, 11).

[3] 'And us, like evil, hateful enemies / Our own soldiers murdered' (Pk, 14).

[4] 'You are neither an idler nor a liar. You are a free Belarusian. / Put some thought to how we can live better in future: / Mushrooms don't grow on a fence, people don't sow on a bog, / And ruling a country is not the same as giving milkmaids a squeeze' (Pk, 16).

Талерантнасць — гэта смак, будзь на троне хоць дурак,
Усё дазволена народам. Што: насамрэч гэта так?[5]

Finally, 'Himn paŭstancaŭ' (Hymn of the insurgents, Pk, 20–21) is a stirring call
to rise up, led by the 'ancient Pahonia'.

Amongst poems celebrating Koŭhan's family and Belarusian traditions, may
be mentioned a devoted tribute to his spouse 'Majoj žoncy' (To my wife, Pk 10),
a village scene in 'Šerych chmarak roj husty …' (A thick bunch of grey
clouds …', Pk, 13), village winter celebrations in 'U chacie pad novy hod' (At
home on New Year's Eve, Pk, 17) and 'Zamiala miacielica dvary i paletki …' (A
snowstorm has covered the yards and fields…, Pk, 18). More gloomy is 'Vioska
maich prodkaŭ' (Village of my forefathers, Pk, 22) in which the poet returns to
his ancestral village where, talking to an old woman, he finds that time seems to
have stood still.

To conclude, 'Zapaviet' (Testament, Pk, 23) spells out what the poet thinks
necessary for wellbeing, ending, characteristically, on the word 'free':

Запавет

У полі — травінка,
У лесе — галінка,
Ля рэчкі — крынічка,
У небе — зарнічка.

Усё гэта — ужо свята.
Зямелька багата,
Жыві толькі годна,
Прыгожа, свабодна.[6]

Koŭhan's verse, though technically unsophisticated, is strong in content, and
he is very adept at expressing his feelings about modern Belarus and its leader
with pithy, often acerbic wit. It must be hoped that his first steps are not his last
in poetry, for such a voice is distinctive and, perhaps, even necessary at the present
time.

Kuźmienka

Žmitrok Kuźmienka is clearly an intensely patriotic poet, and the hope in the title
of his first collection, *Pakuĺ žyvu, spadziajusia …* (So long as I live, I shall hope …,
2012), reflects his longing for a better future for Belarus. Many of the poems

---

[5] 'Tolerance — it has good taste, even if there is a fool on the throne. / Everything is sanctioned
by the people. What: is it really so?' (Pk, 16).
[6] 'Testament // In the field is a little grass, / In the forest a little branch, / Near the river a little
spring, / In the sky a little star. // All this is definitely sacred. / The land is rich, / Just live
worthily, / Decently, freely' (Pk, 23).

express disillusion, bitterness and anger, whilst his strong interest in history appears to be particularly in its relationship to the present. Kuźmienka, unlike many young poets, is rather reticent in writing about himself and his experience as a creative writer.

In the opening verse, 'U labiryncie' (In a labyrinth) he describes himself as trapped by high, blank, mocking walls, and in 'Šmat hadoŭ mnie nikoli ličyć ziaziulia …' (Many are the years that the cuckoo has not counted to me …) he describes his beleaguered Belarus and, anticipating his end, hopes to preserve to his death a sparkle in his eyes, and then to lie down quietly:

Ціха легчы пад сціплы свой крыж беларускі,
Што нясу ўсё жыццё на зацятых плячах. (Pžs, 11)[7]

In 'Apakalipsis' (Apocalypse) he anticipates such a catastrophe, but more moving is a poem on the devastation of Chernobyl, 'Dušy ŭ vyraj daŭno …' (Their souls have long since migrated …), of which this is the third stanza:

Нежывая ануча
На мёртвым загнеце.
У куце адпакутаваў
Цацачны прас.
Смерцю дыхае нават
Абрывак газеты,
На якой прыпыніўся
Няўрымслівы час.[8]

Several of Kuźmienka's poems about the past go far further back than the twentieth century, and some of them compare historical Belarus with the present time. For example, in 'Prytulilisia chaty adna za adnoj lia kaściola …' (The houses one after another squeezed close to the church …), the poet looks back to the history of Navahrudak and imagines his ancient predecessors drinking from the same stream as he was doing. In another historical verse, 'Kurhany-valatoŭki' (The burial mounds of heroes), he recalls valiant deeds by the river Dźvina, and in 'Tak zdaralasia ŭ viek niespakojny…' (It happened this way in an unquiet age …), with an epigraph from Bahdanovič, the poet imagines setting off for a medieval battle led by the Pahonia, whilst 'Čarhovy dzień. Biezradasny, pusty …' (A day like any other. Joyless, empty …) describes a bleak period in the history of Polacak, where Princess Anastasija languishes in prison after a forced marriage. A particularly unromantic view of history as a whole is the vitriolic 'Historyja. Ruiny, abieliski …' (History. Ruins, obelisks …), of which the second stanza is typical:

---

[7] 'To lie down quietly under my modest Belarusian cross, / That I have borne all my life on stubborn shoulders' Numerical references preceded by Pžs are to *Pakul žyvu, spadziajusia …*
[8] 'A lifeless footcloth / Is in the dead metal of the oven. / A toy iron / In the corner continued to suffer / Death breathes / Even from a scrap of paper / On which impetuous time has paused' (Pžs, 16).

Прыдворныя віруючыя кодлы.
Уладныя князі. Аматары інтрыг.
І побач з годнасцю — атрута, здрада, подласць.
Паклёп і сцэны звернутыя ў слых.⁹

Some other poems relate to more recent history, namely Stalin's era. Such are 'Katyń. Ad slova kat …' (Katyń. From the word executioner …), 'Naviednikam Linii Stalina' (To those who experienced Stalin's Line), about the murder of the Belarusian intelligentsia and the burning of many of their manuscripts in 1937, and 'Načnyja hości' (Night guests), which describes an incident typical of Stalin's repressions.

Language is part of Belarus's historical heritage, as Kuźmienka states bitterly in 'Chto takoje skazaŭ?..' (Who said such a thing?..), repressed like so much of Belarus's heritage. In a similar vein are 'Ja maŭču …' (I am silent …), where he compares his language to a bird in difficulties (Pžs, 80), and 'Nas rabavali, dušyli i zabaraniali …' (They plundered, crushed and suppressed us …). In the latter verse the poet points out that, although this is a frequent theme in Belarusian literature, it must be repeated. Here is the closing stanza:

Нехта мне кіне папрок: "Колькі можна пра мову.
Гэта не модна. Чытач да такога прывык".
Быццам бы можа быць модным адчайнае слова,
Вырваны з сэрца ў пустэчу аглухлую крык.¹⁰

Things do not have to be so: in 'Českim budzicieliam' (To Czech builders) he praises his fellow-Slavs for the way they resurrected their language and fortified national consciousness through it.

Kuźmienka's verse is full of despairing lament and indignation at the state of his country's national life, and he often wishes that Belarusians had more national pride and could laugh at their detractors, as, for example, in 'Praśpiavajcie mnie, drevy, zadumennuju vašuju pieśniu …' (Sing to me, trees, your thoughtful song …, Pžs, 71–72). Silence of the metaphorical Belarusian national bells will lead to mockery by outsiders, as we read in 'Advučyŭsia dumać u p'janym durmanie …' (Having forgotten how to think in a drunken stupor …, Pžs, 78). Indeed, loss of memory is a major theme, expressed by the poet with great force, using the powerful image of mankurts:¹¹ 'Evaliucyja mankurctva, abo Čatyry

---

⁹ 'Seething palace factions. / Ruling princes. Lovers of intrigue. / And alongside honour are poison, treachery and baseness, / Slander and walls turned into rumour' (Pžs, 45).

¹⁰ 'Someone will cast at me the reproach: "How much more can one say about the language. / It is not fashionable. The reader has got used to such things." / As if a despairing word could be fashionable, / A cry torn from my heart and cast into a deaf desert' (Pžs, 82).

¹¹ According to a novel by Soviet Kyrgyz writer Chingiz Aitmatov, *Buranny polustanok* (*I dol'she veka dlitsia den'* (Burannyi halt [And a day lasts more than a hundred years], 1980), a mankurt was a man who has been captured into slavery and remembers nothing of his previous life.

razmovy z pramiežkami ŭ hady …' (The evolution of mankurtism, or Four conversations with gaps in the years …), suggesting ironically the disavowal of country, people and parents in turn with the bleak response: 'Добра, мой дабрадзей, я згодны' (Very well, my benefactor, I agree, Pžs, 76–77). The last stanza is particularly bitter:

—Адцурайся самога сябе —
Не бывае асобай бязроды!
Дык забудзься, што ты — чалавек,
Што і ты быў калісьці свабодным.
Стань рабом, хоць душой быў мастак,
Стань бяздумным рабом, бездакорным!

А ў адказ — безуважнае "Так"
І ківок галавой пакорны…[12]

Kuźmienka writes relatively little about his craft and position as a poet, but the danger of slavery is ever-present in his mind. In 'Handliuje navat tvorčaśiu naš śviet …' (Our age even trades in creativity …), for instance, he suggests that talent were better buried in the ground than sold into slavish captivity. Here are the first stanza and the last two lines of the poem:

Гандлюе нават творасцю наш свет,
Як і ўсім, што існуе наогул.
Вось выклаў на латок гандляр-паэт
Шаблонныя элегію, санет,
Паэму, эпітафію і оду.

[…]

Лепш закапаць свой талент у зямлю,
Чым запрадаць у рабскую няволю.[13]

Four lines from the middle of another poem, 'Stol. Pliama žoŭtaha śviatla …' (The table. A puddle of yellow light …) expand further on Kuźmienka's view of venal poetry:

Вядома, мог за чыстую манету
Стаць творцам панегірыкаў і од,
Але як быць прыслужнікам-паэтам,
Калі ў пакутах гіне твой народ.[14]

---

[12] 'Disavow your very self / The stateless cannot be individuals! / So forget that you are a human, / That once you too were free. / Become a slave, although in your soul you were an artist, / Become an unthinking, irreproachable slave! // And in reply comes an indifferent "Yes" / And a submissive nod of the head …' (Pžs, 77).

[13] 'Our age even trades in creativity, / As in everything that exists. / Now the trader-poet has put on the counter / His hackneyed elegy, sonnet, / Narrative poem, epitaph and ode. // […] // It is better to bury your talent in the ground / Than to sell it into slavish captivity' (Pžs, 33).

[14] 'Of course, for cash I could / Become the creator of panegyrics and odes, / But how can you be a lickspittle-poet / When your people is perishing in torment' (Pžs, 36).

The poet feels himself a neglected prophet, and in 'Kudy b šliachi ziamnyja ni viali ...' (Wherever the earthly paths might lead ..., Pžs, 38–39) he rephrases the famous words of Matthew 13. 57: 'A prophet is not without honour, save in his own country'. In 'Havorać časam tak, što prosta tlumna ...' (Sometimes they talk simply incomprehensibly ...) the poet rails against the way anybody who expresses national consciousness is immediately labelled a 'nationalist' (Pžs, 74). In 'Nas dzialili zdaŭna ...' (We were divided up long ago ...) he seems to rejoice in being called an *adščapieniec* (renegade). Here, for example, is the third stanza:

> Адшчапенец ... Ну, так.
> Бо змаглі "адшчапіцца" адкрыта
> Ад дрымучага здзеку,
> Нахабнай казённай хлусні.
> Лепей быць адшчапенцам,
> Чым спаць халуём пры карыце
> I ніколі ў жыцці
> Нават сноў аб свабодзе не сніць.[15]

A final example of the poet's disgust is 'Skroź i zaŭždy bielarus vinavaty ...' (The Belarusian is always thoroughly blamed ...), which begins:

> Скрозь і заўжды беларус вінаваты
> Ў тым, што насмеліўся выбіцца з хаты.[16]

After enumerating some of the many regimes that have oppressed and imprisoned Belarusians, from the Russians and Poles to Hitler and Stalin, he ends with three telling lines about the fact that it is not only foreigners who repress his countrymen:

> Толькі хто мог бы такое прадбачыць,
> Што давядзецца сядзець яму хутка
> За Беларусь у турме беларускай.[17]

Quite different from the poems cited above are a number of verses about the poet's youth and family. 'Ja pomniu addaliena dzień vieraśniovy ...' (I distantly remember a day in September ..., Pžs, 23), for example, is dedicated to his first teacher of Belarusian, for him inextricably linked with the sound of a cockerel in the nearby market. 'Tut dvaccać hadoŭ tamu ...' (Here twenty years ago ...) recalls his grandparents' house, and another poem, 'Pojdziem, siadziem na

---

[15] 'Renegade... well, so be it. / For people could break off openly / From the ancient mockery, / The brazen official lies. / It is better to be a renegade / Than to sleep like a lackey by the trough / And never in your life / Even have dreams of freedom' (Pžs, 42).

[16] 'The Belarusian is always thoroughly blamed / For the fact that he dared to break out of his house' (Pžs, 91).

[17] 'But who could have possibly foreseen / that he would soon find himself imprisoned / For the sake of Belarus in a Belarusian gaol' (Pžs, 91).

lavaččy toj …' (Let us go and sit on that bench …, Pžs, 28), dedicated to his father, praises the simple pleasures of home. Also domestic, 'Suaŭturka' (My co-author, Pžs, 31) describes his cat which, uninterested in questions of versification, greatly prefers to curl up and sleep.

Žmitrok Kuźmienka, however, could not be called a sentimental poet. His great strength lies in the depth of his patriotism and the eloquence with which he expresses indignation at the fate that has befallen his country.

Ivaščanka

Anatol' Ivaščanka is both scholar and poet, the first thanks to his thesis-based book on the distinguished poet Aleś Razanaŭ (b. 1947), which was published in 2008.[18] His own poetry is translated into at least six foreign languages, including German and Russian, and his present reputation rests mainly on two verse collections: *Vieršnick*[19] (2006) and *Chaj tak* (So be it, 2013). He is an enterprising and consistently stimulating poet, whose first two books reflect considerable maturity of thought and a lively imagination, not least in his poems about writing itself. His attitude to his city and to the state of Belarus is often critical, if not despairing, something also found in several other poets of his generation. In ease of technique, he developed considerably between his first publication and the second, but naturally some themes are common to both.

The topic of writing and the forms and reception of poetry arise frequently in the work of young Belarusian poets. Ivaščanka is no exception, and he reflects on the relationship between his computer and muse in several poems: for example, the humorous 'Z čornaha ŭ bielaje' (From black to white, Cht, 7),[20] and 'u tvorčych pakutach …' (in the torments of creation …); in one of his 'Vosieńskija tanki' (Autumn tankas): 'niavažna …' (it does not matter …, Cht, 106) it is suggested ironically that the medium is more important than the message. In a witty longer poem, 'The song — son (Ž niepračytanych listoŭ mistera Bliuma)' (The song — a dream [From some unread letters of Mr Bloom], Cht, 101–02), he mistakes two keys on his computer, producing a green muse instead of a greenfly.[21] Several of his poems on writing poetry, however, are utterly grim: in 'čaho varta vierš?..' (what is a poem worth? …) he answers the question by saying

---

[18] *Paetyka Alesia Razanava: miž medytacyjaj i racyjaj*, Miensk, 2008. In this he was following the ground-breaking work of leading literary critic Hanna Kiślicyna: *Aleś Razanaŭ: problema mastackaj śviadomaści*, Miensk, 1997.

[19] This title, whose first four letters (meaning 'poetry') are in Cyrillic and last four are an English personal suffix, does not lend itself to easy translation. Part 7 of his book, however, is headed 'Vier[š]nik': *viernik* means a religious believer, although the very short poems here do not appear to have any particular spiritual connotation.

[20] Numerical references preceded by Cht are to *Chaj tak*.

[21] This episode cannot be translated.

that, in a 'regime of waiting', it is the equivalent of a gobbet of spit on the pavement (Cht, 22). In another poem, 'ja nie paeta …' (I am not a poet …), it seems to be the whole literary environment that disgusts him, as we read in the opening lines:

> я не паэта
> о крый мяне … матам
> паэзія гэта спорт
> паэзія гэта эстрада
> паэзія гэта пот
> і нясьвежыя швэдры
> не ведаю як каму
> а мне тут бракуе паветра
> скокі й пырсканьне сьлінай
> пад чэргі забойных тырадаў
> яна ўсё болей нагадвае
> сумную клаўнаду[22]

In 'Naradzić radok' (Giving birth to a line) the poet suggests that anybody can write verse, some keeping them close to themselves like doting mothers or fathers of single children, whilst others boldly release their 'little verses' (*vieršaniaty*) into the wide world (Cht, 11). His tone here is scornfully dismissive, as it is in another witty poem 'Liohkaść byćcia' (The lightness of being) where he twice suggests that poetry has died, while fuckwits (*mudzily*) take note (Cht, 29–30). Similar ideas are expressed at the end of '"Bitva pamiž rozumam i dumkami …' ('The battle between reason and thoughts …), of which these are the last five lines:

> Па горадзе ходзіць п'яная Плачка,
> ловячы гукі сваёй мовы …
>
> Моўчкі назіраем,
> як канае на нашых руках
> паэзія. (Vier, 27)[23]

In 'pamiž dvuch' (between two) he describes himself as being

> у вязьніцы радкоў
> і пратухлых цытатаў[24]

---

[22] 'I am not a poet / oh, cover me with … swear words / poetry is a sport / poetry is a variety show / poetry is sweat / and smelly pullovers / I don't know how it is for others / but I feel a lack of air here / the jumping around and scattering spit / accompanied by a series of murderous tirades / it increasingly resembles / miserable clowning' (Cht, 13).

The opening line recalls that of Aleś Harun in his emblematic poem, 'Liudziam' (To people).

[23] 'There walks about the city a drunken Crybaby, / catching the sounds of her native language … // We observe silently / as in our arms there dies / poetry' Numerical references preceded by Vier are to *Vieršnick*.

[24] 'in a prison of lines / and of mouldy quotes' (Cht, 78).

In another poem, 'tvorčaski napal(m)'[25] the creative drive is cleverly associated with violence (Cht, 85). The poet is always clearly aware of the (potential rather than real) danger of writing ephemeral verse like multitudes of poetasters. As an illustration here is an excerpt from '72 hady' (72 years):

чытаеш вершы
(праўдзівей — тое
што вершамі названа) —
радкі-дзеля-надзеі
й бачыш як нішчыцца тое
што ледзь не напісаў
сам[26]

Free verse, according to 'Vierš niesvabody' (A poem on lack of liberty) only appeals when he has free hands and a splenetic mood (Cht, 16). Finally, critical generalizations can be a hazard to poets, as we read in a witty short verse, 'Ja napišu: žyćcio — dziarmo …' (I write: life is shit …):

Я напішу: жыцьцё — дзярмо.
Прачытаюць ды скажуць: дэкаданс.
Я напішу: жыцьцё — казка.
Прачытаюць ды скажуць: папса.
Я напішу: жыцьцё — казачнае дзярмо,
і яны ў адзін голас рэкнуць:
постмадэрнізм![27]

Several young Belarusian poets introduce the theme of alcohol into their works, although none to the extent of Anatoĺ Sys nor, indeed, with anything like his talent. In a curious poem, with a prose interlude, 'Siaredzina' (The middle), Ivaščanka considers filling and swigging down a large glass before spending half an hour writing on a clean sheet of paper (Cht, 46). Of more general interest is a poem, 'T', which enumerates the ways in which he does not need to write in order to affirm the deep longing he feels for his beloved:

я не ведаю
навошта мне шукаць адмысловую рытміку
ствараць нечаканыя вобразы
эксперыментаваць арыгінальную форму верша
выдрочвацца з рыфмоўкай
прыдумляць наватворы

---

[25] The title, with its play on 'napal' (drive) and the international word 'napalm' cannot be translated.
[26] 'you read poems / or rather what are called poems / lines written in hope / and you see how is destroyed that / which you almost wrote / yourself' (Cht, 61).
[27] 'If I write: life is shit / They will read it and say: decadence. / If I write: life is a fairy story. / They will read it and say: pop. / If I write life is fairy tale shit, / they will with one voice announce: / postmodernism!' (Vier, 33).

займацца іншай падобнай лабудой

...

каб проста сказаць,
як моцна сумую па табе,
Каханая[28]

In his first book Ivaščanka refers to love in a variety of strange, even bizarre ways. For instance, in 'ty zahadala vysiečy drevy ...' (you ordered me to cut down trees ..., V, 10) he appears to have only discovered love when the addressee changed some money for him. In 'Idu nasustrač viaśnie ...' (I am going to meet spring ...) his girl is barely mentioned, though apparently present, and in 'demijurh' (demiurge, V, 61) what seems at first to be his beloved turns out to be his paranoia. One pure *jeu d'esprit* about love is 'jon kachaŭ jaje ...' (he loved her ...):

ён кахаў яе
але не ўзаемна
і яна кахала яго
але не ўзаемна[29]

In *Chaj tak* the poet's love is for his wife and family. In, for example, 'vosiem miesiacaŭ' (eight months) he notes that he has written eight poems in that time, and is with his partner, after being away, adding, bizarrely, 'until the jazz starts' (Cht, 52). More straightforward are several affectionate poems to his children, including 'Jana' (She, December 2005), 'Ty' (You, 6–7 November 2006), 'Pa vypiścy ź liakarni' (On being discharged from hospital, October, 2007), and 'Naziraju za svajoj ...' (I watch over my ...), the latter concerning his young daughter, Nastunia.

As has been mentioned, Ivaščanka's poetry gives a far from sanguine picture of the place where he lives and, indeed, his fellow countrymen. Calling Belarus 'краіна сэканд-хэнду' (a land of the second hand, Cht, 28)[30] he offers an even more bizarre picture in 'U krainie blakitnych badchisatvaŭ ...' (In the land of gay people with awakened consciousness ...), the first poem of a small section called 'čornyja vieršy' (dark verses), of which these are the opening lines:

---

[28] 'Т // I do not know / why I should look for special rhythms / create unexpected images / discover by experiment an original poetic form / wank around with the rhyme scheme / think up neologisms / bother with other such bullshit / ... / simply in order to say / how strongly I miss you, / my Beloved' (Cht, 56).

[29] 'he loved her / but not mutually / and she loved him / but not mutually' (Vier, 79).

[30] Interestingly, in the same year as Ivaščanka's book came out, the russophone Belarusian writer Svetlana Aleksievich published in Moscow *Vremia sekond hend* (Time second-hand), translated into Belarusian in Miensk also in 2013 as *Čas Second-Hand: Kaniec čyrvonaha čalavieka* (Time Second-Hand: The end of the red man).

У краіне блакітных бадхісатваў
у горадзе кардонных мянтоў,
на вуліцы гумовых жанчынаў
жыве чалавек з бусьлінымі крыламі.[31]

Ivaščanka suggests in 'Adrynuty(-ja)' (The rejected one[s]) that the entire Belarusian people are locked up (Cht, 37), and indeed imagines rather whimsically in 'Vyvodziš ijerohlif supakoju …' (You bring out the hieroglyph of peace …) life in a prison from which there is no escape (Cht, 46). Particularly telling is 'Žančyna z šklianymi vačyma' (The woman with glassy eyes) where he highlights the dishonourable role of many journalists, particularly those who work in television. Here are four lines from the middle of the poem:

Жанчынаў з шклянымі вачыма
становіцца болей штодня.
Іх памнажае з айчынных
тэлеканалаў хлусьня.[32]

It is therefore not surprising that the poet can exclaim in the first line of one untitled verse: 'паўсюдна манкурты' (everywhere are people with no memory).[33] His comment on boorishness in '?.,' though dry, is heartfelt, as is clear from the opening stanza:

Намагаўся пабачыць розьніцу
між хамствам і выхаваньнем
ды не пасьпеў
пасталеў[34]

'Tack Stokholm' describes a visit to the Swedish capital, where the poet finds that his fellow Belarusians have been unable to throw off some of their bad Soviet habits (Cht, 73–75). In the already mentioned 'Vierš na niesvabodu' the poet rails against ignorant fellow-citizens, going on to mention his own Orthodox beliefs which, he asserts, are often misunderstood. The last six lines of the poem end with a weak macaronic rhyme of resignation:

хтосьці скажа, што ад майго праваслаўя
добра патыхае забабонамі …
хай так
хай так
what the fuck[35]

---

[31] 'In a land of gay people with awakened consciousness / in a city of cardboard cops, / on a street of rubber women / there lives a man with the wings of a stork' (Vier, 44).

[32] 'Every day there are more and more / women with glassy eyes. / They increase in number multiplied by the lies / of the state TV channels' (Cht, 86–87).

[33] For the origins of the word *mankurt*, see note 11 in the previous (Kuźmienka) section.

[34] 'I strove to see the difference / between boorishness and good breeding / but did not manage it in time — / I grew up' (Vier, 16).

[35] 'Someone will say that from my Orthodoxy / there is a strong stink of superstition … / so be

In poems such as these there is obviously a feeling of strong dissatisfaction with life 'у гэтым бяздарным / бязрадасным часе' (in this untalented / joyless time, Cht, 99).

To themes such as those of writing, love, and disquiet about Belarus and the fate of its language, treated by many other young poets, Ivaščanka brings a distinctively original manner, aided by fluency of verse in various prosodic forms, inventive word play and challenging, sometimes provocative, but never dull imagery. It is worth sketching a few other aspects of his first two books. Antagonism towards some of his compatriots is offset by poems such as 'pra "siabroŭstva"' (on 'friendship') and 'braterstva' (brotherhood); his closeness to other writers is shown by the number of dedications to them, particularly in *Chaj tak*. Nature is not often the subject of his poems; notably, however, his picture of a season loved by several other young poets, 'Vosień' (Autumn), is remarkably bleak. An early example of his poetic mastery worth mentioning is the elegant 'Sufijski taniec' (Sufi dance). His poems generally reveal an ambivalent attitude to public protest, but 'Plošča' (The square) is a strong poem recreating some of the atmosphere of one of the youthful demonstrations that have been such a feature of Belarus in the early twenty-first century.

Several of Ivaščanka's poems are semantically challenging, and at times bizarre. Two examples will suffice: 'Ja — slup' (I am a pillar) ends with the hope that someone will point a passenger liner at him (Vier, 13); in 'Historyja śvietlych časoŭ — 2' (The history of radiant times — 2)[36] the following descriptive passage is distinctly surreal:

> Даставалі з капелюшоў станікі
> пялюшкі зубныя пратэзы
> Выцягвалі вонкі свае вантробы
> Дыхалі фарбай кніжным пылам
> вільгацыю намётаў
> Ніколі не ўжывалі туалетню ваду![37]

Finally may be mentioned the poem or song 'Pieśnia pra ciabie' (Song about you), which is directed to be performed to the tune of the well-known group Akvarium's song, 'Kozly' (Goats, Vier, 62–63). Very much a man of his time, the poet translates not only classical literature but also the words of pop singers and groups, as in the important free version of Boris Grebenshchikov's 'Dubrovskii'

---

it / so be it / *what the fuck*' (Cht, 17). An equally weak macaronic rhyme (навобмацак — good luck) ends the poem 'usio tak dobra ...' (everything is so good ..., Cht, 93), but the poet is more successful in 'koly iduć ad poŭni ...' (circles go from the full moon ...): дрэваў — forever (Vier, 82), and in 'usionievypadkova ...' (completelynotbychance ... Cht, 99) : тую — to you.

[36] There does not appear to be a first part, at least in this book.

[37] 'They got out of their hats bras / nappies false teeth / They pulled out their intestines / They breathed paint and the dust of books / the dampness of snowdrifts / They never used toilet water!' (Vier, 37).

as 'Kalinoŭski', in which Belarusian place names replace Russian ones, and the hero becomes the celebrated Belarusian leader of the mid-nineteenth-century anti-Russian uprising, Kastuś Kalinoŭski, who inspired many other poets, old and young.[38]

Ivaščanka does not dwell on himself greatly, but several poems relate to his search for identity and a path through life, although not always seriously, for instance, in 'Ad tyhra da maĺpy' (From tiger to monkey) when this is the path on which he is setting out (Cht, 68); in another poem 'na seansie ekzarcyzmu …' (at a session of exorcism …) he looks at himself and sees signs that he may be a werewolf. Also worth mentioning is 'korpajemsia ŭ sabie…' (we poke around in ourselves …), in the hope of digging up 'some justification for our existence' (Vier, 34). 'Let it be' (an apparent reference to the 1970 Beatles' song) is a call to accept fate (Cht, 100). Less sanguine is the stressful 'razarvać noč …' (to tear night apart …), as he seeks to mask his face from the gaze of alien eyes (Vier, 5). More charming, and peaceful, is (Maŭ i Liaŭ), apparently the names of two Siamese brothers who help the poet to find his way in life (Vier, 8).

Whatever he writes about himself, Anatoĺ Ivaščanka is certainly, if not an outsider, then, in his own words, 'outside the context' of contemporary Belarusian life.[39] He has, nonetheless, in his first two books made a genuine contribution to contemporary Belarusian literature.

Prylucki

Siarhiej Prylucki is an undoubtedly distinctive and talented writer: very modern, unromantic, even bleak and brutal. Unsurprisingly, his first book, *Dzievianostyja forever* (The nineties forever, 2008) attracted some quizzical critical attention when it first appeared. Highly referential and making many links between past and present, it includes 'typical' 1990s phenomena, often described with heavy irony. Prylucki has been active in numerous literary competitions and a finalist in several of them. He also writes prose and has published translations from English, Polish and Ukrainian.

Dzievianostyja forever is, indeed, a rather extraordinary book. It is divided into seven sections, with a two-part postscript, and the sections have striking titles: 'Vierteryjada' (Wertheriada), 'Dyviertyśmienty, napisanyja pad kajfam' (Divertimentos written when high on drugs), 'Dušeŭnyja prykuty vychavanca S.' (The spiritual torments of the pupil S.), 'Liohki žanr' (A light genre), 'Tajm-aŭt' (Time out), 'Modern wars' and 'Pilarama žarści' (A sawmill of passion). Many of the poems, most written in blank verse or prose set out as verse, are dedicated to

---

[38] For more examples of this see Arnold McMillin, "'Where Are You, Kastuś Kalinoŭski?": Overt and Covert References to Kalinoŭski and His Fate in the Work of Young Belarusian Poets"', *Studia Białorutenistyczne*, 8, 2014, pp. 107–16.
[39] See 'pa-za kantekstam' (outside the context, Cht, 18–19).

living and dead cultural figures, and even places. As the title implies, this book is something of a manifesto, a declaration of beliefs, and the lyrical hero seems at first to associate himself with Goethe's young Werther, although in 'Mroi, mroi' (Daydreams, daydreams) the musings are not of a young man in his early twenties, but of a youth of sixteen half obsessed with glamorous fast cars, night clubs and, of course, girls. It may be noted that the decade Prylucki's lyrical hero is ostensibly celebrating seems to be that of a semi-imaginary West, since in Belarus it was a decade split almost in two, by a change of regime, a time of 'blind amnesia of nerves' (Df, 16).[40] When, rarely, the poet turns to the more distant past it is to imagine how great men of other cultures might have coped in his country. For example, in 'Dekart pa bielarusku' (Descartes in Belarusian), he dismisses the relevance of 'cogito ergo sum' and ponders on how the Frenchman would fare as a light-fingered Belarusian factory worker with the characteristic interests of that social class (Df, 13). Before turning to some of the views of Belarus expressed in the book, it is worth noting that later, in 'Dyviertyśmient dlia IK' (A divertissement for IK), he defines himself slightly more specifically:

Я — арфей, словаблуд, мацюгальнік заўзяты —
у памежнай правінцыі краю абсурду,
час і розум марнуючы ў порна і чатах,
паратунак знаходжу у словах.[41]

Prylucki's work reveals a dyspeptic and scornful view of his native land. Amongst much criticism may be mentioned two poems titled 'Randevu z krajavidam' (Rendezvous with a landscape). In the second of them, alighting at the last bus stop, the hero meets a pitiful crowd hoping to return home:

пад вокнамі сотняў палат,
напоўненых процьмай астматыкаў,
паўінвалідаў, неўротыкаў,
сімулянтаў і сіфілітыкаў
што чакаюць вяртаньня назад.[42]

In 'U darozie pad kajfam' (Travelling when high on drugs, Df, 28) he calls Belarus a country of irony and fear, and in the same poem writes of ubiquitous loneliness:

Тут самота — паўсюдны галімы рэфрэн:
ён гучыць у размовах, ліецца са сцэн
непаўторным айчынным дэфектам.[43]

---

[40] Numerical references preceded by Df are to *Dzievianostyja forever*.

[41] 'I am Orpheus, a driveller, a fierce swearer / in a borderland province of a land of absurdity / I waste my time and brain on porn and chat rooms, / I find salvation in words' (Df, 134).

[42] 'under the windows of hundreds of wards / filled with a host of asthmatics, / semi-invalids, neurotics, / malingerers and syphilitics / who are waiting to go back' (Df, 33).

[43] 'Here loneliness is the ubiquitous miserable refrain: / it is heard in conversations and pours from the stage / as a unique defect of our native land' (Df, 30).

Critical as Prylucki's view of his country may be, when he turns abroad to real rather than imaginary places, he is hardly complimentary, describing Riga as 'Еўрапейскі заднi дворык' (Europe's little back yard) with not long to live,[44] and another ancient city in 'начны кракаў' (cracow at night) as like a Broadway musical (Df, 36), although in both cases his overall pictures of the towns are far more alive and interesting than those in most guide books. Somewhat different is 'black sabbath in lemberg', at the opening of which Prylucki's lyric hero not only names a Scottish writer of comparably uncompromising prose, but also describes himself and his friends as like desperate young dervishes, supporting the suggestion of the main critic of his work, Iryna Šaŭliakova, that Prylucki's work is shamanistic.[45] Here is the opening of the poem:

Усё было брутальна i прыгожа
як у кнігах Ірвіна Ўэлша
мы хадзілі па дахах i вуліцах
адчайнымі маладымі дэрвішамі.[46]

The tone of 'azija dlia biednych' (Asia for the poor) is rather calmer than that in the poems about Western countries such as the first of the two poems entitled 'Randevu z krajavidam', where the interests of capitalist visitors are shown as being 'Толькі "money" and "fuck"' (Only 'money' and 'fuck').[47] Another poem, 'Intercity', describing a wildly drunken railway journey, ends with images from the Western cinema:

А жыццё, нібы гангстэрскае кіно,
перамешвае ў купу дабро i лайно.

таму цела й душы тваіх Бонi i Клайд
уцякаюць пасьпешліва за далягляд.[48]

Prylucki's lyrical hero often seems to suffer from *Weltschmerz*, which sometimes, but not always, is linked to his hostile attitude to religion. Even in 'piena budniaŭ' (the foam of everyday life), he sees alcohol and pain as the only relief from (presumably religious) 'illusions', because they do not work like a cleaning rota in the public lavatory of the world, with the living to the left and

---

[44] 'Ryžskija siekstety' (Df, 35).

[45] Iryna Šaŭliakova, *Sapraŭdnyja chroniki Poŭni: artykuly i recenzii*, Miensk, 2011, 130.

[46] 'Everything was as brutal and beautiful / as in the books of Irvine Welsh / we walked over the roofs and in the streets / like desperate young dervishes' (Df, 44).

[47] This assertion recalls the title of another controversial British writer, Mark Ravenhill and his *Shopping and Fucking* (1996). It is notable that Prylucki makes free with English expletives, but uses rather transparent contractions of Belarusian non-normative words, such as 'jo…' (fu…) (Df, 80) and 'zas…ancy' (shi…heads) (Df, 31); the last of these nominal contractions also occurs at several other places in the book.

[48] 'And life, like a gangster film, / mixes into a lump goodness and shit, // therefore the bodies and souls of your Bonnie and Clyde / quickly disappear over the horizon' (Df, 39).

the dead to the right, and with the traditional injunction to 'please leave the place as you found it' (Df, 26). In '11-ja zapavieḋ' (The eleventh commandment), after a lament about his married life, he finally ends with characteristically dismissive blasphemy:

> і што б ні казалі
> апосталы бацькі альбо твой участковы
> забудзь усе запаведзі
> і пастарайся палюбіць
> гэты кашмар[49]

'Vigilia' is a rambling anti-religious diatribe, but perhaps more imaginative is the picture of the world as a shooting range in 'Vintoŭka' (The rifle), of which these are the last two stanzas:

> Бо сьвет — нібы вялікі цір,
> дзе кожны заслужыў па кулі.
> Мой Бог — мой кілер і кумір —
> вальні па мне зь нябеснай рулі.
>
> Быў паляўнічы — стаў трафей.
> Мне ўсё адно: піры, малебны …
> Бо доўгі патранташ падзей
> пусты і болей непатрэбны.[50]

'Siastra Darota' (Sister Darota) is a semi-narrative poem about a venal nun, apparently sexually attractive to the lyrical hero, who hides a copy of *Cosmopolitan* under her ample vestments and compares the ten commandments unfavourably to the menu on the wall of a café she frequents, for at least the menu varies (Df, 127–29). Finally, in this account of consistent hostility to religion is an imaginative alternative take on the Christmas story, dedicated to Andrej Chadanovič (b. 1973), 'Navahodnie-kaliadnaje regi' (New Year — Christmas reggae). The last stanza is typical of the whole:

> Паднясе тройца магаў дары-абярэгі
> немаўляці. І зменяцца ўсе *status quo*.
> Ды пачуецца зь неба анёльскія рэгі
> і ты радасна ўсклікнеш: <Во-бля-ха-ра-ство!>[51]

---

[49] 'and whatever is said by / the apostolic fathers or your local policeman / forget all the commandments / and try to love / this nightmare' (Df, 25).

[50] 'For the world is like a huge shooting range. / where each of us has earned a single bullet. / My God — my killer and idol — / take a shot at me from the barrel of a heavenly gun. // I was a hunter — and became a target. / It is all the same to me: feasts or public prayers … / For the long ammunition belt of events / is empty and no longer needed' (Df, 65).

[51] 'The three magi will present their gifts and charms / to the babe. And the entire status quo will change. / And from the heavens will be heard angelic reggae / and you will exclaim joyfully: "That was bloody beautiful!"' (Df, 88).

The lyric hero's problems with love, already indicated in '11-ja zapaviedź', are also reflected in other poems. The ending of 'adysieja-2007' (odyssey-2007), for instance, is unromantic by any standards:

сьвет расплываецца бензінавай плямай
па возеры тваёй сьвядомасьці

навокал лайно ты гэта выдатна ведаеш
але ўжо ня ў стане адчуць дзе яно дакладна[52]

'Saniety da Frančeski' (Sonnets to Francesca) is a very graphic, relatively straightforward, description of sex and, it seems, completely unromantic in its crude account of physical relations (Df, 76–77). Quite different is 'Dziońnik mieduzy' (Diary of a jellyfish), in which the hero holds onto the past by his reason, which is bound by his love (Df, 133). One of Prylucki's most conventional poems in terms of prosody is the deeply passionate 'Sientymientalny ramans' (Sentimental romance), in which there is a quantity of interesting imagery as well as the characteristic linking of good and evil. Here is the second half:

наша жарсьць і каханьне выходзяць звонкі
як выходзяць на волю вязьні і ўсё што стане

нашым прыватным апокрыфам я гатовы
перажыць з табою і жыць адною табою
дзеля цябе я згодны на перамовы
зь любою зь дзьвюх сіл — добраю і ліхою[53]

As will already be apparent, Prylucki is a very individual and exclusive writer, despite the plethora of sometimes elaborate dedications and a wide range of intertextual references in his first book. For all the exoticism of real and imaginary foreign adventures and the bleak vision of many aspects of the lyrical hero's country and life, the mixing of prose and verse is, so to speak, tempered by the poet's clear enjoyment of sometimes extravagant rhymes. He also comments occasionally on his craft as a poet. In 'Dźvie eliehii' (Two elegies), for instance, intractable creative problems are brought to the fore at the end of the second of them:

Таму мой розум па сьлядах Адама
шукае код-пароль твайго Эдэму:
брыдзе на мулах думак, экіпажах
метафараў, гіпербалічных баржах
ды па сканчэньні бачыць: вынік — лажа[54]

---

[52] 'the world is afloat with an oil slick / on the lake of your consciousness // all around is shit as you well know / but you are in no condition to smell where it is exactly' (Df, 45).
[53] 'our passion and love making emerge outside / like prisoners emerging into freedom and all that will become // our private apocrypha I am prepared / to experience with you and live with you alone / for you I agree to negotiations / with either of the two forces — good and evil' (Df, 139).
[54] 'Therefore my mind following the footsteps of Adam / seeks the code or password to your Eden: / it wanders on mules of thought, carriages / of metaphors, hyperbolic barges / but in the end sees that the conclusion is a mess' (Df, 123).

The last poem in the book, 'Budzień paeta' (The everyday life of a poet) describes some banal everyday events and how after breakfast he crosses out two lines from his poem of the day before, going on to what by his own standards is an optimistic thought:

> Дзень выдаўся надзвычай паэтычны
> увечары трэба будзе пачаць новы верш
> пра гэтую клятую красу сьвету[55]

Siarhiej Prylucki's ostensibly enthusiastic tribute to the decade of his childhood and teenage years, though sometimes brutal and even crude, nonetheless shows him as a poet of rich imagination and genuine talent. So much has been included in this book that it almost seems like a final testament, which makes it all the more interesting to see how his talent develops.

Ścieburaka

Usievalad Ścieburaka, a promising poet and prose writer, has to date produced two books: *Krušnia* (A pile of rocks, 2007) and *Bieh pa samaadčuvańni* (Running on how I feel, 2013). The first consists of some prose work and a quantity of occasionally unrhymed, but always rhythmical and punctuated poetry, mainly about history, nationality and family; other themes include disappointed hopes, and death and mortality; optimism and pessimism are often found together in his verse, and poems about writing itself are frequently concerned with originality, some linked to the poet's personal issues. The book is divided into five sections, the last consisting of prose. The first is 'Kraj' (Country), and the opening poem, 'Jak parviecca …' (When tears away …, Kr, 5–6)[56] describes setting out from a boring, hateful land on a night time quest for freedom (from sun, earth and sky, from belief and self-deception), but the objective turns out to be a great storm. This negative description of the poet's native land has relevance to several other poems in the first section, although 'Bielarusi' (To Belarus) in its total commitment to the country perhaps recalls some of the impassioned work of young poets like Janiščyc and Škliarava in the 1960s. A particularly strong poem, 'Nu što ž śnišsia tak pahana mnie Radzima?..' (Well, why do you seem so disgusting to me in my dreams, Native Land? …) contrasts a Heine-like dream of his country with the traditional idealized one of villages with storks and ponds, which, at the end, the poet says, if he found them, would cause him alarm and the need for some water. Here are the first two stanzas:

---

[55] 'The day turned out to be exceptionally poetic / in the evening I must begin a new poem / about this accursed beauty of the world' (Df, 144).
[56] Numerical references preceded by Kr are to *Krušnia*.

Ну, што ж ты сьнішся так пагана мне, Радзіма?
У вачох заплюшчаных, праз шрыфт CyrillicOld
я бачу, як ў разоры бульбяной Місіма
сьцізорыкам тупым успорвае жывот.

Я сплю цябе парваным фатаздымкам
у шыбіне замерзлай на гаўбцы.
Закінутым аўтобусным прыынкам,
дзе, як ў ваду, зьнікаюць усе канцы.[57]

No less bleak is 'Stary Miensk' (Old Miensk, Kr, 10), which laments that after all the damage inflicted on it by foreign invaders, at the present time it consists largely of glassy, faceless buildings. Other interesting poems are 'Dziady' (Grandparents, Kr, 8) in which he laments their loss, feeling acutely the passing of time; 'Liasun' (The wood goblin, 2001), a rather folksy poem about this creature's death; and 'Jana byla babkaj Praslavy' (She was Praslava's granny), a verse rich in national feeling about St Euphrosyne, who 'unites all who are faithful to their country' (Kr, 12). Finally may be mentioned a verse with the same first line as a celebrated poem by Bahdanovič, not, however, an example of plagiarism, but of respect for the classics: 'Ja chacieŭ by sustrecca z vami na vulicy …' (I should like to meet you in the street …') in which Ścieburaka's lyrical hero wishes to escape from all who shout about beliefs and fears, hoping to meet them only with his eyes, and then just walk along the street.

The next section 'Horad' (The city) depicts Miensk in various seasons and types of weather. One of the best poems is the first, 'Viecier huliaje ŭ naparstki …' (The wind is playing at thimbles …, 2004) in which the squalor of plastic cups and floating cigarette ends on a wet evening is covered up by darkness, as people settle down to meals and the TV, before rain descends, confusing the wind and preventing any further games of thimbles (Kr, 23). In 'Ranišni bliuz' (Morning blues) he insists that five in the morning is a time when creation is possible, as is made clear in the penultimate stanza:

У пяць гадзін раніцы, ў пяць
можна сабе дазваляць
простыя рыфмы ствараць
У пяць гадзін раніцы, у пяць.[58]

A curious feature some of Ścieburaka's early poems is that at times sense appears to be led by rhyme. For instance, in 'Nie viedaju, jak u Landonie …' (I don't know

[57] 'Well, why do you seem so disgusting to me in my dreams, Native Land? / Through my closed eyes in CyrillicOld font / I see how in a furrow of potatoes Mishima / with a blunt pen knife cuts open his stomach. // I dream of you as a torn photo / on an icy pane of the balcony. / As an abandoned bus stop, / where, as into water, all traces disappear' (Kr, 9).

[58] 'At five-o-clock in the rnorning, at five / one may allow oneself / to create simple rhymes / At five-o-clock in the morning, at five' (Kr, 24).

how it is in London, 2004), the unusual spelling of the name of the British capital seems to be led by a rhyme with 'palonie' (captivity);[59] comparably, in 'Kaliady' (Christmas, 2004), in which he describes the pleasure of being far away from the wind and the cold and 'our universal Sodom', he feels himself both Mozart and Salieri (rhyming with 'kvatery' [apartment], Kr, 34).

The third section 'Vieršy pra vieršy' (Poems about poems) affords some insight into the poet's creative processes. In 'Nad stalicaju noč …' (It is night above the capital …), for instance, he acclaims, in a characteristically whimsical way, July as the most propitious month:

> З ненадзейных сяброў
> ліпень першы і апошні
> за пісьменным сталом —
> за мяне піша вершы.[60]

Two more verses on this theme are 'Rastlumačyć, jak pišucca vieršy …' (To explain how poems are written …, 2002) and 'Dumki liotajuć dy nie pišucca …' (Thoughts fly but cannot be written down …). In the first of these, the poet explains in the final stanza his theory with considerable clarity:

> Я ўглядаўся ва ўсё ў задуменьні,
> покуль там, недзе над галавой
> нараджалася паразуменьне
> паміж вершам, натхненьнем і мной.[61]

The other poem uses some of the language of an intimate relationship with autumn, hoping to repair the damage of stealing rhymes by making a present of sweets:

> Думкі лётаюць ды ня пішуцца,
> На паперы аловак крышыцца.
> Я скраду колькі рыфмаў у восені,
> сапсую нашы з ёю адносіны.
> А пасьля аднаўляю з ёй стасункі,
> прэзентуючы вершы-ласункі.[62]

---

[59] Although there seem to be two widely used spellings of this city in Belarusian: Londan and Liondan, one traveller asserts that the only spelling should be Landan: see Aleś Paškievič, *Sim pobediši*, Miensk, 2012, p. 207.

[60] 'From amongst my unreliable friends / July is the first and the last / it sits at my writing desk — / and writes poems for me' (Kr, 28).

[61] 'I gazed at everything pensively, / until there, somewhere above my head / an understanding was born / between a poem, inspiration and me' (Kr, 42).

[62] 'My thoughts fly but do not write themselves down / the pencil is crushed on the paper/ / I shall steal a few rhymes from autumn, / and ruin our mutual relations. / But later I shall renew my connexion with it, / by making a present of poetic sweets' (Kr, 44).

The gentle humour, not far from the surface of many of the poems in Ścieburaka's first book, is prominent in the last of the verse sections, 'Žarści i žarty' (Passions and jokes). It begins with a triolet about intimacy, 'Kali ty pryjdzieš da mianie ...' (When you come to me ...), and shortly afterwards another triolet sensibly suggests that a little alcohol serves as a better prelude to love than a full glass: 'Nia licie hety kielich poŭny ...' (Do not pour me this full glass ...). There are several more triolets in this section, not, one might have thought, the ideal form for expressing passion or making a joke. An interesting poem, 'Nie hliadzi ...' (Do not look ..., 2003), consists of a series of prohibitions, ending with a bizarre stanza about taking offence:

Не крыўдуй.
Пасядзім удвох.
Паглядзім як у вочы ў неба.
Гэта ўсё, што я для цябе зьбярог...
Не крыўдуй, можа, хоць і трэба.[63]

It is followed by another poem of everyday life and morality in the form of seeking and finding, 'Šukać: dzie troški mienšy dzień ...' (To seek: where is there a slightly shorter day ...). Some of the jokes are very brief and quirky; here are three examples:

Пройдзе гадкоў дзесяць,
стане гадкоў з трыццаць —
будзе і ў нашым сьмецці
досыць цікава рыцца.[64]

Які сам ты —
Такі й твой Санта![65]

Ціха!..
Сядзі
й не будзі
ліха.
Можа
яно
і не прыйдзе
само ...[66]

---

[63] 'Do not take offence. / Let us sit together. / Let us look at the sky, as if into each other's eyes. / That is all that I have kept for you ... / Do not take offence, although, perhaps, you should do' (Kr, 64).
[64] 'About ten years will pass, / and I shall be about thirty — / and even in our rubbish / it will be interesting enough to rummage' (Kr, 73).
[65] 'What you are / is what your Santa will be' (Kr, 74).
[66] 'Quiet! ... / Sit / and do not arouse / misfortune. / Maybe / it / will not come / of its own accord ...' (Kr, 75).

Finally, after the poems about city life, two simple verses offer descriptions of life in the country and amongst the natural world: 'Noč u majontku' (Night on the homestead) and 'toj, chto čakaje daždžu ...' (he who waits for rain ...).

Ścieburaka's second book, in some ways more sophisticated than the first, is also far from devoid of humour. It may moreover be noted that he uses more regular prosody, particularly rhyme. *Bieh pa samaadčuvańni* comprises four parts: the first 'Jak jość' (How it is) is followed by some poems from the first book; the third section 'Jak maje być' (How it ought to be) is followed by 'Remarki'[*sic*], a selection of philosophical short prose, often humorous or quaint. Many of the first poems describe the poet's disappointment with his country. For instance, 'Ty viedaješ, ja dziŭliusia ...' (You know, I shall be surprised ...) in which he suggests that Belarus has everything, but that the poet's desire for freedom does not melt. (Bps, 7).[67] Another gloomy picture is 'Nia horšy čas, nia horšy lios ...' (Not a worse time, not a worse fate ...) in which attempts to escape only lead to an overgrown path. A tender poem is 'Jana viedaje movy i modu ...' (She knows both languages and fashion ...) but the following, presumably unrelated, verse is devoted to the poet's spaniel Emilija for whom true devotion is taken to a further level in 'Moj sabaka razumieje bielaruskuju ...' (My dog understands Belarusian ...), in which the animal is shown not only to know Belarusian (like, by implication, the girl in 'Jana viedaje movy i modu ...') but to be a true patriot in other ways:

> Мой сабака разумее беларускую…
> Ён сядае, лапу падае.
> З асаладой вантрабянку трускае
> і шануе месцы, што свае.
>
> Ад усіх дзьвюхногіх суайчыньнікаў
> ён адрозны з той адной прычыны,
> што і ў процьме неспрыяльных чыньнікаў
> ён адданы сукін сын сваёй Айчыны![68]

As was also the case in *Krušnia*, dreams play a considerable role in Ścieburaka's second book, and two contrasting examples indicate something of their range. The first, addressed to his beloved, 'Kali ty pierastanieš śnicca ...' (When I stop dreaming of you ...), expresses the freedom that can come only when dreaming ceases:

> Калі ты перастанеш сьніцца,
> я зноўку паспрабую жыць.[69]

---

[67] Numerical references preceded by Bps are to *Bieh pad samaadčuvańni*.
[68] 'My dog understands Belarusian ... / He sits, gives his paw. / He shakes his stomach with relish / And values his own territory // From all his biped contemporaries / he differs for one single reason, / that amidst the multitude of adverse factors / he is a devoted son of a bitch to his Fatherland' (Bps, 17).
[69] 'When I stop dreaming of you / I shall again try to live' (Bps, 63).

In the other poem, 'Miedykam śniacca šprycy i chalaty …' (Doctors dream of syringes and house coats …) the poet reflects humorously and with some exuberant imagination on the dreams of various workers and professionals, before thinking about his own dreams:

Сьніцца акуле аквалангіст,
доўгачаканы палкоўніку ліст.
Сьніцца мічурынцам хрэн на сасьне,
што мне пабачыцца сёньня у сьне?[70]

The poet's comment on his beloved above does not reflect his relationship in general. For instance, there is genuine regret in 'Ja nia vieru, što budzieš čakać …' (I do not believe that you will wait …) and 'Ciažka pisać pra vočy …' (It is difficult to write about eyes …) makes clear that being together is better than any description. Finally, and more extravagantly, is a fantasy of love, 'A niekali budzie tak …' (And one day it will happen …) in which a girl with a large scythe visits the poet, and he throws everything up to go with her in search of happiness; here is the last stanza as they meet in the clouds and melt:

І ў вэлюме белых сноў
ля рысы апошняй станем —
абрысамі з туманоў
хітнемся і ўшчэнт растанем.[71]

The waking world continues to be a source of anguish for the poet, and a particularly strong poem is 'Pakajaĺnaja spravazdača naščadkaŭ ajcam nacyi' (A confessional report by their descendents to the fathers of the nation). Here are the last eight lines:

Мы ратуемся ад безвыходнасці
нежаданьнем прымаць усур'ёз
панаваньне хлусьні і подласці
і абрыдлы гаротны лёс.

І фарбуючы скроні сівыя
на падлеткавай галаве,
на уласнай зямлі — чужыя,
не бароnім гнёзды свае …[72]

---

[70] 'The shark dreams of an underwater swimmer, / the colonel of a long-awaited letter. / Followers of Michurin dream of horseradish on a fir tree, / what will I see tonight in my dreams?' (Bps, 67).

[71] 'And in a veil of white dreams / near the last boundary we shall stop — / like the contours of mists / we shall stir ourselves and melt away completely' (Bps, 62).

[72] 'We save ourselves from hopelessness / by unwillingness to take seriously / the rule of lies and baseness / and our hateful, bitter fate. // And painting grey temples on a youth's head, / in our own country — we are aliens, / we do not defend our nests …' (Bps, 68).

Equally powerful is 'Źmitru Daškievču da 31-ha dnia narodzinaŭ' (To Źmicier Daškievč on your thirty-first birthday), addressed to a well-known political prisoner who is a near coeval of the poet but, as is implied in the last three lines, somewhat better off locked up:

> Аднагодкі мы зь ім —
> тры дні розьніцы,
> але ён свабаднейшы ў турме...[73]

In 'Jedu dachaty ...' (I am going home ...) he is affronted at the total indifference of the other passengers to his reading an outstanding book of poetry.[74] The fact is, he suggests in another verse, 'Pakryjdžanaj muzie' (To my offended muse, Bps, 33), his time is not one for poetry, if there ever was one; this verse shows Ścieburaka's desire to come to terms with the ambient reality. As a poet, he declares it difficult to be original. Here is the end of 'Kali boĺšaja śvietu palova ... ' (When the greater part of the world ...), with a decidedly original rhyme:

> калі пошукі — самамэта,
> калі шлях замыкае кола,
> я сваё дваццаць шостае лета
> дажываю на грані фола.[75]

Age is also a factor in 'Ja nie maru — nia toj uzrost ...' (I do not daydream — it is not for my age ...), a poem that links the 'crucified language' (a fairly common image) with the crosses he has to bear, although the poet feels that he can rise above the *pakora chieŭra* (submissiveness of the crowd, Pbs, 70) in what he refers to in a somewhat didactic poem, 'Liubomu pakaleńniu pryśviačajecca' (Dedicated to any generation) as *śviadomy bardak* (conscious chaos, Bps, 22). In a rather jaunty verse, 'Bielaruskaja kliasyka' (Belarussian classics), he appears to conflate *taraškievica* with *trasianka* (not to mention grammar with orthography), although his (far from unique) desire to use classical spelling rather than the more russified *narkomaŭka*, is clearly related to a broader aspiration for freedom:

> Беларуская клясыка
>
> Я цьвёрда стаўлю мяккі знак
> ва ўсіх належных словах!
> Бяз знаку гэтага ніяк
> Мая ня можа мова!
>
> У <эўропе> — сьмела стаўлю <Э>
> і <Я> — пішу у <клясе>.
> Такой граматыкі стае
> На думкі ў кожным часе!

---

[73] 'We are coevals . / three days apart, / but he is freer in prison ...' (Bps, 69).
[74] Uladzimir Niakliajeŭ's *Prošča*, 1996.
[75] 'if searching is an aim in itself / when the path closes a circle. / I to the end of my twenty-sixth year / shall live on the verge of a foul' (Bps, 26).

Баронім <Ё>, кароцім <Ў>,
трасянку робім моваю.
Звычайную
маю
тваю
мы робім адмысловаю!⁷⁶

Like several other young Belarusian poets, Ścieburaka combines religious faith with a light-hearted attitude to God, as may be seen in the following lines from 'Zimovaje' (Winter) in which he rhymes God (*Boh*) with grog (*hroh*):

Давай, акдрыўшы насьцеж дзьверы,
чакаць — госьць ў хату —
ў хату Бог,
давай мы кропляю даверу
гарачы замацуем грог.⁷⁷

Despite the various comparisons with others made here, Ścieburaka is an original voice and a poet of considerable and varied technique, whose more despairing poems appear to come from an intelligent head and rational heart.

Ryžkoŭ

Vitaĺ Ryžkoŭ is a distinctive and talented young poet and translator who has won a number of prizes for his skilfully written and thematically varied verses, which are often humorous, and rather worldly and unsentimental. They include several about the past: World War II, medieval times, and the age of the samurai, at least in his imagery. His love poems are frequently indirect and unhappy, whilst his writing about creativity itself often seems light and, sometimes, oblique. The moral poles of good and evil, however, are more explicitly postulated than in the poetry of many of his contemporaries. To all these themes Ryžkoŭ brings a rich imagination and an easy technique that is never facile.

Dźviery zamknionyja na kliuču (Locked doors, 2010) comprises three parts: 'Čorna-bielyja vieršy' (Black and white poems), 'Spravazdača pa rospačy' (A report on despair) and 'Bliuz uciekačoŭ (pieraklady)' (Refugee blues [translations]). Attached to the book is a CD of readings by the author,⁷⁸ which serves as a reminder that several young writers, as well as many of the preceding

---

⁷⁶ 'Belarussian classics // I firmly place a soft sign / in all appropriate words! / Without this sign there is no way that / my language can manage! / In "Europe" I boldly put a reversed "E" / and I write "IA" in "class"! / We defend "IO", shorten "Ŭ", / we make *trasianka* into a language. / The normal one / of me / and you / we make deliberately!' (Bps, 25).

⁷⁷ 'Let us, throwing the doors wide open, / wait — for a guest in our house — / into our house, God, / let us strengthen / hot grog with a drop of faith' (Bps, 79).

⁷⁸ The disc contains five original verses and translations from the work of three poets, accompanied by a small but obtrusive musical ensemble that at times almost drowns the words.

Bum-Bam-Lit generation, envisage their poems in performance and well as on the page.[79] The relationship between versions of foreign poets and Ryžkoŭ's original work will be touched on later.

In the book's opening poem, 'kali padajem, zory …' (when we fall, the stars …, 2009), he declares that from childhood his wish was to be happy and become a poet. Many of his poems on writing, however, seem to be less than completely serious or self-obsessed: in 'Tramvajny šum' (The noise of trams, 2009), for instance, he warns against taking him at face value, noting 'усё, што пішу / нагадвае толькі трамвайны шум';[80] in an interesting verse, 'Unisonnyja z vietram' (In unison with the wind, 2008), poems are born in a manner comparable to an epileptic fit, and can be so small as to get in your eye, which leaves the poet with the choice of washing them out with tears or attempting to understand what they are (Dznk, 29). More serious is 'tapahrafičny kretynizm' (topographical cretinism, 2009) where he writes about seeking for rhymes, while aware of the danger of slapdash versifying (schalturyš), and the loneliness of such searches. Here is the fourth stanza and the beginning of the fifth:

> бывае, падоўгу ледзь не па мапе шукаеш рыфму —
> і тое не так, і гэта не палезе,
> потым паставіш што-небудзь, схалтурыш крыху
> і думаеш: паэзія гэта ці не паэзія?
>
> бывае, у стане творчага пошуку адчуваеш самоту[81]

Finally may be mentioned a surreal, potentially blasphemous, poem, 'Zialiony čalaviečak' (The little green man, 2003), in which the eponymous creature is crucified on a traffic light, and where one line links composing poetry with reproaches: 'і складаеш вершы, забыўшыся на дакоры' (and you compose poetry, forgetting about reproaches, Dznk, 33); the topic of criticism of poets is echoed in another, later, poem, 'Śviatočnyja ahni' (Holiday lights, 2009): 'выйдзеш прайсціся — уважліва да дакораў і рыфмаў' (you go out for a walk — attentive to reproaches and rhymes).[82] Later it will be possible to mention fulsome praise rather than reproaches.

---

[79] Two overt examples of a contemporary poet's works clearly meant for performance may be found in Anatoĺ Ivaščanka's 'Pieśnia pra ciabie', Vieršnik, 62–63 and in his 'Kalinoŭski', Chaj tak, 117–18.

An interesting poem comparing snowflakes to lines of verse that cannot be spoken is 'Śnieh' (Snow, 2003) (Dznk, 53). Numerical references preceded by Dznk are to Dźviery, zamknionyja na kliučy.

[80] 'everything I write / recalls only the noise of trams' (Dznk, 15).

[81] 'it happens that for a long time, almost using a map, you look for a rhyme — / and that won't do and that doesn't fit, / then you put in something or other, a bit slapdash / and you think: is that poetry or not poetry? // often in a state of creative search you feel loneliness' (Dznk, 8–9).

[82] Vierasień, 1, 2009, 12.

Like the theme of writing, that of love is naturally frequent in the work of young poets. In Ryžkoŭ's first book, however, it does not occupy a central place. In 'Śnieńni padčas paliavańnia' (Dreams while hunting, 2010) he imagines a chase after a female goat (in which he compares himself to a samurai),[83] which seems to last such an eternity that relations between him and his dearest have to be re-established by post:

Я тут настолькі даўно,
што лісты ад маёй адзінай сталі раптоўна пачынацца з <мы>:
маўляў, мы пішам табе толькі ў надзеі
даць адпачынак падчас палявання, твой запаволіць бег,
бо, так бы мовіць, хоць ужо не чакаем, любім цябе і помнім.

Калі я казаў
<Я кахаю цябе>
І чуў адказ
<Я кахаю цябе>,
Я ніколі не забываў, што гэта — амонім.[84]

'Balada niepadzieĺnaha' (Ballad of the inseparable, 2003) is an oblique, inventive love poem, full of painful images, such as that of two hearts being thrown against a sheet of glass (Dznk, 36); the ballad ends by repeating the first and second stanzas, providing some relief after what had gone before. Here is the final stanza:

Бы абраныя,
ад жыцця адарваныя,
бы адзіныя і суцельныя.
Закаханыя,
адно аднаму адданыя,
неаслабныя, непадзельныя.[85]

A particularly striking image concludes another poem about separation from his lover, 'Pakuĺ ciabie nie bylo, skončylasia viasna …' (While you were away, spring came to an end …, 2003):

---

[83] An earlier poem that, inter al., suggests that writing poetry is not a manly occupation, 'vierš kaliasamurajskaj tematyki' (a poem on Samurai-related themes, 2007), ends with four lines about catching a goat.

[84] 'I have been here so long / that letters from home from my dearest one have suddenly started beginning with "we" / you would say, we are only writing in the hope / of giving you a rest during the hunting, slowing your pace, / for, so to speak, although we are not expecting you, we love and remember you. // When I said, / "I love you" / and heard in response, "I love you" / I would never forget that these are homonyms' (Dznk, 14).

[85] 'Like chosen ones, / torn apart from life, / as if we were the only ones and sufficient unto ourselves. / In love / devoted to each other, / constant, undivided' (Dznk, 37).

Пакуль цябе не было, скончылася вясна,
лета, восень, зіма, вясна, лета …
Вусны развучыліся вымаўляць *мы, нас, нам.*
Дзе ты

была?
Усміхнешся ў сваёй звычайнай манеры
Бля
я — громаадвод, які заземляе нервы.[86]

Finally may be mentioned a curious poem, 'Nasupierak' (Contrary, 2005, 2008), in which a 'bitch' is constantly called contrary, until she gives birth and everything changes, so that the poet is now the one who is out of step (Dznk, 41–42).

The word 'despair' is highlighted in Ryžkoŭ's first collection, and one poem, 'Spravazdača pa rospaču' (A report on despair, 2004), as mentioned above, gives its name to a whole section of the book; also striking is 'Rospač na prodaž' (Despair for sale, 2005). In the first of these poems the theme broadens from the individual poet to everybody (all Belarusians?) when he writes: 'Бог глядзіць на нас — толькі дзівіцца' (God looks down on us and is simply amazed, Dznk, 48). At the end of the second poem, which is rich in assonance and interesting harmony, we learn that creative people have despair for sale. In the middle of this work the poet, characteristically, broadens the theme to encompass the whole country:

Выспела роспач,
У краіне адчаю,
пераважна населенай беларусамі,
Чалавек з вусамі шлёпае вуснамі,
і слова яго —
                    не дапамагае …[87]

In 'Zahinajučy paĺcy' (Bending one's fingers, 2009) the poet twice addresses Belarusians as 'his people', offering to lead them to a nameless mountain, at the foot of which mostly shitty villagers are grazing shitty cows (Dznk, 17). The poet's dislike of the triviality of modern life may be reflected in the rhyming of '*boh*' (God) with '*bloh*' (blog) in 'da pabačeńnia!' (goodbye!, 2008). Finally, on this topic may be mentioned a challenging poem, 'Bielaruś siamivokaja' (Seven-eyed Belarus, 2007), of which these are the last two lines:

У нас усё добра — мы ў атачэнні патрэбнага радыуса
у самым смярдзючым цэнтры чагосьці жывога[88]

---

[86] 'While you were away, spring came to an end / summer, autumn, spring, summer … / My mouth forgot how to say, *we, us, to us.* / Where were // you? / You smile in your usual way, / Damn it, / I am a lightning conductor that brings nerves to earth' (Dznk, 51).

[87] 'Despair has matured. / In the country without hope,/ mostly inhabited by Belarusians, / The moustached man talks and talks, / and what he says — does not help …' (Dznk, 45).

[88] 'everything is good here — we are surrounded by a necessary radius / in the most stinking centre of something living' (Dznk, 54).

Moral questions are addressed in several of Ryžkoŭ's poems, often, but not always, with humour. The nature of evil, and the question of laws and their effects compared with experience form the subject of a curious poem, 'U temie vady plavajuć navat ryby' (In the topic of water even fish swim, 2009); these are the third and fourth stanzas:

бо калі жыццё па коле ўспрымаць як такое
і калі пакінуць як ёсць гэты вулей,
варта прыдумаць, як пазбягаць усяго, што непакоіць,
што раздражняе і што нервуе.

месца подлых, вядома, наводдаль,
ды заўсёды зарана ўздыхнуць з палёгкай —
бо калі законы жыцця афармляюць ў зводы,
дослед пасля гартавання робіцца крохкі.[89]

Also interesting is 'Čorna-biely vierš' (A black and white poem, 2009), some of which consists of definitions of *praŭda* (truth) including 'conscience pulled into a bundle on the neck of a dumb person', 'that which is slapped on the face like a rag', 'a boring heavily advertised piece of goods', and many more (Dznk, 6). The opening stanza reflects on morality as it relates to contemporary politics:

… тых, хто замахаўся на тыранаў, ці аўтарытарных лідараў,
далёка не ўсе — і справядліва — лічылі героямі,
бо прапаганда зла не пакідае выбару,
як і любая зброя.[90]

Quite different in tone is 'Śviataja praŭda' (The sacred truth, 2008), a humorous poem about a priest stopped by the police for drunken driving who for all his holy rank curses his arresters in extremely vulgar terms; the poem ends with God being thanked for the great entertainment, for life and love, and freedom and truth (Dzkn, 21). Truth, generally, considered to be on their side by those who write about war, is rather sidelined in Ryžkoŭ's two poems set in wartime, 'dva skrypačy praz polie vajennych dziejańniaŭ …' (two violinists crossing a field of military action …, 2009) and 'samaje cikavaje' (the most interesting thing, 2010). In the first, the violinists flee from their orchestra when the Germans come, one having to carry the other, but soon they quarrel bitterly; at the end of the poem the wounded man taunts Symon who is planning to abandon his colleague:

---

[89] 'for when life in its circle is taken as such / and when this hive is left as it is, / it is worth thinking how to avoid everything that worries, / that aggravates and sets one's nerves on edge. // as is well known, the place of despicable people is not far off, / and they will always breathe a sigh of relief too early — / for when life's laws are formulated in documents, / experience, after being forged, becomes feeble' (Dznk, 16).

[90] '… those who struck out against tyrants, or authoritarian leaders, / were not considered heroes by everyone — and quite right — / for the propaganda of evil leaves no choice, / like any other weapon' (Dznk, 6).

ты слабак, сымон, таму ты мусіш бегчы адзін
і сына свайго абдымі і скажы, што ён мой сын

ты мамчын сынок,
сымон! —
чулася наўздагон[91]

'samaje cikavaje' tells of a promiscuous woman who goes through a series of wartime affairs and disappointments, ending up sleeping next to a kind and generous, but in her view 'idiotic' wounded soldier, who is described with revulsion. Though credible, neither of these poems contains any of the heroism and pathos associated with most Belarusian writing about the war; the anguish is individual and purely personal. Finally, from a different historical era, may be mentioned 'Maja karalieva, mama, praŭdzie, ja prosta raźbity, ja liedź tryvaju …' (My queen and mother, in truth I am simply crushed, I can hardly bear it …, 2010), in which a young prince begs his mother to cancel all the noisy celebrations and spare him from being sent to war (Dznk, 28). In other words, Ryžkoŭ's poems about war might be said to range from the peripheral to pacifism.

Premature elegiac notes are not rare in young Belarusian poetry, but Vitaĺ Ryžkoŭ depicts the passing of time and ageing with particular sensitivity. In 'Čas praz svaju piedantyčnaść našmat mudrejšy za pamiać …' (Time with its pedantry is far wiser than memory …, 2009), for instance, falling leaves remind the reader that people are constantly coming into the world as others leave it. Particularly touching is the poem that gives the book its title, 'Dźviery, zamknionyja na kliučy', which opens with a picture of human frailty and decay, and ends with almost complete silence. Here are the opening and closing stanzas of a fine poem:

старая страціла розум, яе стары
хутка губляе зрок. і слых. на ўсё наваколле
па тэлефоне намякае на розныя нумары
збольшага выпадковыя.

[…]

увечары дзверы замкнёныя на ключы.
стары ўголас чытае, пераказвае байкі.
радыё па начах маўчыць, увогуле ўсё маўчыць,
акрамя сабакі.[92]

---

[91] 'you are a weakling, symon, and therefore you must run on alone / and embrace your son and tell him that he is my son // you are your mother's little darling, / symon! / were the words that followed him' (Dznk, 25).

[92] 'the old woman has lost her mind. her old husband / is rapidly losing his sight. and hearing. to all around / he dials various telephone numbers. / for the most part chance ones. / […] / in the evening the doors are locked with keys. / the old man reads aloud, repeating stories. / the radio is silent at night, in general everything is silent, / apart from a dog' (Dzkn, 22–23).

Another kind of loss is of a bird flying away from the poet's window to freedom, expressed in a seemingly heartfelt and vivid poem, one of the earliest in the book, 'Uzmach krylami' (The flapping of wings, 2006). Both comparable and at the same time quite different is 'darožnyja zdareńni' (events on the road, 2009), which describes running into an elk during a night-time journey, and the driver's sincere horror, ending with a reflection on the unpredictability of life:

> ніколі не ведаеш што з табой здарыцца
> ў наступны момант што цябе напаткае —
> прыгажосць
> каханне
> лось[93]

'Adzinoki vierš' (A lonely poem, 2008) describes the poet's relationship to his indifferent shadow; here are the opening lines:

> Ілбом грукаю ў сцены —
> замест дыялогу з ценем.[94]

The wide variety of Ryžkoŭ's undoubtedly gifted work throws some doubt on his loneliness, but his is a remarkable talent and he has had the rare honour of being acclaimed by a prominent poet of an earlier generation, Leanid Halubovič (b. 1950), who suggests that the writers Ryžkoŭ has translated influenced his own original poetry, not automatically for the better (for example in the use of non-normative language).[95] The translations in this book include one from W.H. Auden, 'Refugee Blues' (which gives this section of the book its title), one from the Polish of Ryszard Krynicki, five from the Georgian of Georgi Nahutsryshvili, five from the Ukrainian of Serhij Zhadan, and five from the English of Americans Michael Salinger and Taylor Mali. The success of these ambitious versions of contemporary poetry further enhances the early achievements of Vitaĺ Ryžkoŭ, who, to judge by his first book, is certainly one of the most promising poets of his generation.

Mancevič

Nasta Mancevič's first book of prose and verse, *Ptuški* (Birds, 2012), caused a considerable stir in Belarus's patriarchal society by its sometimes frank descriptions of lesbian sex. In the same year she published an electronic book, *Heta nie ličycca* (That does not count). What follows will be based on *Ptuški*.

Mancevič is clearly a talented writer of both prose and verse. The blurb suggests that occasionally these two cannot be distinguished, and they are certainly linked

---

[93] 'you never know what will happen to you / what will meet you in the next moment — / beauty / love / an elk' (Dznk, 12).
[94] 'I bang my head on the walls — / instead of holding a dialogue with my shadow' (Dznk, 43).
[95] Leanid Halubovič, 'Vakol pieršaj knižki Vitalia Ryžkova: Tezisy da nienapisanaj recenzii', *Dziejasloŭ*, 53 (2011),277–82.

in some places, although the poems are clearly set out as verse. Prose is, by its very nature, usually more explicit than poetry, and this applies here, so that the attacks on the book as 'pornography', for example, have been mostly based on the short prose narratives.

The exiguous poems in *Ptuški* begin more than halfway through the book with 'Viliejka. Dubaŭka. Ranica …' (Viliejka. Dubaŭka. Morning …), an existential poem that is quite different from the plot-rich prose. Simple in content, it contains an elaborate rhyme in ll. 3 and 4:

> Вілейка. Дубаўка. Раніца.
> Ён сказаў у нудзе:
> <Сэ ля ві>,
> і мы селі ля Віліі.
> Запалілі.
> Каменчыкі ў рэчку кідалі,
> глядзелі, як паспаўзаюцца
> круті ад іх па вадзе … (Pt, 32)[96]

In 'Halava-žban' (Jug-head) she describes her head as an empty jug, and regrets that she has done nothing in life, insisting that she was not born, but that someone gave birth to her, without thinking. The last four lines indicate her real problem:

> Галава — жбан,
> галава — бот,
> балюча галаве, бо
> галава навучылася марыць.[97]

An example of the poet's frankness about her sexuality where it is no less clear than in her prose is 'Niepazbiežna viasny nastupstva …' (Inevitable is the coming of spring …), which combines intimate feelings with humour:

> Непазбежна вясны наступства:
> што ні дзеўчына, то распуста,
> з Менску, з Горкі, з-пад самай Ніцы
> што ні дзеўчына, то ў спадніцы.
> Захіснула вясна мне вочы —
> агаляюць паненкі грудзі.
> І з цырульні паволька крочыць
> ці то дзеўчына, ці то пудзель.[98]

---

[96] 'Viliejka. Dubaŭka. Morning. / Bored, he said: / "C'est la vie", / and we sat by the Vilija. / Lit up. / Threw pebbles into the little river, / and watched how circles / from them spread over the water …' Numerical references preceded by Pt are to *Ptuški*.

[97] 'My head is a jug, / My head is a boot, / my head hurts, because / my head has learnt how to think' (Pt, 33).

[98] 'The coming of spring is inevitable: / every young girl means debauchery, / from Miensk, from Horka, from the environs of Nice itself, / every young girl is in a skirt. / Spring covered my eyes — / the young ladies' breasts were laid bare. / And from the barber's shop was slowly stepping / either a young girl or a poodle' (Pt, 36).

Despite such moments of ecstasy, love seems to bring the poet as much pain as joy. In 'Što mnie rabić z taboju …' (What am I to do with you …), a poem addressed to her lover, she describes looking at her, embracing her, sleeping with her, and simply being with her. The last stanza, however, is far the most indirect, free of logic and impermanent (*niaviečnaja*) (Pt, 37–38). Lighter in tone is 'Milan. Viečar' (Milan. Evening) in which, sitting in the La Scala café, she manages to outrage the people at the next table by fondling her lover's knee (Pt, 39). When the affair has come to an end, in 'My kročyli pobač …' (We walked side by side …) all closeness is systematically reversed, and the heroine is in despair at their alienation (Pt, 40–41). Another poem, 'Ja nazyvaŭ ciabie zajac …' (I used to call you my hare …), is even more touching as she reflects on the loss of their pet names for each other (Pt, 42). Lack of recognition as an artist is the theme of 'Maliavać usio noč …' (To paint all night …), in which, after saying that nobody cares a toss (усім да задніцы) about her painting, she plans her gravestone (Pt, 34). Less creatively, in 'Siadžu kalia telievizara …' (I sit by the television …), she sits in front of the television, eating sweets, aimlessly scribbling and picking a hole in her socks, as she waits in a state of fierce anguish for the telephone to ring (Pt, 35).

The poet's pain and grief is not at all simple, as we learn from 'Zabiary moj boĺ …' (Take away my pain …): if it all goes, there will be nothing left. Here are the last four lines:

Забяры мой цень
Забяры мой сум
Забяры мой боль

I мяне не стане[99]

Some of the harsh naturalism of her stories comes out in 'Kali niedaskanaĺnaść śvietu …' (When the imperfection of the world …) and 'Ja viedaju, što tak budzie …' (I know that is how it will be …). The latter gives a dyspeptic description of a New Year's Day, with all its drunkenness and feelings of loneliness: the heroine has seen it all before, and her country and vodka seem to be closely related. Here are the last three lines:

Я і гарэлка <дзяржава> —
такое вось дэжа вю,
такі, бляха, новы год.[100]

The last two poems slightly relieve the gloom: 'A mnie chočacca žyć, navat kali mnie nie chočacca žyć' (But I want to live, even when I do not want to live), ends with the positive assertion, 'хочаш жыць' (You want to live, Pt, 47). In 'Kali ŭ

---

[99] 'Take away my shadow / Take away my sadness / Take away my pain // And I shall cease to exist' (Pt, 43).
[100] 'I and 'State' vodka — / such déjà vu, / the same frigging new year' (Pt, 44).

vačoch ciamnieje …' (When my eyes grow dark …) the heroine wishes to return to childhood when she was happy, disturbing the picture, however, in the penultimate line with a curious 'formal' variant of the most common mother oath in the language:

> Калі ў вачох цямнее,
> мне хочацца проста ўкленчыць:
> <О Божа, хачу да мамы!
> да таты хачу на плечы…>
> каб апынуцца ў дзяцінстве,
> як колісь —
> хавацца ў шафе
> сярод кажухоў і шапак,
> цукеркі цягаць з буфета
> ды красці ў суседа слівы
>
> і быць маленькім і лёгкім,
> і, ёб вашу маць,
> Шчаслівым.[101]

Nasta Mancevič has successfully introduced new themes and a new narrative manner to Belarusian prose and verse, in so doing arousing a storm of protest. It may be hoped that she will continue to write, for she has a distinctive literary voice.

---

[101] 'When my eyes grow dark, / I want simply to kneel: / "O God, I want to go to my mother / I want to get up on my father's shoulders …" / in order to remain in childhood, / as it once was — / to hide in the wardrobe / amongst the sheepskin jackets and fur hats / to pinch sweets from the sideboard / and steal our neighbour's plums // and to be small and light, / and, goddamn you all, / Happy' (Pt, 46).

CHAPTER 4

≈

Use and Defence of the Language

The language like the history of small countries needs to be actively defended against erosion. Although young Belarusian poets are on the whole not as emotive as some poets of the 1960s in lamenting the fate of the national tongue, nonetheless a number of strong words are used to express dismay at the Belarusian language's current plight, including, 'crushed', 'crucified' and 'trampled down'; some believe that it can best be saved from its russifying enemies by young people. Additionally, the way the Czechs successfully used language reform to cement their national identity is noted with admiration by more than one poet.

Attempts are made by some to create their own version of the language, using archaic or even invented forms in addition to the, presumably involuntary, Russian lexical influence in the verse of some poets. Less important, perhaps, is the variation in spelling between two orthographic systems (the so-called taraškievica and the officially approved *narkomaŭka*). Of the young poets, some write specifically of the advantages of the former, whilst others reject or ignore the rules of both. Macaronic writing is popular, sometimes but not always used wittily and with the essential proper knowledge of both languages. Non-normative language or swear words appear in the work of several poets, mainly but not only men, sometimes using a transparent mask of ellipses. Taćciana Niatbaj, whose poems do not fit into any other category, is included here for her free use of this linguistic freedom. Another aspect of language is the absence of punctuation and capitals in about half of the young poets, a tendency championed by some and criticized by others. The very future existence of the language is questioned in at least one recent novel.[1] Naturally, use of the language in contemporary verse is in itself a step towards its preservation, and the nature of writing is also a major theme in young Belarusian poetry.

---

[1] Viktar Marcinovič, *Mova*, 2nd edition, Miensk, 2014,

Kulikoǔ

Ihar Kulikoǔ, author of *Pavarot na mora* (A turn to the sea, 2011) and *Svamova* (2013),[2] is a popular poet, with a keen interest in living and dead languages as well as Oriental cultures. Many of his untitled poems are written in stanzas, as if verse, but essentially prose,[3] and there is much imagery, rhythm and internal rhyme. A humorous poet for whom Salvador Dali appears to be a hero, he relishes incongruity, though the genre of his verse is far from nonsense poetry. Kulikoǔ's love poems are particularly distinctive, often bizarre. In his second book he constantly attempts to create his own 'pure' language, which combines exuberance with obscurity, although it is not quite as opaque as, for instance, Joyce's *Finnegan's Wake*.

One boldly extraordinary love poem, in what will be called here poetic prose, begins as follows:

> Закіньма ўсё на сьвеце — у твой і мой рукзак,
> а мо прайдзем на лыжах усе на сьвеце тэксты. (Pnm, 13)[4]

At the end the poet and his lover see the same dream, and warm themselves on an electric stove ... of black chocolate.[5] Somewhat less romantic is 'U jejnych vačoch niamožna sieśći na meĺ ...' (In her eyes it is not possible to land on a sandbank...) which ends with a remarkable and unflattering image:

> Твой лёс неадольна
> выпівае цябе да дна — і ты вар'яцееш, як рыба,
> якая ідзе на нераст.[6]

Another poem, 'Bo kožnamu ǔ hetym śviecie chočaca byč z taboj ...' (For everyone in this world wants to be with you ...), offers a slightly oblique but

---

[2] The title is one of Kulikoǔ's neologisms, not, however, included in the extensive glossary at the end of the book.

[3] In quoting such works I have retained the line breaks of the original, but broken the translations only where there is a new stanza.

    The intermingling of prose and verse by setting the former in, for example, stanzas, and the latter without conventional lines has already been seen in some of the work of Siarhiej Prylucki and Nasta Mancevič and will be seen to be especially common in the work of Maryja Martysievič. A further step down this road is taken by a young writer, Žmicier Bajarovič, (d.o.b. unknown). He describes his 2012 collection *Šali* (Libra) as 'Liryčna-pobytavaja proza' (Lyrical-everyday prose), although some of the pieces seem more like a kind of free verse, without metre or rhyme. They are not discussed further in this book.

[4] 'Let us throw everything in the world into your and my rucksacks, / and maybe we will ski through all the texts in the world' Numerical references preceded by Pnm are to *Pavarot na mora*.

[5] This line is not exactly like a picture by Dali, however, for the words for stove and bar (of chocolate) are the same in Belarusian. There are many puns in Kulikoǔ's work, but to explain each one would be laborious indeed.

[6] 'Your fate irresistibly / drinks you right up — and you go crazy, like a fish / that is going for spawning' (Pnm, 14).

touching depiction of love. Being lovers in the modern world seems not to be easy and may even be absurd, as we read in 'pahonia za budučym časam zajšla kančatkova ǔ tupik …' (the chase after the future has finally come to a dead end …). A final example of Kulikoǔ's extensive love poetry is 'Usio, što my adšukali na doǔhaj darozie dadomu …' (Everything that we sought out on the long road home …), which ends with some quasi-scientific imagery, a recurrent feature of this poet's work:

> Усё, што мы адшукалі на доўгай дарозе дадо-
> му, і усё, што сабе прысьнілі калісьці на нашай
> эры, цяпер прарастае аортамі ў касьмічныя
> магістралі, змагаючыся са стомай — палачкамі
> халеры.
>
> Усё, што было між намі, ня зьнікне ў азона-
> вых дзірах, і новае пацяпленьне ў нашым з та-
> бой рамане растопіць сьнягі Антарктыды і зь
> неба складзе арыгамі, а я паднясу табе золата,
> сьмірну, грыбы и ладан.
>
> Ты станеш новым прарокам і будзеш хадзіць
> па вясёлцы, ты станеш сьвятлом і сьветам у
> нетрах усіх тунэляў, і дзеля ўсяго чалавецтва
> мы сплавімся разам пад токам і зьдзейсьнім,
> зазьзяўшы, бы сонцы, гідроліз душы і цела.[7]

Most of Kulikoǔ's poems on language are in *Svamova*, but there is also a somewhat bizarre piece, with rhyme and a quantity of neologisms, in his first book: 'Halosnych dni padličany. Ich śviet čakaje zhniba …' (The days of vowels are numbered. Mould awaits their world …). Here are the last four lines:

> Мы будучыні носьбіты, мы рэзьбіты дарогі,
> варажбіты прасьцягу, валадары ўсіх сьніб.
> Нас будуць прапускаць, не спатыкаючы, парогі,
> апошніх перакладзьбітаў у мову лёткіх рыб![8]

---

[7] 'Everything that we sought out on our long road home and and everything that we once dreamed up in our era, now grows like aortas on the cosmic highway, fighting again exhaustion — with cholera bacilli. // Everything that was between us will not disappear in holes in the ozone layer, and the new warming in our romance will melt the snow of the Antarctic and will form origami from the sky, and I shall bring you gold, myrrh, mushrooms and incense. // You will become a new prophet and we shall walk along a rainbow, you will become lighting, light in the depths of every tunnel, and for the sake of all mankind we shall fuse together under the current and will bring about, bursting into light like suns, hydrolysis between body and soul' (Pnm, 15).

[8] 'We are bearers of the future, we are the carvers out of the path, / foretellers of continuity, lords of all the disabled. / They will let us in at the thresholds without meeting us, / the last translators into the language of flying fish!' (Pnm, 44).

In 'Nieruš' (Nirvana) the poet describes in his second book how his 'mature language' (*stalaja mova*) constricts his breathing, and how light bursts in his chest. Hardly less strange are the last two lines of the work's title poem:

воля да руху вядзе нас празь невымоўны дождж
зноем сваемным таемнай Свамовы (Sv, 27)[9]

Finally may be mentioned the familiar topic of the way the language has been woefully neglected, described by Kulikoǔ here with almost frivolous irony in a prose poem about his education, 'U pierapisach nasieĺnictva, nie kažučy …' (In the people's correspondence, not to say …), of which this is the third stanza:

Казалі, што ты разумова адсталы і доўга
не пражывеш, што сядзеш на голку, ў тур-
му або, ня дай божа, паткнесься ў баптыстыя.
Але насамрэч цікавіў ты іх ня болей, чым
нейкі там Бангдядэш, Зымбабвэ, родная мова,
гомасэксуалістыя.[10]

Not all Kulikoǔ's poems about his past are so dismal. Far more upbeat, for example, is the first piece in *Pavarot na mora*, a prose poem with consistent internal rhymes, that evokes his childhood, 'Heta nieĺha nabyć na rynku abo ǔ kramie …' (This cannot be got at the market or in a shop …), although 'Tamu što jano — dziacinstva niemahčyma …' (Because it is childhood, which cannot be …), suggests that childhood is immortalized in life 'by inscriptions on desks, nuclear disarmament and the fresh smell of ozone' (Pnm, 16). Of broader span are 'adnojčy ty praśnieśsia čalaviekam …' (one day you will wake up as a person …), which traces life from the uncertainty of birth to the decay and misery of death (Pnm, 69–70), and, a prose poem with intermittent rhymes but no stanzas, 'Ja vypraviǔsia z domu, niavyspany i biaśsiĺny …' (I set out from home, sleepy and weak …), which describes his own life hitherto including teenage years and his experiences as a dissident, as an undisciplined young man and as a *iurodzivy* (simpleton) (Pnm, 41). Many poems concern Kulikoǔ's search for fulfilment: in 'Padojm' (The rise), for instance, the opening is despairing, but by the end there is a 'brazen rise' (*nahly padojm*) into the embrace of the Native Land. Here are the first two and last lines of this poem:

---

[9] 'the will to move leads us through inexpressible rain / with its own sultriness of the mysterious Svamova' Numerical references preceded by Sv are to *Svamova*.

[10] 'They used to say that you were intellectually backward and would not live long, that you were taking drugs, and would go to jail or, God forbid, blunder into the Baptists. But in reality you interested them no more than some places like Bangladesh or Zimbabwe, or your native language or homosexuals' (Pnm, 25).

Народжаны без народу, нязнаўшы свайго імя,
насельнікі сьветлай будучыні, няўхваленай Богам.

[…]

Наш наглы падойм у абдымкі Радзімы.[11]

'Horac' (The highlander) consists of a series of injunctions (to himself and his partner) as to what should and should not be done, many of them humorous, with the logic of nonsense. Here are the first two and last two lines:

Не прачнуцца на досьвіту, каб адстаць ад атраду.
Не сагрэцца ля вогнішча, каб згарець у пажары ўзысьця.

[…]

як суцешлівы напамін:
не агораць гары аднаму, каб ня зьвершыць удвух вяршыні.[12]

The path of life is further discussed in 'Puć' (The path)[13] each of whose four stanzas begins with a definition: 'пэўніць' (it assures); 'поўніць' (it fills); 'напінае' (it dons); 'спыняе' (it halts). Here, as an example, is the third stanza:

Пуць — напінае.
Цеціва. Надзетая на вось быцьця.
ён — лук, што нацягваецца пуцявітам,
выпростваючы пакручастых,
напружваючы слабкіх.
Ён — страла, выпушчаная у неварець,
што не згубілася ў быльнягу.[14]

Comparably to 'Puć', 'Viera' (Faith) begins each verse with a definition of the word of the title, all but the last preceded by *zaйsiody* (always): *выбар* (choice); *гарачыня* (passion); *вязьмо* (a tie); *воля* (liberty). The last stanza makes its point with two concise images:

Як зь сьнегу струмень дыханьнем горца,
як з прадзіва нітка верацяном
снуецца з ісьвету ісьціна
верай.[15]

---

[11] 'Born without a people, not knowing our own name, / inhabitants of a radiant future, unblessed by God' // […] // Our brazen rise into the embrace of the Native Land ' (Sv, 17).

[12] 'Do not wake up at dawn in order to be late for your brigade. / Do not warm yourself by a bonfire, in order to burn up during the fire of the ascent. // […] // as a consoling reminder: / do not climb mountains on your own, in order not to reach the peaks together' (Sv, 21).

[13] In his glossary Kulikoў gives various additional meanings for *puć*, including harmony.

[14] 'The path strains. / A bowstring. Placed on the axis of existence. / It is the bow that is pulled taut by the traveller, / straightening the winding, / bringing firmness to the weak. / It is an arrow fired into oblivion, / that does not get lost in the mugwort' (Sv, 36).

[15] 'Like a stream from the snow, which is the breath of a mountaineer, / like a thread from the spindle of a loom, / so truth is formed from the world / by faith' (Sv, 39–40).

On the subject of religious faith, it may be mentioned that God is referred to quite frequently in Kulikoŭ's poetry, but often with whimsy rather than piety, for instance in 'Prosta zaŭždy šukaj — navat u čystym poli …' (Simply always seek — even in an open field …), which ends with 'Аўтар ідэі — нехта Бог' (The originator of the idea was a certain God, Pnm, 50).

In a surreally fanciful poem about his aspirations, 'Chacielasia b: a/ papylyści kudy-niebudź kroliem …' (I should like to a/ swim crawl somewhere …), Kulikoŭ enumerates thirteen very varied wishes, including eating sweetmeats from the hands of young schoolgirls to reading an as yet unknown draft of a Sacred Document, and ending with a phone call to heaven to ask God whether it is true that apples contain heroin (Pnm, 20).

Kulikoŭ is far from sanguine about his country's authorities, which he describes in 'Jany adnavili budoŭli, dzie my praviali z taboj …' (They have renovated the building where you and I …) as 'viečnaja mierzlata' (eternal frost), adding 'pajšlo na chuj' (everything went to shit, Pnm, 27). His disgust is very personal in 'Ja chadziŭ halyšma pa skalach, razbeščany Krymam …' (I walked naked over the cliffs, depraved by the Crimea …): 'Вярнуўся ў краіну, што такіх, як я, пасылала ў жопу' (I returned to the country that would tell people like me to get screwed, Pnm, 54). For all his interest in Sanscrit and ancient culture, Kulikoŭ is clearly also well aware of attempts to destroy Belarus's own historical heritage, as may be seen from a highly ironical poem about the need to forget and completely free oneself from the past, 'Razvieścisia z minulym, padać u sud na pamiać …' (To divorce oneself from the past, to take memory to court …).

The sky and heaven feature extensively in this poet's verse, and an interesting meditation on weather and ecology, 'niechta pastaviŭ nadvor'je…' (somebody has set the weather…), begins with snow and ends with hailstones in a particularly local image. Here are the last lines:

> і расчулены норд-вэст ужо ня можа
> стрымаць градзіны сьлёзаў чуючы як
> выбухаюць атамныя станцыі
> чалавечага сьмеху[16]

It is not possible to give a full account here of the rich corpus of Ihar Kulikoŭ's first two books, but they certainly reveal a strong imagination, and considerable mastery of his selected genres; his attempts to create a new or resurrect an old language in *Svamova* is ambitious and, perhaps worthwhile. There appears to be much to look forward to.

---

[16] 'and the tender northwester can no longer / hold back the hailstones of tears hearing how atomic power stations / of human laughter are exploding' (Pnm, 62).

Upala

Anka Upala is a considerable figure amongst young Belarusian writers, known mainly for her prose, for which she has won several prizes. Her first book, *Dreva Entalipt* (The Enthalyptus tree, 2012) contains mostly prose, but there are a few poems, and it is these that are considered here. The majority of them are comic, with spelling deliberately 'wrong' (perhaps a reaction to the 21st-century orthographical debates?), and rhyme and prosody are very loose, with the sense often seeming to be guided by tempting rhymes.

'Trypcich' (Triptych) comprises three poems, followed by a fourth, which ends the book. 'Levy bok' (The left side) is a comic poem about a woman wearing a bucket for a hat in a mode akin to that of Daniil Kharms,[17] with shades of Oliver Sacks. The eccentric (largely but not only russified) spelling and inconsistent rhyme scheme emerge clearly in the first two stanzas:

Жэншчына зь вядром на галаве,
Вы каво удумалі пугаць ім?
Мы віць вам за эпатаж ня плацім,
Жэншчына зь вядром на галаве.

Вам ано ідзёт, я і ня спору,
Галаўной убор страйніт вас так!
Нет, не каждаму прыйдзёцца ўпору
Этат моды вычурный пусьцяк! (De, 84)[18]

'Siaredzina' (The middle) starts boldly by declaring Dunin-Marcinkievič to be a brother, saying that the Taraškievič orthographical system was not compulsory for either of them.[19] In her opinion the language of the street, the vox populi, is the only true guide to language, and she believes that truth is more important than grammar. The poem ends with her imagining Bahdanovič, Pushkin and Mandel'shtam turning crazily in their graves. Two lines from the first stanza illustrate her belief:

---

[17] In 2007 Upala won the Daniil Kharms literary prize in St Petersburg.

[18] 'Woman with a bucket on your head, / Who did you think you would frighten with it? / After all we do not pay for being shocked, / Woman with a bucket on your head. //It suits you, I do not even dispute it, / The headdress makes you look so shapely! / No, it would not suit everyone to wear / Such is the artsy frivolity of fashion!' Numerical references preceded by De refer to *Dreva Entalipt*.

[19] Upala, of course, knows that Dunin-Marcinkievič lived in the middle of the 19th century when it was forbidden to publish in Belarusian at all.

Another, older, poet shares Upala's dissatisfaction with linguistic norms: Jaryla Pšaničny (pen name of Uladzimir Bańko, b. 1973), in his verse collection, *Piščavyja liški* (Scraps of food, 2011) deliberately uses *trasianka*, a mixture of Russian and Belarusian often heard in Belarus.

Ÿместа правілаў забытай мовы
Мне майго народа вескі глас[20]

'Pravy bok' (The right side) is a nonsense poem about an English officer, whose name incidentally is (probably deliberately) spelt inconsistently. Putting far too much sugar in his Ahmed tea, he is punished not only by being called a bad kangaroo, but also by having coffee rubbed into his bald pate and sugar poured in his ears (De, 86). As in many nonsense poems, the rhymes are very important, though here somewhat erratic. The last poem, 'Krasny dzień kaliendara' (A red letter day in the calendar), set in a chicken farm, shows the takeover of Easter by May Day. This lively piece ends with the lyrical heroine's heartfelt words to her mother:

Красная пасха, пракцічаскі
        з лозунгамі, трудавая!
Картошку сеяць не магі, мама.
Ў дзень труда грэх трудзіцца,
        пасядзім дома.
Пціцэфабрыке первай спасіба скажам
За яйца, за патрасаюшчых курыц,
За чалавечаскае вніманіе.[21]

It is a pity that Anka Upala wrote so little verse, as an Important Person may have subsequently thought about Vasiĺ Bykaŭ on the day of his funeral, when, seeing the massive crowd, he said, 'I have always loved Bykaŭ's poems', a gaffe that has become legendary. Luckily, Upala is far from both the Important Person and, indeed, her funeral, so it is only appropriate to wish her strength in her chosen field, whatever it is.

Hanna Novik

Hanna Novik is a poet of considerable talent and great imagination, whose interests in painting and music add to her very individual nature poems, the majority of which explore various aspects of autumn. Her first book, *Sumioty ahniu* (Piles of fire, 2010),[22] is a promising debut, valuable for its rich imagery and humour, as well as a clear-eyed view of the world around her. An unusual aspect of the poems is that some of them appear to have a poetic hero rather than heroine.

---

[20] 'In place of the rules of a forgotten language / For me the voice of my people has real weight' (De, 85).

[21] 'Red Easter, activist units with slogans, a labour day! / One can't plant potatoes, mummy. / On a day of labour it is a sin to labour, let us sit at home. / We will say thanks to the First Chicken Farm / For eggs, for fantastic chickens, / For their humane attention' (De, 87).

[22] The translation of the title may be misleading, as the meaning here is literally snowdrifts; fallen leaves are consistently referred to as fire in this book.

Like most young poets Hanna Novik writes about the search for her own voice, taking in not only inspiration, loneliness, pain and dissatisfaction, but in her case also humour in her handling of the subject. Pain, from the scars of wings on the poetic heroine's back (an image that is repeated more than once in other poems), features at the end of a delightfully wry verse when she is addressed by her muse:

… На спіне шнары. То ад крылаў.
Я ведаю: табе баліць. (Sa, 11)[23]

Simpler, but strong in content as a poetic credo is the triolet 'Zapaviet' (Testament):

Запавет

Вазьмі асадку і пішы
Насуперак вятрам і змроку.
Ты не адзін ў мгле глыбокай,
Вазьмі асадку і пішы.
І розгалас нясе далёка
Малітву змучанай душы.
Вазьмі асадку і пішы
Насуперак вятрам і змроку.[24]

Before returning to the more serious aspects of writing, two poems linking poetry with food are worth mentioning. In 'Adrežcie mnie kavalak syru …' (Cut me off a piece of cheese …), for instance, poetry is set aside for merrymaking; here is the last stanza:

Я на цвічок павешу ліру
І ў кут адпраўлю німб стаяць.
Адрэжце мне кавалак сыру,
Давайце будзем баляваць.[25]

In 'Hurmanskaje' (Gourmandizing) there is at least the promise of a long poem about the refreshments. More humour is found in 'Liasnoje liusterka' (The forest mirror) where poets in February apparently sit around on their haunches (Sa, 96). An interesting poem written from the point of view of a disturbed male writer's unsuccessful search for self-knowledge is 'Ja byŭ paet natchnionaha śvitannia …' (I was a poet of an inspired dawn …), of which these are the last two stanzas:

---

[23] 'There are scars on your back. They are from wings. / I know: you are in pain' Numerical references preceded by Sa are to *Sumioty ahniu*.

[24] 'Take a pencil and write / In the face of winds and darkness. / You are not alone in the deep murk, / Take a pencil and write. / And the echo carries far away / The prayer of a tortured soul. / Take a pencil and write / In the face of winds and darkness' (Sa, 13).

[25] 'I shall hang my lyre on a nail / And send my nimbus to stand in the corner. / Cut me off a piece of cheese, / Let us make merry' (Sa, 103).

Быў патрыётам. Хлусіў мо замала,
Ахвяраваў мо мроям лішні міг …
Надзея нескароная канала.
Спасціг усё. Спакою не спасціг.

Быў шэрай і бяспамятнай істотай,
Пазычанай з ненапісаных кніг.
…І часта дакараў сябе
Употай,
Што сам сябе я так і не спасціг.[26]

In 'Vosień' (Autumn) the lyrical heroine wonders what medium of art is most suitable for an elegy (chalk or pastels) while dreams shower down from the branches (Sa, 60).

Autumn features in many of Hanna Novik's poems, often using personification, but less romantically than many other poets describing this season, although she does feel loneliness at its departure, judging by the following words from 'Rostani' (Crossroads):

Бы жоўтае лісце, шапочуць імгненні —
Дыван адзіноты, сумёты чакання.[27]

Similar loneliness expressed through images of personified nature is found in several other poems including 'Huliaje pa aliejach doždž …' (Rain plays in the avenues …), 'Doždž paciery šepča. Ružancam biaskoncym …' (The rain whispers its beads. An endless rosary …), and 'Sumuje za aknom kaštan …' (The chestnut is melancholy outside the window …), the latter verse inspiring the poet to dip her paintbrush into the mist, borrowing colours from the fallen leaves (Sa, 59). In the book's title poem, 'Sumioty ahniu' she paints a grim, occasionally banal picture of autumn; here are the last two of the four stanzas:

А пасьля будзе дождж. Назаўжды
Ці на некалькі дзён — невядома.
І на хвалях загаснуць сьляды,
І імгненні асыплюцца долу.

Каб праз сотні дажджынак — ня менш —
Засмуціліся думкі употай.
І азяблы кастрычніцкі верш
Грэўся ў яркіх, стракатых сумётах.[28]

---

[26] 'I was a patriot. Perhaps I lied too little, / Perhaps I wasted my spare moments in daydreaming … / The undefeated hope of a channel through. / I reached everything. I did not reach peace. // I was a grey being who had forgotten the past, / Borrowed from unwritten books. / … And I often reproached myself / Secretly, / That I had simply not reached my own self' (Sa, 66).

[27] 'Moments whisper like yellow leaves — / A carpet of loneliness, piles of waiting' (Sa, 63).

[28] 'And later there will be rain. Whether permanently / Or for a few days is unknown. / And

In 'Viečareje ... Za šerym aknom ...' (Evening is falling ... Outside the grey window ...) she writes not of unwritten but of neglected books, many of them hardly relevant or interesting to the poet, as may be seen in the last stanza:

> Прагнуць стосы нячытанных кніг
> Для самлелых старонак свабоды.
> ... Ты ж за сотні імгненняў спасціг
> Толькі сэнс сакавітых назавай.[29]

Likewise, in 'Odum' (Meditation) 'we' keep playing at postmodernism, while Hlobus's books gather dust on the shelf (Sa, 61).[30]

Amongst the numerous examples of Hanna Novik's mastery of imagery may be mentioned only a few: raindrops are related to time in several places in addition to 'Sumioty ahniu', for instance in 'U parku' (In the park) where, to the tolling of a clock tower, moments quiver on the branches of trees (Sa, 52); in 'Praz sotniu daždžoŭ zaduchmianicca vosień ...' (Through hundreds of rainfalls autumn becomes fragrant ...) evening makes the trees blush red (Sa, 15); and finally, two images of the full moon, first as playing ball with the clouds (in 'Na horad naš, suzdrom pazbaŭleny ahniu ...' [Onto our town, completely deprived of light ...]), and secondly in 'Dumak zabytych, skamiečanych reštki ...' (The remains of forgotten, crumpled thoughts ...) the full moon wanes like wax melting on a candle, whilst the clouds resemble ghosts (Sa, 28).

The topic of language is raised both directly and indirectly throughout the book, one strong illustration of the poet's concerns being 'Mova' (Language):

Мова

> Распляжылі. Патрушчылі.
> Знявечылі. Забыліся.
> Аскепкі неўміручыя
> Усё-ткі зліцца сіляцца.
>
> Пакуль не могуць. Множацца
> І ў сэрцы колюць дзідамі.
> Аж покуль дыхаць можацца,
> Не забывай радзімую.[31]

---

[29] 'Piles of unread books thirst for / Freedom for their worn out pages / ... But for hundreds of moments you have achieved / Only the sense of juicy titles' (Sa, 75).

on the waves traces will die, / And moments scatter downwards. // So that through hundreds of raindrops — no less — / Thoughts are secretly saddened. / And a chilled October poem / Was warming itself in the multi-coloured piles' (Sa, 18).

[30] Adam Hlobus (b. 1958) was described as a cult figure in the independent journal *Arche*, which in the year 2000 devoted an entire issue to his work.

[31] 'Language // They smashed it. They crushed it. / They forgot it. / Nonetheless surviving fragments / Are striving to fuse together. // For the time being they cannot. They swell in numbers / And poke staves into their hearts. / But for as long as you can breathe, / Do not forget your native heritage' (Sa, 31).

In 'Imkliva' (Headlong) we are told that it is young people who with time will rescue the language from the oblivion that its enemies wish on it (Sa, 87). The poet's personal aspirations are expressed in a poem 'Atreści z krylaŭ lusku' (Shake the scales from your wings), which ends thus:

> Ды адно вашы душы запалім
> Святой
> Забытаю мовай.[32]

For all the romantic imagination shown in her nature imagery and the frequent appearance of ghosts in her work, Hanna Novik has a modern sensibility and awareness of the good and bad sides of the world around her. She is particularly dismayed by the glorious history of her country that is now in ruins, as is described vividly in 'Viaśliar nad Sožam dzień strakaja novy …' (An oarsman on the river Sož meets the new day …); here is the last stanza:

> Спініся на якую хоць хвіліну.
> Мінае ўсё? Мой сябра, толькі глянь.
> … Раса сьцякае зь клёнавых галінаў.
> Па сьцежцы цьмянай шпацыруе здань.[33]

Also worth mentioning is a subject that is surprisingly rare in this book, namely that of love; it is treated very unconventionally in 'Liryčnaje' (Lyrical), a poem narrated by a failed nihilist and 'worthy mocker' who ends by calling his beloved his antipode and himself ('in love') a demon from the second circle of hell (Sa, 35).

Finally, the wider world is addressed directly in a nightmarish poem about moral decline and social breakdown, 'Atliantyda' (Atlantis), from which the following are a selection of particularly potent lines:

> Тут кожны жыве апрыёры
> І ў сеціве тоне павольна.
>
> Тут трызняць спакоем балотным,
> Тут кожны — і кат і ахвяра.
>
> […]
>
> … І крыўдай забытаю мора
> Ля сценаў ля самых бушуе …[34]

Hanna Novik is a remarkably promising poet, whose vivid and varied imagery and unconventional approach to potentially hackneyed themes, as well as her

---

[32] 'And the only thing that we can set your souls alight with / Is the Sacred / Forgotten language' (Sa, 30).

[33] 'Stop for a moment any time. / Is everything passing? My friend, just look. / … The dew drips from the maple branches. / Along the dark path strolls a ghost' (Sa, 68).

[34] 'Here everyone lives a priori / And slowly drowns in the internet. // Here they dream of the peace of the marsh, / Here everyone is both an executioner and a victim. […] … And a sea of forgotten resentment / rages against the very walls' (Sa, 29).

fierce defence of her native language, makes her a worthy contributor to the flourishing literary scene in Homieĺ.

Niatbaj

To date, Taćciana Niatbaj has published a book under her real name, Nietbajeva, about Belarusian provincial chronicles in the 17th–18th centuries,[35] but, so far, no collections of her own verse, so that what follows is based on a cycle of a dozen poems published in the enterprising East Polish journal *Termapily* in 2012, 'Žyćcio praciahvajecca' (Life goes on).

Niatbaj's cycle comprises very modern poems with a strong narrative sense, and some romanticism, although romance is not usual in relation to the physical love that her lyrical heroine encounters in some unattractive forms, including drunkenness and cynical attempts at seduction. Another strong theme is that of boundaries and frontiers, perhaps reflecting the poet's own recent emigration. The first poem, 'napivacca ŭ ziuziu …' (to get completely sozzled …) shows a woman, constantly pestered by men, who gets completely drunk four times a month (one of them to coincide with her period); the setting moves imperceptibly to wartime, where she is a field cook and soon seduced by a 'very practical' officer with various bribes, including, amongst other things, a month's leave with ice hockey matches, the world cup, and a warm climate with siestas. All she can do, however, is revert to her original pattern of drinking. Here is the end of the poem:

Дзела-
віта:
я люблю цябе, дзетка,
усё акей,
хакей
на лёдзе
ў нясцерпную спёку,
кактэйль,
даніна модзе,
чэмпіянат свету па футболе, сіеста,
казырныя
словы й ніякіх вестак
з фронту чарговы месяц —
юзер! лузер!
адно што паспееш зноў чатыры разы —
у зюзю (Žp, 159–60)[36]

---

35 Taćciana Nietbajeva, *Čalaviek i historyja ŭ bielaruskich miascovych chronikach XVII-XVIII stst*, Miensk, 2012.
36 'Business- / like / I love you, kid, / everything's OK, / hockey / on ice / in unbearable heat, / a cocktail, / a tribute to fashion, / the world football championship, a siesta, / the trumping / words and no news at all / from the front for another month — / user! loser! / the only thing

Men also feature in 'mužčyny razvaročvajucca roŭna na sto vosiemdziesiat …' (men turn exactly a hundred and eighty degrees …), which details their skill at making alcohol, but ends with an impressionistic account of love making. More romantic is 'tak pachla lipami z usich haradskich dvaroŭ …' (it smelled so strongly of lime trees from all the courtyards of the town …) where the lyrical heroine is overjoyed at the coming of her lover like a Viking, and their intimacy.

In 'heta jak zasynać, hliedziačy telievizar …' (it is like falling asleep in front of the television …), however, time passes by and she feels abandoned, aside from life and bereft of people to communicate with, as we read in the first stanza:

> гэта як засынаць, гледзячы тэлевізар
> жыццё працягваецца, а ты саступіў на ўзбочыну
> дзе ніхто не пытаецца ні квіткоў, ні візаў
> але і няма каму зазірнуць у вочы[37]

The only person worse off is a prostitute at the end of the poem who is prepared to sell herself for a bottle of beer. Also downbeat is 'Sonca na padvakoṅni…' (Sun on the windowsill…) which describes waking up on a summer's morning when life seems reducible to coffee, black or with little poems:

> Сэнс жыцця — побач з намі,
> Ён згортваецца да кавы —
> Чорнай або з вяршкамі.[38]

The poem 'Miorznuć ruki, a dychać niama čym — dušna, i …' (My hands are frozen and there is nothing to breathe, it is stuffy, and …) depicts miserable surroundings and the heroine's aspiration for a better life. Here are the first stanza and the last two lines:

> Мёрзнуць рукі, а дыхаць няма чым — душна, і
> Мы, здаецца, яшчэ не скончылі размаўляць:
> Калі ўсе мужыкі — свалата, казлы і блядзішнікі,
> То тады і я — не больш і не менш, чым блядзь.
>
> […]
>
> Я жывая тады, калі ёсць у каго верыць,
> І далёка-далёка праглядаецца далягляд.[39]

---

you can manage is again four times — / completely sozzled' Numerical references preceded by Žp refer to 'Žyćcio praciahvajecca'.

[37] 'it is like falling asleep in front of the television / life goes on, but you have moved onto the side of the road / and no one asks about tickets and visas / but also without anyone with eyes to look into' (Žp, 164).

[38] 'The meaning of life is alongside us, / It is reduced to coffee — / black or with little poems' (Žp, 161).

[39] 'My hands are frozen and there is nothing to breathe, it is stuffy and / we, it seems, have not yet finished our conversation: / If all the guys are swine, johns and whoremongers, / Then I too am, neither more nor less than a whore. […] I am alive when there is something in which to believe, / and far, far away can be seen a horizon' (Žp, 163).

The first line of 'Zabiraj mianie ad mianie i ratuj ad skruchi …' (Take me away from myself and save me from melancholy …) introduces a strong poem of passion and escape; here the theme of visas is quite different from that in 'heta jak zasynać, hledziačy telievizar …':

Забірай мяне ад мяне і ратуй ад скрухі —
Аддавацца салодка ў моцныя рукі. Рухі
Да мяжы, праз мяжу, паўз мяжу, у памежжа, дзе
Я сабе не належу і ты сабе не належыш.
Аўтамат замíж кавы налівае каньяк (і зьлізваю
Да кроплі апошняй), і памежнік пускае без візаў
І бяз мытных збораў, ап'янелы ад шчасця нашага,
Замест штампаў ён піша верш на старонках пашпарта.
Мы ўсё цалаваліся, як Харон праплываў байдай,
Ён быў пэўны, што бачыў сапраўдных Боні і Клайда.
Мы з табой на мяжы, дзе нішто больш ня мае межаў,
Дзе пачуцці сягаюць вышэй найвышэйшых вежаў,
І вільготныя ночы поўняцца дзіўнай музыкай,
Твае рукі імкнуцца хутчэй распіліць гузікі,
І туманнымі ранкамі — пад гострымі лёзамі лёсаў —
Там самотны рыбак ловіць цені хмарачосаў.[40]

Niatbaj's poetry has a strong sense of detail and narrative. It must be hoped that, despite living and working in Warsaw, she will continue to contribute to Belarusian literature.[41]

---

[40] 'Take me away from myself and save me from melancholy — / It is sweet to give oneself into strong arms. Moves / To the border, across the border, over the border, into the border area where / I do not belong to myself and you do not belong to yourself. / The dispenser pours cognac instead of coffee (and I lick it / Until the last drop), and the border guard lets us through without visas / And without inspecting our luggage, intoxicated by our happiness, / Instead of stamps he writes a poem on the pages of my passport. / And we were still kissing , when Charon sailed by in his boat, / He was sure that he had seen the real Bonnie and Clyde. / You and I are on a frontier where nothing has frontiers any more, / Where feelings reach higher than the highest frontiers, / And the damp nights are filled with wondrous music, / Your hands strive to undo my buttons / And in the misty mornings — under the sharp blades of fates — / There a lonely fisherman tries to catch the shadows of skyscrapers' (Žp, 166).

[41] In 2014, too late for inclusion in this study, Taćciana Niadbaj [sic], published in Warsaw a short collection of verse: Sireny śpiavajuć džaz: vieršy (Polackija labirynty).

CHAPTER 5

~

The Lyrical Impulse

Many young poets pay homage to the bucolic idyll, and some have produced excellent nature poems. Relatively few, however, make Belarusian flora and fauna the centre of their poetic world, and even the three women chosen for this chapter, despite the primacy of nature in their work, are certainly not monothematic.

Siviec

Taćciana Siviec's first book was *Lipieńskaja navaĺnica* (A July storm, 2003), followed in 2008 by a book of verse, prose and drama, *Tamu, chto znojdzie … Kachańnie dy inšyja kazki* (For whoever finds … Love and other fairytales). It is on her first book that what follows will be based. Her verse is formally traditional, though her best pieces show a strong individual voice. Very few of the poems in this collection are more than three or four stanzas in length, but the genuine feeling within them is beyond doubt. She seems attracted to the classical forms first introduced by Maksim Bahdanovič over a century earlier, including the rondeau, ritornello, rondelle and, particularly, triolet. The latter form is used for a wide range of subjects including an actor dying on stage (Ln, 6),[1] a prayer incorporating words from the Catholic service (Ln, 21), sentient flowers (Ln, 32), physics (Ln, 64), and a sunset (Ln, 68). Perhaps one of the most interesting of her triolets is the pessimistic 'Kryžy nad ploščaj — heta naš kaniec …' (Crosses over the square — that is our end …), which, like the above-mentioned prayer, incorporates Catholic words, albeit here written in Cyrillic:

'Трыялет'

Крыжы над плошчай — гэта наш канец
Або працяг атрутнага шаленства?
Кантату крокаў граюць струны лесвіц…
Крыжы над плошчай — гэта наш канец?!

---

[1] Numerical references preceded by Ln are to Siviec's *Lipieńskaja navaĺnica*.

Мне сэрца не сагрэе Ваша <не> —
На вуснах стыне <Кірые элейсан...>.
Крыжы над плошчай — гэта наш канец
Або працяг атрутнага шаленства?.. ²

Almost all the poems in Siviec's first collection employ rhyme, although it is
sometimes slightly strained, for instance in 'Prychadzień-zmrok ...' (The newly
arrived sunset ..., Ln, 12). Her infectious sense of humour emerges in several
poems, one instance being 'Ranej pisali ...' (Earlier they used to write ..., Ln, 42),
in which she wonders whether triolets written with a pen are more likely to be
light and winged, but ends by asking why they should be. Beyond the form of
triolets, 'Natchnieńnie' (Inspiration, Ln, 66) gives an imaginative but far from
over-serious description of her craft, whilst in 'Ci treba?' (Is it necessary?, Ln, 49)
she suggests that poets should write about everyday phenomena, not just the more
obvious sources of inspiration. A fine poem about the fate of poets, 'Tyja, što
chodziać pa drocie' (Those who walk on a high wire) compares being a poet to
balancing high in the air, while the crowd below wait for a fall:

Тыя, што ходзяць па дроце

Паэт не проста піша —
Ён ходзіць па танюсенькім дроце:
Чым вышэй,
Тым большая адказнасць
За кожны крок.
Тым болей сціскаецца сэрца
І халадзеюць рукі.
А натоўп пад ім усё чакае,
Калі ж ён не вытрымае
І ўпадзе.
Тады яны змогуць лічыць сябе разумнейшымі,
Бо не палезлі на гэтую вышыню.

Калі паэт не можа болей пісаць,
Гэта тое ж самае,
Што зрываецца ўніз канатаходзец,
Яны чакаюць ... А Ён ідзе ...³

---

² 'Triolet. // Crosses over the square — that is our end / Or the continuation of poisoned
madness? / The strings of ladders play a cantata of footsteps ... / Crosses over the square —
that is our end?! // Your "no" will not warm my heart — / On my lips the "Kyrie eleison" grows
cold ... / Crosses over the square — that is our end / Or the continuation of poisoned
madness? ...' (Ln, 81).
³ 'Those who walk on a high wire. // The poet does not simply write — / He goes along a slender
wire: / The higher, / The more responsibility / For each step. / The more your heart tightens /
And your hands grow cold. / And the crowd below him keeps waiting / For him to stand it no
more / And fall. / Then they will be able to consider themselves more sensible, / For they did
not climb to this great height. // If a poet cannot write any more, / It is the same as / When a
high wire artist loses his grip, / They are waiting ... But He goes on ...' (Ln, 41).

A less dramatic view of her own poems is to be found in 'Paślia prasluchoŭvańnia niekatorych sučasnych piesień' (After listening to certain contemporary songs, Ln, 18), where the eponymous songs are felt to be over-emotional, while, by contrast, she writes (perhaps in vain) of stars, dreams, snow and rowan berries. She does not want to go backwards with these popular singers, but claims her independence in the poem's last three lines:

> Назад? Гляджуся ў цемру ночы …
> Я не хачу! Я не павінна збочыць
> З нікім не пратаптанай пуцявіны …[4]

'Manaloh na liodzie' (Monologue on the ice, Ln, 62) is delightfully humorous, whilst 'Susiedu źvierchu' (To my neighbour upstairs, Ln, 66) treats an everyday problem with more good humour than the subject probably deserves. On the other hand, whether a description of Minsk when it rains becoming 'almost Paris' is meant to be humorous or not is unclear: 'Za veliumam daždžu' (Behind the veil of rain, Ln, 13).

Many of Siviec's poems are concerned with flowers and other features of nature including the seasons, weather, especially storms, clouds, dawn and dusk. Other recurrent themes include dreams, music, miracles, faith and religion. The latter theme is not always treated seriously, as in 'Da Boha' (To God, Ln, 5), in which God is imagined as living at the top of a ten-storey building, while the poet is on the ground floor, wondering whether to go up and how she would get back.

Several of the nature poems are sad such as, for instance, 'Liliei plačuć …' (The lilies weep …, Ln, 32) or 'Liście' (Leaves, Ln, 51), in which fallen leaves are compared to people, and the poet asks who will weep for them? Similarly, in 'Vosieńskija miražy' (Autumnal mirages, Ln, 51) nature and human fate are linked, and in 'Adplata' (Repayment, Ln, 21) joy is repaid by a rather alarming full moon that obstructs the poet's path. Two poems about storms and the thoughts they arouse deserve mention here. 'Navaĺnica'(Thunderstorm) gives a very personal response to a storm that appears to burn away a 'black wing' over Belarus, as may be seen in the last stanza:

> Заходзься, гром! Лютуй, маланка!
> Спаліце чорнае крыло!
> Над Беларуссю звонкім ранкам
> Заззяе новае святло![5]

In 'Rozdum paślia navaĺnicy' (Reflections after a thunderstorm) the poet reflects on earlier days when people superstitiously believed storms to be divine

---

[4] 'Backward? I look into the dark of night … / I do not want to! I am not obliged to turn aside / From my completely untrodden path …' (Ln, 18).

[5] 'Rage, thunder! Flash wildly, lightning! / Burn the black wing! / Over Belarus on a clear morning / Will shine a new light!' (Ln, 58).

punishment, and notes that nowadays they pay no attention to them. She, however, has many unanswered questions as we see in the poem's last stanza:

... На тысячы запытанняў
Адказаў мне не знайсці.
Ніколі
        Не будзе
                 рання
Тым, хто не змог дайсці ...[6]

Music plays a considerable role in Siviec's poetic world. In 'Muzyka'(Music) she describes it as 'Пяшчотнае дакрананне, / Як дотык гарачых вуснаў ...'[7], and in 'Pakuĺ tvaja ruka caluje stromki klaviš ... (Whilst your hand kisses the flowing keys ..., Ln, 17) her response to music is to that of a beloved performer. In another poem, 'Na skryžavańni, by na skraźniaku ...' (At a crossing, as if in a draught ..., Ln, 80), musical imagery is used that is mainly about loneliness. The latter feeling is also prominent in her poems about religion and the Church, another setting where negative feelings might not be expected. For example one of the triolets begins:

Мне сніцца аскамітны неспакой,
Настоены на смутку рэлігійным ...[8]

In 'Šliachi' (Paths, Ln, 56) a stark choice is presented: whether to take the road to the devil or to God. An important work connected with religion is 'Liturhičny trypcich' (Liturgical triptych, Ln, 78–79): the first poem suggests that 'Dona nobis pacem' sounds like an exhausted liturgy (знямоглае літанне), and the second poem to 'Gothic unhappiness' (гатычная туга), whilst the third stanza of the third of the poems expresses the hope of salvation by religion from the darkness of earthly loneliness and sickly dreaminess:

О, Lux aeterna, выратуй мяне
Ад мораку зямное адзіноты,
Ад хворай летуценнасці блакнотнай,
О, Lux aeterna, выратуй мяне![9]

Several of Siviec's poems appear to express feelings of depression, particularly about Belarus's national situation, for instance 'U palonie' (In captivity):

---

[6] 'To a thousand questions / I can find no answers. / There will never be morning / For those who could not reach it ...' (Ln, 54).

[7] 'Gentle touching, / Like the contact of hot lips ...' (Ln, 16).

[8] 'I dream of velvet disquiet / Infused with religious sadness ...' (Ln, 22).

[9] 'O, Lux aeterna, save me / From the darkness of earthly loneliness, / From the sickly dreaminess of my notebook, / O, Lux aeterna, save me!' (Ln, 79).

У палоне

Мы жывём, бы схаваныя ценямі кратаў,
Вечна ў цемрадзі згубаў і лютасці катаў.
Да бясконцай хлусні і пакутаў
Мы здаўна кайданамі прыкуты.

Колькі год мы блукаем, шукаючы раю,
Пад праклён і прароцтва ваўчынае зграі:
Мо не трэба шукаць і не варта ісці,
Бо ўсё роўна нічога не зможам знайсці?

І змяняўшы пакуты на вечны спакой,
Будзем спаць пад гатовай упасці страхой,
Будзем спаць і пабачым ўсё, бы ўва сне.
І памром ... Ды навошта, скажыце Вы мне?[10]

The word imprisonment also occurs in 'Naša historyja' (Our history) where the words for prison bars (кратаў) and executioners (катаў) are again rhymed. Another poem, with a potentially deeply depressing title, has a subtitle that presages a redeeming sense of humour at the end, '"Vychadu niama", ci Rozdum u mietro' ('"No exit", or Thoughts in the underground') The second stanza, however, expresses true despair:

Забываем паняцце <шчырасць>!
Навакола — бястварая шэрань.
Праўдзе час адлятаць у вырай,
А паэтам — паліць паперы ...[11]

The themes of ageing and mortality, though more common amongst older poets, are not unknown in the work of the youngest generation, including Siviec. In one such verse, 'Ja snoŭ viasiolkavych nie bačyla daŭno …' (I have not seen rainbow dreams for a long time …, Ln, 35), she points out that most people choose to ignore mortality, living like soap bubbles. In 'Randeľ' (Rondelle, Ln, 14) she compares the temporariness of human life to the falling blossom of chestnut trees, whilst the quatrain, 'Iduć hady i dumki ŭsio radziejuć …' (The years pass and thoughts keep thinning out …), confronts the theme of ageing very directly:

---

[10] 'In captivity // We live, as if hidden by the shadows of prison bars, / Always in the darkness of losses and the fierceness of executioners. / To the endless lies and torments / We have long been bound by chains. // How many years we have been wandering, looking for heaven, / Under the curses and prophesy of a wolf pack: / Perhaps we should not seek and it is not worth going forward, / For in any case we cannot find anything? // And exchanging our torments for eternal rest, / We shall sleep under a roof that is ready to fall in, / We shall sleep and see everything as if in a dream. / And we shall die. And for what, will you tell me?' (Ln, 52).
[11] 'We are forgetting the concept of "sincerity"! / All around is faceless greyness. / It is time for truth to emigrate, / And for poets to burn their papers …' (Ln, 57).

Ідуць гады, і думкі ўсё радзеюць,
Як валасы на галаве сівой.
І ў дом ужо не клічаш ты надзею,
Баронішся сустрэч з самім сабой …[12]

To end on a national rather than purely human issue, Siviec responds to the characteristically inspiring topic of one of Belarus's true heroes with a question, a feature of many of her poems. In 'Dzie ty, Kastuś Kalinoŭski?' (Where are you, Kastuś Kalinoŭski?) she relates his heroic example to the present day, as we read in the last stanza:

Годзе гібець нам у крыўдзе і горы!
Час ужо кропкі ставіць — не коскі!
Хтосьці іншы ты быў яшчэ ўчора —
Сёння ты — мужны Кастусь Каліноўскі![13]

Tacciana Siviec's poetry, formally simple, frequently marked by exclamation and question marks, is at times very memorable, not least by the combination of passion and humour.

Sidorka

Naścia Sidorka's first book of verse, *Pialiostki* (Petals, 2013) has a short autobiographical Introduction, and some words of encouragement from poet Aleś Kasko (b. 1951). Sidorka is a very young writer whose work is both thematically and formally in the classical Belarusian tradition, at the peak of which stands her favourite poet Maksim Bahdanovič. Religion and, particularly, the natural world are prominent in her work, as is the past — both of her family and her country. Her fondness for alliteration is manifest, although the rhyming, particularly in poems consisting of couplets, shows room for further development.

A good example of Sidorka's romantic nature poems, here with a sense of living history, is 'Niaśvižski park' (The park at Niaśviž):

Нясвіжскі парк

Я блукаю па восеньскім парку
Пад нагамі ўсё болей лісця.
Гэта клёнаў апалыя крылы
Старажытны цуд-парк залацяць.
Абсыпаюць сцяжынкі і лаўкі,
Камяні і азёрную даль.
Тут эпохаў былых адгалоскі,
Тут свае і пяшчота, і жаль.

---

[12] 'The years pass, and thoughts keep thinning out, / Like hair on a grey head. / And you no longer call hope into your home, / You defend yourself against meetings with your own self …' (Ln, 34).

[13] 'We have been ruined enough with wrongs and grief! / It is now time to place full stops, not commas! / You were somebody else even yesterday — / Today you are the bold Kastuś Kalinoŭski!' (Ln, 53).

Як жа шмат і легенд, і паданняў
Сведчаць тут аб сівой даўніне!
Вось і постаці статуй маўклівых
Таямніцы нашэптваюць мне … (Pia, 10)[14]

Similar romanticism is found in 'Žnička' (A falling star, Pia, 23) in which she
dwells on the value of these comet-like phenomena, feeling that their loss will
make the world a poorer place, and also in a poem acclaiming the arrival of
spring, 'Apranulisia višni va ŭbory bialiavyja …' (The cherry trees have dressed
themselves with whitish adornment …), of which these are the first four lines:

Апрануліся вішні ва ўборы бялявыя,
І прырода звініць, ажывае яна.
Усміхаюцца промням сасонкі смуглявыя —
Навакол бярэ ўладу красуня-вясна.[15]

Another nature poem, centring on a butterfly and its dreams, is 'Byŭ padviačorak;
promni viesnavyja …' (It was towards evening; spring rays …):

Быў падвячорак; промні веснавыя
Паволі ападалі на траву,
На стомленыя крыльцы залатыя;
Спаў матылёк, схіліўшы галаву.

Ён сніў палі, што ўлетку каласяцца,
Чуў пах рамонкаў, спеўны шэпт лясоў,
Крыніцы, што паміж дубоў бруяцца,
Гаворку краю — скарб палешукоў.

Так лёгка навакол было і проста,
Так ціха, што кружыла галаву…
Спаў матылёк, бы трапяткі пялёстак,
Які зляцеў раптоўна на траву.[16]

---

[14] 'The park at Niaśviž // I wander through the park in autumn / Under my feet are ever more
leaves. / It it the fallen wings of maple trees / That are gilding this wonderful ancient park, /
pouring onto the paths and benches, / The rocks and the lake in the distance. / Here are the
echoes of past epochs, / Here is our comfort and pity. // How very many legends and tales /
Here bear witness to its grey antiquity! / Here the figures of the silent statues also / Whisper
their secrets to me …' Numerical references preceded by Pia are to *Pialiostki*.

[15] 'The cherry trees have dressed themselves with whitish adornment, / And nature rings out,
it is coming to life. / The swarthy pine-trees smile at the sun's rays — / All around beauteous
spring is coming into its own' (Pia, 19).

[16] 'It was towards evening; spring rays / Were slowly falling on the grass, / Onto weary little
golden wings; There slept a butterfly, with head bent. // It dreamed of fields that in summer
grew ears, / It sensed the smell of camomile, the melodious whispering of the forests, / The
springs that bubble amongst the oak trees, / The language of the region — the treasure of
Polessians. // It was so light and simple all around, / So quiet, that it made one's head spin …
/ The butterfly slept, like a trembling petal, / That had suddenly flown down onto the grass'
(Pia, 16).

This reference to language is taken further in one of Sidorka's historical ballads, 'Varta' (The guard), where fear that the native tongue may be forgotten, and thoughts of how it may preserved by writing become prominent at the end; this is the third part:

Коціцца дзень … На мяжы небяспечнай
Цвёрда і мужна змагаецца воін …
А на паперы, на полі адвечным,
Абараняе краіну бяззбройны.[17]

In similar mode is 'Skaz pra Kalinu' (A tale of Kalina), about a fiery maiden's wait for her heroic husband, although, after her final oath if he were to die, the narrator's ending is almost throwaway:

І клятву дала:
<Над магілай яго
Калінаю стану, калі я агонь!..>
Ці стала калінай нявеста, ці не,
Даруйце, пра гэта няведама мне.[18]

A more serious reflection on modern times is 'Serca' (Heart), set on an old country road, and based on the conceit that people find it convenient to leave their hearts by the wayside in order to have easier lives. This is the final stanza, describing a particularly heartless person:

Цвёрды. Дужы. Халодны, Чужы.
Абыходзіць надзьмута сустрэчных …
Колькі ж іх на гасцінцы старым,
Непахісных, глухіх, бессардэчных?[19]

Poetry is the eternal opposite of life's prose, as Sidorka writes in the simple poem that begins her book (as well as adorning the cover), 'O świet! Ciabie nituje advarotnaje …' (O, world! You are united by opposites …):

О свет! Цябе нітуе адваротнае.
Зімы і лета дзіўная інверсія.
Усмешка і сляза. Чужое й роднае.
Жыццёвай прозы вечная паэзія![20]

---

[17] 'the day is coming to an end … On a dangerous border / the warrior fights firmly and bravely … / But on paper, on an eternal field, / He defends his country without weapons' (Pia, 29).
[18] And she made an oath: / "Over his grave / I shall become a guelder rose, if I am fire! …" / Whether the bride became a guelder rose or not, / Forgive me, that is something I do not know' (Pia, 27).
Another example of Sidorka's humour is 'Žart' (A joke), a poem apparently addressed to her friend Ivan, about how their lives might be magically transformed (Pia, 18).
[19] 'Hard. Strong. Cold. Alien. / He haughtily avoids the people he meets … / How many there are on the old road / Stubborn, deaf, heartless people' (Pia, 11).
[20] 'O, world! You are united by opposites. / The amazing inversion of winter and summer. / A smile and a tear. What is alien and what is dear. / The eternal poetry of life's prose!' (Pia, 3).

The rest of Sidorka's verse touches on familiar themes, such as rays of light, as in 'Na tkaninie hetaj čornaj …' (On this black cloth …) and, particularly, 'Soniečny šliach' (The sun's path), or Belarus's historical heritage, as in 'Ikona' (about Saint Euphrosyne) and 'Paetu' (To a poet) devoted to the short but immensely creative life of Maksim Bahdanovič, her chief inspiration. The Afghan war figures in two poems: the first, 'Jon pajšoŭ na vajnu …' (He went to war …, Pia, 13), ends with something known to soldiers everywhere, namely that fighting is easier than waiting for something to happen; the second, 'Čakańnie' (Waiting, Pia, 14) describes a mother anxiously anticipating news of her conscripted son. In 'Matuli' (To my mother) Sidorka paints a very affectionate picture:

Матулі

Твае вочы — блакітныя зоры,
У якіх акіян дабрыні,
Твае рукі і ў шчасці, і ў горы
Ахінуць, быццам промні вясны.

Найдарожшая ў свеце жанчына,
З тваёй ласкі — так радасна жыць!
Слова <мама> павек немагчыма,
Як і слова <Айчына>, забыць.[21]

Probably closely related to this poem is 'Toj čas, što ŭ pamiaci haryć …' (That time that burns in my memory …) describing her recent happy childhood:

Той час, што ў памяці гарыць
Святлом яскрава-залацістым,
Што смехам сонечным звініць,
Завецца цёпла так —
Дзя-ці-і-нствам …[22]

Naścia Sidorka's first book is clearly a youthful debut, and only time will bring greater experience and creative maturity. At present it may be said that she is a fluent poet at her own level, with a pleasant sense of humour, and a sane outlook on the world.

---

[21] 'To my dear mother // Your eyes are light blue stars, / In them is an ocean of goodness, / Your arms, both in happiness and in sadness / Embrace, like the rays of spring light. // Dearest of all women in the world, / With your affection, it is such a joy to live! / The word "mother", like the word "fatherland"/ can never ever be forgotten' (Pia, 7).

[22] 'The time that burns in my memory / With a shining golden light, / That rings with the laughter of sunshine, / Is warmly called — / chi-i-ld-hood …' (Pia, 20).

Kaciurhina

Anastasija Kaciurhina before reaching the age of twenty had published two collections of verse, both in 2011: *Pad vietraziem ranku* (Under the sail of morning) and *Parason* (Umbrella). Almost all the poems in these books are about love, which is passionate, but very often associated with pain of various kinds, especially that of parting and frustration. Frequent themes are dreams and memory, and the poet's feelings are often related to natural phenomena, especially autumn and winter, with bonfires serving as an occasional metaphor for passion. It is, however, her personal anguish that dominates over nature and the rest of the outside world. Exclamation marks and final ellipses are widely used to emphasize emotion and suspense.

In the opening poem of *Pad vietraziem ranku*, 'I budzie vosień, mily, nazaŭždy …' (And there will be autumn forever, my beloved …) the poet shows belief in and hope for a future with her loved one, and in the next, 'Padary mnie vosień' (Give me autumn) she rejoices in their shared identity. In 'Kachanamu' (To my beloved) she reveals that he believes in dreams and God, and hopes he may come to her with his dreams (Pvr, 7).[23] Somewhat different is 'Naradžeńnie' (Birth), which gives a passionately romantic description of pregnancy and birth. An example of a love lyric that combines religion (or marriage), dreams and pain is 'Ty mnie kazaŭ: "Nikoli"' (You said to me 'Never'):

> Ты мне казаў: <Ніколі>
> <Ніколі> … Як яно гучыць?
> Ні пацалункаў, ні сустрэчы.
> І не заплач, не закрычы,
> Не ўсміхніся цэлы вечар …
> <Ніколі> — з тым не пазнаюць
> Жыццё што стала мне табою …
> І толькі сэрца так нясуць
> Да алтара, да сноў, да болю …[24]

Pain is also to the forefront in several other poems, including 'I toĺki boliu vysachlyja vočy …' (And only my eyes dried up with pain …) and 'Oda pacalunkam' (An ode to kisses), a fiercely romantic poem. In 'Oda boliu' (Ode to pain) the last two lines compare love to wormwood:

> — Мой боль, як і мая любоў, —
> Палын зямны — таму і горкі …[25]

---

[23] Numerical references preceded by Pvr are to *Pad vietraziem ranku*.
[24] 'You said to me "Never" // "Never" … / How does it sound? / Neither kisses nor a meeting. / And do not cry, do not shout, / Do not smile the whole evening … / "Never" — with that word people would not recognize / What life has become for me with you … / And only in this way do they bear their hearts / To the altar, to dreams, to pain …' (Pvr, 13).
[25] '—My pain, like my love, — / Is earthly wormwood — and therefore bitter …' (Pvr, 36).

'Nie adzaviecca recha boliem ...' (The echo does not respond with pain ...),
referring to her lover's waiting wife, begins:

Не адзавецца рэха болю
Мой сум схаваўся ў цёплы шаль.[26]

Another strong poem on the subject of betrayal and disillusion begins with the
following two lines:

Колькі дзён адышло толькі болем,
Колькі здрадлівых стала надзей![27]

Particularly affecting are Kaciurhina's poems of parting. One of the best,
'Raskryju parason ...' (I shall open my umbrella ...) also raises the question of
her position as not merely lover but also poet. In the lines that follow, this subject
affords a vivid picture of physical separation:

—Хай твар зямны любоў
Кладзе на аркуш белы!
—Пячатка для ахвяр!
Смяешся ў процьме. Дзе ты?
Ніхто не цалаваў
Каханку як паэта.
Цягнік халодны крык
Кідае ў твар перону —
І ты, як сон мой, знік
У вусені вагонаў ...[28]

In 'Adychodziačym ciahnikam' (To departing trains) she feels as impermanent
as the snowflakes that swirl around the train taking her lover away, with even
memory lost, as we read at the end of this poem:

Будуць самотныя мухі кружыцца
З новай халоднаю вераю зноў:
Гэта не спраўдзіцца ... Можа, прысніцца?
Можа, без памяці гэта любоў?..[29]

---

[26] 'The echo does not respond with pain / My sorrow has hidden itself in a warm shawl'
(Pvr, 49).
[27] 'How many days have passed in pain alone, / How many treacherous hopes have arisen!'
(Pvr, 51). The poem ends with the same lines, replacing hopes (*nadziej*) with people (*liudziej*)
[28] 'Let love place an earthly face / On a white sheet of paper! / A signet for sacrifices! / You
laugh in the darkness. Where are you? / Nobody kissed / A lover like a poet. / The train throws
a cold cry / In the face of the platform — / And you, like my dream, disappeared / In the
caterpillar of carriages' (Pvr, 21).
[29] 'The lonely flies will circle / With a new cold belief once again: / This will not happen ...
Perhaps it is a dream? / Perhaps this love is without memory? ...' (Pvr, 47).

A new disquieting theme is of the lover as a judge in 'Minulaje, i ty skanala znoŭ!..' (The past, you have died again! ...). The following five lines will give an impression of its contents:

Мне страшна, ды іду на гэты суд.
І Вам, Суддзя, у твар крычу, што тут,
Не Вы адзін, каханы мой, зацяты!

[...]

Ёсць месца для кахання і нуды,
Суддзя Вы мой, и Вы не без заганы...[30]

The poet's feeling of being let down is expressed with great clarity in the last two lines of 'Biez žurby — ŭsio adno spačuvańnie ...' (Without grief — sympathy is empty ...):

Дайце выпіць самоту з падманам,
Каб яго пераблытаць з каханнем[31]

Although there is a great deal of passion, pain and disappointment in a book with what appears to have a soothing title, *Pad vietraziem ranku*, and more examples could be given, it comes as almost relief when one of the love lyrics, 'Byla liuboŭ, bylo i licha ...' (There was love and there was also misfortune ..., Pvr, 40), is semi-humorous, as the poet loses all joy in life when she takes the wrong bus.

*

Kaciurhina's second book of 2011, *Parason*, naturally, shares many of the features of the first, as well as including a few of the same poems. Introduced by Nina Škliarava, it mainly continues the theme of frustrated love, and the first poem, 'I ja hliadžu, hliadžu Vam naŭzdahon ...' (And I gaze and my gaze follows you ...), is an impassioned poem dedicated to the older poet, which contains the rather pathetic line, 'А дзе ж яны, мужчыны?' (But where, oh where, are the men?, Pa, 5).[32] The next poem, 'Ptuški Paleśsia' (Birds of Polesia) celebrates the life and work of Nina Škliarava, Jaŭhienia Janiščyc and Raisa Baravikova, describing them as a collective firebird released into the country, treasures of the Palesian lands. The main part of the book is divided into two parts, 'Caluju kropieĺki daždžu' (I kiss drops of rain) and 'Ničoha boliej' (Nothing more).

---

[30] 'I am terrified, and I am going to this court. / And, Judge, I shout in your face that I am here, / You are not alone, my stubborn beloved! [...] there is a place for love and longing, / You, my Judge, you too are not without fault ...' (Pvr, 30).
[31] 'Let me drink loneliness with deceit, / In order to mix it up with love' (Pvr, 48).
[32] Numerical references preceded by Pa are to *Parason*.

Nature, implied loosely by the title of the first part, is, although described delicately, almost always the background to the lyrical heroine's anguish and frustration. Umbrellas, unsurprisingly, feature in several poems, sometimes symbolically, but the sense of inequality, pain and unsatisfied love is ubiquitous, as are reproaches, despair and self-pity. Some of these may be seen in the following short extracts. The first two lines of 'I viernaja, zdavalasia, starannaja ...' (And faithful, it seems, and caring ...), for example:

> І верная, здавалася, старанная ...
> Ды толькі стала прыкраю і горкай.[33]

or, as a victim, in 'Kachaŭ da samych tonkich strunak ...' (He loved me to my most delicate heart strings ...):

> Кахаў да самых тонкіх струнак,
> А вось забыўся пра мяне...[34]

'Niežadanyja stomiacca hości ...' (Unwanted guests become weary ...) expresses vividly in its final stanza the loneliness of her situation:

> Пакахаю чужога я ўпотай,
> Маладосць у любосці ў даўгу.
> І такая бярэ адзінота,
> Што, здаецца, і жыць не магу.[35]

Finally, here is a perhaps emblematic poem of the lyrical heroine's misery, 'Usio ŭžo vyśpiela. A serca ...' (Everything has come to fruition. But my heart ...):

> Усё ўжо выспела. А сэрца
> Збалела прыкрасцю, на жаль,
> І не паспела адагрэцца...
> Накіну смутак, як вуаль,
> Ці шалік. Так, было і годзе.
> Адно — адчай. І тут — знявер.
> Не зманіш львінае пародзе:
> Каханы мой — драпежны звер.[36]

Since these books were published in the same year, it is not possible to speak of development as such, but both feature not only a tormented lyrical heroine, but also show that Kaciurhina is a poet of undoubted talent at the start of her career.

---

[33] 'Both faithful, it seems, and caring ... / But I only became vexed and bitter' (Pa, 17).

[34] 'He loved to my most delicate heart strings, / But then he just forgot me ...' (Pa, 26).

[35] 'I secretly love another's man, / My youth is in debt to my feelings of love. / And such loneliness takes hold of me, / That, it seems, I cannot live' (Pa, 29).

[36] 'Everything has come to fruition. But my heart / Is unfortunately sick with vexation / And has not yet become warm again ... / I shall put on sadness, like a veil / Or a shawl. So it has happened and enough of it, / All that is left is despair. And now disbelief. / You cannot deceive the leonine breed: / My beloved is a beast of prey' (Pa, 39).

CHAPTER 6

~

Humour

The seven poets in this chapter are far from being the only ones to reflect the comic side of life in their work. Some of the humour derives from a light-hearted attitude to the Deity, but more arises from a sarcastic attitude to the current regime and its representatives; purely ludic verse is also not rare, and puns or macaronic jests are evident, particularly in some rhyming poems.

Martysievič

Maryja Martysievič plays a very active role in contemporary Belarusian literature, as a lively journalist and critic in addition to her highly imaginative prose and poetry. The subject of what follows will be the verse found in her first two books, *Cmoki liatuć na nierast: Ese ŭ vieršach i prozie* (The serpents will fly to spawn: Essays in verse and prose, 2008) and *Ambasada: Vieršy svaje i čužyja* (Embassy: Original and translated poems, 2011). To begin with the earlier book, in both prose and verse Martysievič has produced a veritable salmagundi with various forms of fun from absurdity to subtle irony, clear enjoyment of the possibilities of rhyme and repetition, and a variegated collection of themes and stories. There is, however, also a serious side to many of her reflections, not least in No. 1 of the book's ten sections,[1] 'Frynas' (Threnody), which has an epigraph from the words of the religious scholar Mialieci Smatrycki (1572–1630) in a modern Belarusian version by Aleś Razanaŭ. The following lines end the poem's first paragraph:

> Бог праз мае пустыя вачніцы
> выцякае па кроплі, ўцякае. Яму наўздагон
> дзікай ружай вятроў у званіцы выю праклён.
> І скрозь прарэхі муроў, у якія відно душу,
> зруйнаваную ўшчэнт, па мёртвых сваіх галашу. (Clnn, 8)[2]

---

[1] The numeration begins with 0.

[2] 'Through my empty eye-sockets God / trickles in drops, and runs away. Chasing after him / like the wild rose of winds in the bell tower I wail a curse. / And through the holes in the walls, through which the soul can be seen, / utterly ruined, I lament for my dead' Numerical references preceded by Clnn are to *Cmoki liatuć na nierast*.

Then a young man with a rucksack is introduced, deeply dismayed at finding that everything has gone and that he has missed the holy Grail; he is fiercely hostile to the (Russian) heritage that is left, with its own world, its swear words and 'Whistling By'.[3] The young man is no match for the poet's sorely missed hero, telling the latter, however, 'Я — тое раньш, якога ўжо тут ня будзе.' (I am what I was earlier, and shall never be here again, Clnn, 9).

Section 2 takes as its reference point Mickiewicz's well-known ballad 'Świtezianka' (1821) in Belarusian translation. Martysievič's poem has a similar rhyme scheme, ABAB, but shorter lines, and includes some interesting Polish beauties, Marysia, Hanulia and Zosia, against whom she warns her lover.

'Barbara Radziwił's Livejournal' is the title of Section 3, with the subtitle, 'excerpts from the internet diary —barbara_ru'.[4] It represents a journey undertaken in the 16th century, but with many contemporary elements, as the title suggests, including the metro, oral sex, shift keys, visas and so on, and tells the story of her love for young Žykgimont (from 1547 her husband). The rhyme is intermittent.

The following section, 'Comme il faut', offers a mixture of advice about authentic life styles, including nail care, but in a very off-beat manner. Of the other parts, the theme of 'Jana i Jano' (She and It) returns to distant love and fingers, the She being Penelope, a perfectionist who weaves a map of the Miensk underground; 'Pamiežnyja historyi' (Stories from the border) describe in a mixture of prose and verse various difficult episodes, one of which, 'Havenda' (An unpretentious story),[5] ends with an account of a priest who declares, 'We are all transit in this life' (Clnn, 66). Martysievič's imagery is often strikingly unexpected: for instance, a young man hitching back from Amsterdam to Belarus feels relief, when crossing the frontier, comparable to emergence from the womb. Part 7 of the book, 'Siastra Zoja i Kaniec Svietu', reappears in slightly changed form and with additional material in *Ambasada*; it will be discussed later.

The penultimate part of *Cmoki liacuć na nierast* is entitled 'I Maci ich Safija' (And their mother Safija) which begins mysteriously with 'Yhvh.by' and has epigraphs about God from Karatkievič and Brodsky; here the patriarchal deity is depicted as a beekeeper, and at the end the poet begs forgiveness for urban obsessions: the nationalists for emphasizing language (as they rightly all do), the blue-trousered feminists (although the author herself may be one) for considering all men goats, and anti-globalists for violent behaviour, suggesting that they should all be forgiven, for war is about to break out. The book ends with a poem,

---

[3] Clnn, 9. The Whistling By (*Prosvistela*) may be a humorous version of Russian *Prosvetitelia* (Teacher / Enlightener).

[4] Barbara Radziwiłł (1520–1551) was Queen of Poland and Grand Duchess of Lithuania.

[5] The word in Polish, gawęda, means either free conversation or an unpretentious literary composition in verse or prose.

'A jašče — nieĺha źvieźci z saboj krainu (aziory, reki) ...' (And what is more, you cannot take with you the country [the lakes and rivers] ...). The poem concerns the preservation of national values and the need to be constantly on the alert to defend these values from serpents that may visit.

Ambasada is introduced by a short English-titled essay 'Poets Never Survive', in which she declares that the indifference to poetry of her country and of the Nobel Committee only inspires her to write and translate more (A, 5–6).[6] The original poems in this volume show a sense of fantasy as well as of fun and imagination, introducing a wide range of cultural references. The first of them, 'Sweet Home', describes a modern home but, as it turns out, through the eyes of a burglar, who is invited to steal the quarrels and bitterness as well as his swag (A, 9). Another startling but comic poem is 'Mabilizacija' (Mobilization) on the unlikely theme of Parkinsons, Alzheimers and other ailments with some delightfully unexpected rhymes such as *tupa* (stupid) with *Gvadelupa* (Guadeloupe) and *hiemier* (gamer) with *Alchiejmier* (Alzheimer).

Two poems give very different impressions of schooldays: 'Adnaklasniki.by' (A web-site for finding old school friends) describes, in school slang with many contractions, preparations for meeting in a cafe. The following lines give an impression of the tone:

і такая прыет, пака,
скока лет, скока зім, как там Лёха, а как Максім,
і грыт, у нас тут устрэча ў кафэ ...[7]

The other poem, 'Old School' describes in the first stanza the outdated moral programme, and in the remaining two the ways in which the girls dress, and the effect it has on the male teachers. The poet is more sympathetic to the girls' fashion sense than to the teachers' reactions, as may be seen in the last of three stanzas:

І нарэшце спадніцу — вышэй ад каленяў,
каб географ рэльеф гэты позіркам
не змог абмінуць ніяк,
каб біёлаг згадаў пра пахвіну,
каб настаўнік гісторыі
ўсе сорак пяць хвілінаў
меў гарантаваны стаяк.[8]

---

[6] Numerical references preceded by A are to *Ambasada*.

[7] 'and what a one, 'lo, 'bye, / long time no see,/ how's Liocha there, and how's Maksim, /and, they say there's gonna be a meet-up in the caff ...' (A, 15).

[8] 'And finally — a skirt above the knees, / so that the geography teacher could no way avoid / this contour with his gaze,/ so that the biology teacher mentioned the groin, / so that the teacher of history / for the entire forty-five minutes / had a guaranteed hard-on' (A, 16).

The next three poems all touch on a different kind of adult theme, though not necessarily seriously. 'Miratvorčaść' (Peace making) suggests that if peace makers can really make peace, then miracle workers can create miracles, concluding that, according to this scheme, the Virgin Mary weeps, Judas kisses, and the Buddha smiles (A, 17). Whether football fanaticism is really adult, or not, the poet describes it with several Hebrew words, some producing lively rhymes in 'C'mianyja mieśca TaNaČu' (Obscure parts of the Tanach), whilst 'Praviedniku narodaŭ śvietu' (To the righteous man of the world's peoples) she uses Jews, who sometimes prove stronger than Germans, and their concealment in cellars during hostile occupations, as an image to help people to live a more moral life (A, 20).

Maryja Martysievič is a widely read and very referential poet, as is additionally witnessed by her epigraphs and the poets she translates from Polish, Ukrainian, Russian, English and American.[9] It seems doubtful, however, whether 'Šviejnaja mašynka praŭdy' (The sewing machine of truth), with its long epigraph from Quenteen [sic] Tarantino's film Inglourious Basterds, is meant to echo satirically the moral encomium to sewing machines in Nikolai Chernyshevskii's Chto delat' (What is to be done,1863). Like many of her poems, this one moves between many places and refers to a multitude of things and people, including fellow poet Vital Ryžkoŭ.

The seasons of the year are treated with ebullient humour in 'Vieršavany kalendar' (A verse calendar), combining pastiches of traditional elements with very modern references. In May, for instance, the writer Kastuś Travień (b. 1947) goes to other people's literary evenings, selling his own books in the foyer, after which he goes home, looking forward to a new Thaw, and reads Karl Friedrich May (A, 33).[10] Ksienia August, an organ student from East Prussia, puts on her advertisements, 'Aŭhusta Žnivień' (Augusta August). September (Vierasień) leads to skittish play with the word and particularly viera (belief), including an under-age prostitute, the translator Vera Rich and the religious belief of Abu Dhabi, going on to online dating and other features of modern women's lives (A, 35–36). October and November are devoted to two poets with punning names, K. Stryčnik and L.Istapad (the first wrote about Lenin, the second about autumn), but here Martysievič introduces pathos into her humour, suggesting that victims of oppression need praying for (A, 36). Other unusual treatments of the seasons include the intermittently rhymed 'Serca śviatoha Siĺviestra' (The heart of St Silvester), in which we are given a squalid view of Christmas, though the tree turns out to be hung with various hearts, including those of the saint and the poet herself (A, 39). 'Happy Easter', in rhyming couplets, depicts quarrelling and

---

[9] This distinction might not have been approved by Oscar Wilde who described America and Britain as 'two nations divided by a common language'.
[10] Travień and Maj are two alternative Belarusian words (the first less russified) for the month of May.

fighting in a store for Easter goods (A, 43–44).[11] Customers' behaviour is only marginally better in the ironically titled, 'Expobel mon amour'.[12]

In her first book, Martysievič discussed bad language in Belarusian: 'Pašli mianie pa-bielarusku: Karotki kurs ajčynnaha brydkasloŭja' (Up yours in Belarusian: A short course of native bad language', Clnn, 56–63). Her own use of non-normative words is relatively mild, except where she uses transliterated English in, for instance, 'Belarus — England, Varšava — Minsk', a romp around a train journey where a Belarusian peasant encounters some uncouth Englishmen (A, 52–53). The aim is clearly not to shock, but a revelling in nonsense, often deriving from inventive and sometimes wild rhymes. A change from Slavamir Adamovič's earlier Russian poem, 'Ubei prezidenta' (Kill the president, 1995), Martysievič calls for (new) life in 'Naradzi prezidenta' (Give birth to a president), imagining, rather wistfully, what a new president might do for Belarus:

> Ты кажаш, голкай цэнзуры зашыты твой рот
> і ванітоўней, чым сёння, ужо не будзе.
> А па мне, усё ў тваіх руках, пакладзеных на жывот:
> Нарадзі прэзідэнта, якога хочаш, сабе і людзям.[13]

The first line would seem to refer to the bold act of protest of Slavamir Adamovič (b. 1962), when at a public meeting in 1997 he sewed up his own lips.

'Siastra Zoja i Kaniec Śvietu' (Sister Zoja and the End of the World) is appropriately apocalyptic in form (extraordinary words and fonts, and stranger layout), with random rhymes. Its content is likewise unusual and complex: Zoja, a negro girl, pregnant yet again, wonders whether she is bearing God's child, called Jonah, hearing from her womb, amongst other things, the words, 'Arise and go forth', which she does, but only into a glass factory. There ensue a number of entertaining peripeteias, including a visit to Middle Eastern fruit markets and clinics. There are far too many passing biblical allusions to illustrate here, but Zoja's adventures with Jonah are consistently amusing. In the second section, 'The End of the World', Zoja dreams of God admonishing his flock, like a teacher with parents, for planning an Apocalypse when it was going to happen anyway. It seems to have arrived when, horror of horrors, mobile phones and the internet go down. Gazing into God's eyes, Zoja, pregnant again, wonders if she is carrying His child. When she appears on TV, the rush to be baptized leads to mass drowning in the Tigris and Euphrates. This huge *jeu d'esprit* ends with elaborate mathematical formulae to help people find the Virgin Mary aka Zoja who has

---

[11] This sort of behaviour in shops is a not uncommon theme in modern Russian as well as Belarusian prose and verse.

[12] Expobel is a shopping centre in Miensk.

[13] 'You say that your mouth was sewn up by the needle of censorship / and there will be nothing more sickening than today. / But, in my opinion, it all lies in your own hands, placed on your stomach: / Give birth to the president you want, for yourself and for the people' (A, 55).

disappeared. This romp is not easy to account for, even though it is all in verse apart from the apocalyptic chaos of fun with fonts and formulae at the end.

The eponymous and last work of the book, 'Ambasada', is described as a serial, beginning with words connected with computer discs. The first few lines after the title will give an idea of its form:

README.TXT
Змест тэкставага файлу на першым дыску

Створаны 15.11.2008
Зменены 29.05.2011

Ксеня мілая, як ты й прасіла,
я запісала для цябе <Амбасаду>.
Серыял гэты — страшная сіла,
у вас таксама на яго падсядуць.

Звычайнае тэлевізыйнае мыла,
ружовае жыццёвае мяса
нечакана падалося мілым
рафінаванай інтэлігенцкай масе.[14]

There follow a trailer, pilot series, first season, and another four seasons. This piece does not qualify Martysievič as a playwright, but, like her other work, holds the reader's attention with her lively and inventive imagination.

To conclude this review of Maryja Martysievič's first two very promising books, here are two examples of her use of rhyme from the end of 'Praktyčny dapamožnik pa tancach na stalie: vierš na svabodu'[15] (A practical guide to dancing on a table: A poem for freedom):

Каталонцы даяджаюць да Львова —
гэта клёва,
але
ім не зразумець беларускага танца на хісткім стале.[16]

It must be hoped that this writer produces many more lively books to entertain and delight her readers.

---

[14] 'README.TXT / The content of a text file on the first disc // Created 15.11.2008 / Changed 29.05.2011 // *Ksenija, dearest, just as you asked, / I have written for you "Embassy" / This serial — has terrible power, / people will lie in wait for it with you too. // An ordinary television soap, / pink meat of life / unexpectedly seemed pleasant / to the refined mass of the intelligentsia'* (A, 95).
[15] The subtitle of this poem has nothing to do with Radio Svaboda's anthology, *Vierš na svabodu* (2002).
[16] 'The Catalonians arrive in L'viv — / it's cool, / but / they can't understand a Belarusian dance on a rickety table' (A, 62).

Plian

Žmicier Plian has produced only one book of verse, although he appears to be active in other parts of Belarusian cultural life. *Taksidermičny praktykum* (Taxidermal practice, 2004) seems very much in the iconoclastic tradition of the Bum-Bam-Lit group, as Plian's editor, Žmicier Višnioŭ, notes (Tp, 3–4).[17] Aspects of Plian's postmodern verse that recall the group's ideas and manner are a tendency to fantasy and pure nonsense, allied to exuberant assonance and alliteration, and an apparent desire to shock, not least by the commentaries on his own body, especially his stomach and its entrails. Whether this has anything to do with the taxidermy of the book's title, or whether he is referring to metaphorically stuffing literary tradition or, in Višnioŭ's words, literary bodies which have gone cold, is perhaps a moot point.[18] Plian's work, often melodious and well-balanced, is also highly unconventional in many other ways, with sound frequently dominating semantics, however bizarre the latter may be.

The first poem, 'noč vyjšla na vulicy miensku ...' (night came out onto the streets of miensk ...) combines fantasy with violent imagery and, incidentally, open hostility to Russians:

ноч выйшла на вуліцы менску
ноч з'ела ўсе ліхтары
ноч паглядзела сваімі вачыма
што робіцца ў нашым двары
там нейкія адмарозкі лаяліся
напэўна маскалі
ноч схілілася й паглядзела ў маё акно
сваім адарваным вокам
ноч убачыла праз бруднае шкло
як калоціць мяне токам
я дакрануўся да дроту вялікага напружаньня
і ўся кватэра налілася змрокам
але ноч нічога не зрабіла
і накрочыла далей
і я зноў пачуў ля дому сварку маскалёў[19]

---

[17] Numerical references preceded by Tp are to *Taksidermičny praktykum*.

Katarzyna Bortnowska notes the same affinity, according him considerable attention in her study. For more information on the Bum-Bam-Lit movement see McMillin, *Writing*, 853–934.

[18] All the poems in this book are printed plumb in the centre of the page (and almost entirely without punctuation; here they are printed with a justified left margin.

[19] 'night came out onto the streets of miensk / night ate up all the lights / night looked with its eyes to see / what was going on in our yard / there some thugs were swearing / probably russkies / night leant over and looked in at my window / with its detached eye / night saw through the filthy glass / how my body was being shaken by a current / I had touched a high voltage wire / and the whole flat was filled with darkness / but night did not do anything / and moved on further / and I again heard near my house quarrelling russkies' (Tp, 5).

Another poem, 'kryvi kryvickaj kroŭny kryk …' (the dear cry of Kryvian blood …)
offers an extreme form of alliteration by beginning the words of each line with
the same letter, in a basically nonsense poem, but with elements of reality here
and there. Other highly alliterative poems include 'napalovu razlamaŭšy son …'
(having half smashed my dream …), most of which comprises a list of words
beginning with 's', and 'fanetyka!' (phonetics!), which relies on rhythm, sound
and repetition; also worth mentioning in this connection is the very inventive
'zabarona-abarona-zababona …' (prohibition-defence-superstition …). In
'ramatus …' (a rheumatic …) there is an elementary narrative thread, albeit an
absurd one:

> раматус
> выцягнуў туз
> згуляў партыю ў дурня
> са мной
> і я зьнік
> распусціўшыся ў паветры
> зрабіўся нерухомым дрэвам
> потым прыйшлі людзі
> сьпілавалі мяне
> і зрабілі запалкі[20]

Two examples of totally absurd poems are 'jon' (he) and 'drevy rastuć dahary
karaniami …' (trees grow with their roots in the air…): in the latter, the title needs
no further explanation; in the first, the opening line will suffice: 'ён піў сакэ і
станавіўся самалётам' (he drank sake and began to turn into an aeroplane,
Tp, 21). A feature of some poems is the, often abrupt, switching between
absurdity and what we think of as reality: 'prusak zabraŭsia …' (a cockroach got
itself in …), for instance, provides an example of such a sudden change; in another
poem, 'u sloiku reaktyŭny jod …' (in a jar reactive iodine …), the tragedy of
Chernobyl is, as it were, carnivalized when nature arranges a festival around the
contaminated site; and in 'kvitok …' (a ticket …) Plian introduces three lines of
an earlier poem into the middle of a verse that repeats its opening thirteen lines
after this quotation.

Members of Bum-Bam-Lit were hardly shrinking violets in their attempts to
overthrow old cultural norms, but when they wrote about themselves it was
usually in a very stylized and/or humorous way. The same applies to many of
Plian's verses, but the description of mental illness in 'z maich vačnic ciače
mazut …' (fuel oil runs from my eye-sockets …) seems both more brutal and
personal. Here is the last part of this poem:

---

[20] 'a rheumatic / pulled out an ace / playing a game of Durak / with me / and I disappeared /
dissolving in the air / I became a motionless tree / later people came / cut me up / and made
matches' (Tp, 8).

я прайшоў тэсты
яны прызналі
мяне шызафрэнікам
я ведаў гэта і бязь іх
я кожны вечар
п'ю салярку
вось дзе псыхааналіз
нават фройд павесіўся б
калі б даведаўся
пра мяне²¹

In this connection may also be mentioned 'ja var'jacieju z kožnym dniom …' (I grow crazier every day …), which begins thus:

я вар'яцею з кожным днём
сябе не кантралюю
мне страшна²²

Finally, in 'kryvavyja zdani navakol mianie …' (bloody ghosts surround me …), there appears to be real paranoia, as his nightmare (or a shadow on the wall) seems to be of a soldier bent on murder.

As has been mentioned, Kastuś Kalinoŭski is a major symbolic figure in the consciousness of the Belarusian intelligentsia, and he has been treated in various ways by many poets, including those of the younger generation. Plian's contribution to this theme, 'mianie zlavili …' (they caught me …), is bizarre from beginning to end:

мяне злавілі
адрэзалі вушы
паклалі у рот
батон кілбасы
аперазалі маё цела,²³
туалетнай паперай
зрабілі зь мяне
мумію
пазнаёмілі з
кастусём каліноўскім
ён сьпеў мне песьню
і сышоў²⁴

---

²¹ 'I underwent tests / they identified / me as a schizophrenic / I knew that without them / every evening / I drink diesel oil / so much for psychoanalysis / even freud would hang himself / if he found out / about me' (Tp, 9).

²² 'I grow crazier every day / I cannot control myself / I am terrified' (Tp, 24).

²³ This comma, amidst an otherwise total lack of punctuation, seems to be the result of a mistake at the printers.

²⁴ 'they caught me / cut off my ears / stuffed into my mouth / a long piece of sausage / bound up my body / with lavatory paper / they made of me / a mummy / they acquainted me with kastuś kalinoŭski / he sang me a song / and went on his way' (Tp, 14).

Other themes widespread amongst young poets are pain, concern for their country, affinity with nature, and love. Plian writes in 'biazkoncy bоĺ …' (endless pain …) of suffering and its coordinates, as may be seen from the opening lines:

> бясконцы боль
> бясконцы жах
> бяздонны нэрв
> баліць упарта[25]

In 'ja tak maryŭ pračnucca …' (I so dreamt of awaking …) he describes his life as a rubbish pit, and we (Belarusians) as the rubbish in it, asleep or in a coma, with spectres and ghosts all around. Dreaming and sleeping are more positive in 'zasynać na ložku tvaich maraŭ …' (to fall asleep on the bed of your daydreams …), which is another, rather discursive, poem about his native country:

> засынаць на ложку тваіх мараў
> расьцярушваць словы на склады
> біцца галавой аб сьцены храмаў
> піць віно і прагнуць вады
> атлянтычны акіян
> нёман, прыпяць, сож
> менскае ўзвышша-джамалунгма
> палесьсе — не тыбэт
> дрыгва на небе
> мытнае спагнаньне
> выгнаньне з радзімы
> оды ў гонар амон ра
> арыйскія плямёны
> насялялі беларусь
> апошні боль
> сасьлізвае са столі
> пакідаючы сьляды-шпалеры[26]

Affinity with nature is at its clearest in 'jak ciopla i vіĺhotna …' (how warm and damp …), where the poet seems to collapse into its rich and delicately intricate body. Love is treated by Plian in a quite different way from that in other poetry of his generation. For example, in 'jazyk raściahnuć …' (to stretch one's tongue …), he, amongst other things, plans to print his lips in all journals so that 'the female tribe' (žanočaje pliemia) could kiss him; another poem 'sto kropieliek daždžu …' (a hundred droplets of rain …) is hardly more romantic, associating as it does his beloved with death:

---

[25] 'endless pain / endless horror / bottomless nerves / hurt persistently' (Tp, 26).
[26] 'to fall asleep on the bed of your daydreams / to send out words to the stores / to beat one's head on the walls of a church / to drink wine and long for water / the Atlantic ocean / the rivers Nioman, Prypiać and Sož / the Miensk heights of Everest / Polesia is not Tibet / a quagmire in the sky / a customs penalty / exile from one's native land / odes in honour of Amun-Ra / Aryan tribes / have populated Belarus / a final pain / is slipping off the ceiling / leaving a wallpaper of traces' (Tp, 42).

сто кропелек дажджу
упалі ледзь нячутна
на твае вусны
вусны-маланкі
вусны-труна для лялькі
з тваіх вуснаў
сочыцца сьліна
сьліна пажоўклай цемры
ты пахавала свае рукі
ты пахавала свае ногі
зрабілася пчалой
ты стала гуру
як весела
і я сьмяюся
бо ты ніколі больш
ня будзеш плакаць
над маёй труной.²⁷

The last poem in the book is both strange and sad:

глядезць на неба
крычаць розную лухту
я знайду
свае згубленыя вочы
я прышью
адарваныя вусны
кватэра бяз вокнаў
скляпеньне
луска на твары
на руках — маладзік
серабрысты серп
серп і молат
працоўны і калгасьніца
я не памятаю свайго імя²⁸

Whether or not Źmicier Plian is a late manifestation of Bum-Bum-Lit, there can be no doubt that he is unlike any other poet in the present study. He is clearly a talented, albeit often mystifying, figure, and his humour is of a particularly dark kind.

---

²⁷ 'a hundred droplets of rain / fell almost imperceptibly / on your lips / lightning-lips / lips that are a doll's coffin / from your lips / saliva is seeping / the saliva of yellowish darkness / you have hidden your arms / you have hidden your legs / became a bee / you became a guru / how merry / and I laugh / for you will never more / weep / over my grave' (Tp, 29).
²⁸ 'to look at the sky / to shout various rubbish / I shall find / my lost eyes / I shall sew on / my severed lips / a flat without windows / an arch / scales on my face / in my hands a new moon / a silvery sickle / a hammer and sickle / worker and collective farm girl / I do not remember my own name' (Tp, 46).

Yvanoŭ

Viktar Yvanoŭ, who also writes under his real name, Viktar Lupasin, studied mechanics and mathematics at BDU followed by a degree in philology at the same university. A writer of poetry, prose and drama, he published in 2009 *Asarci* (Assortment), a variegated collection of mainly prose, some Russian poetry, and a limited amount of Belarusian verse. In her introduction to this book, Viera Burlak (pen name Džeci) notes Yvanoŭ's attraction to projects of various kinds, and one of them, entitled 'Tvorčaść Pasiukieviča' (The work of Pasiukievič), forms the greater part of *Asarci*. The other substantial element in the book is a cycle of sonnets, near-sonnets and, in one or two cases, not even near-sonnets, 'Aŭtamabili SSSR' (Cars of the USSR), certainly an original choice of subject, as well as the most interesting part of the book in terms of Belarusian poetry. Yvanoŭ has published quite widely in the periodical press, but what follows will be based on the contents of his first book.

The fictional Paval Pasiukievič (b. 1971) is a performance artist in many genres who is introduced as a young man living with his girlfriend Volia. His first poem in the book is 'Litvolat', in which he splits up words for humorous effect. It defies translation:

> Літволат
> Во лат
> ыніне
> Воля
> наляцінула на
> мяў … НЕ!,
> я ў не-
> сьвядомасьці,
> дома ці
> на дне? (As, 10)[29]

The next example of Pasiukievič's creative work is the slightly less obscure, 'patychaje tvorčaśiu …' (it stinks of creativity …):

> патыхае творчасьцю
> падыхае
> рэдактарка і дыхае
> паэт. Хайль
> Творчасьць! Патыхае
> ёю і хай
> сабе,
> абы кабы мне,
> а ім — не.[30]

---

[29] Numerical references preceded by As are to *Asarci*.

[30] 'it stinks of creativity / the woman editor breathes / and the poet also breathes / Heil Creativity!/ There is a bad stink from her / and so be it, / as far as I am concerned, / for them it is not so' (As, 17).

After an extensive, bizarrely detailed prose description of Pasiukievič's life, including several Russian poems and a few Belarusian *jeux d'esprit* such as 'TRUBAniaDURA' (A PIPEisnoFOOL, As, 91), described as mayonnaise lyrics, the second part of the project comprises this fictional poet's creative work. The content is very strange and the versification eccentrically impressionistic: for example, in one poem, 'Mianie treba čytać padrad ...' (I must be read consecutively ... As, 106),[31] he compares his poetry to building, and writes his verse in the form of two columns of words. Another poem, 'Maja tvorčasć' (My creative work), begins with some advice he has been given by another poet:

Мая творчасьць

Геніяльную характарыстыку
Творчасьці даў паэт:
каб ня йсьці (ня ссы) ў білетрыстыку,
не выціскаць зь сябе
танную калямбурыстыку ...[32]

Yvanoŭ's humour is not mainly derived from punning but from dismantling and rearranging lines and words, as in 'Litvolat'; also important is repetition, as may be seen in a bizarre love poem, 'Paema avala' (Poem of an oval, As,109), or in 'Pieśnia pra škodu seksualnaj rasputy' (Song about the harm of sexual profligacy, As, 113–15), a semi-rhymed poem about an eighty-two-year-old man who dreams of sex, and goes through various adventures in search of a partner in, amongst other places, a police helicopter and an orchestra.

The next cycle, 'Aŭtamabili SSSR', takes an original theme that is interesting for its element of nostalgia. Since the poet was only four-years-old when the Soviet Union began to crumble, the vehicles featured in this cycle must have either survived well or been known to him from his early studies at university. Yvanoŭ offers imaginative, sometimes witty poetic portraits of cars, minibuses and vans, buses and trolleybuses, lorries, sports models and cars of high off road ability. The first, 'Haz-20', begins with the excitement of spring, setting it in Stalin's time when people could be shot for a chance remark, and ends with a description of the middle-class fastback, rhyming victory (*pieramoha*) with old (*staroha*). The next vehicle, 'ZIS-102' is most suitable for flirting — here the rhyme is with auto and chateau, whilst 'ZAZ-968M' is a deceptively swift car that looks better in a village than a town. 'VAZ-111' gives a mocking picture, in two sets of three lines,[33]

---

[31] The translation aims to reflect the poem's apparently misprinted pronouns *mianie* rather than *mnie* (me rather than I). There is another misspelling in the third line of 'Maja tvorčasć' (see *infra*).

[32] 'My creativity // A brilliant description / of Creativity was given by a poet: / not to go (or piss) into belles-lettres, / not to squeeze out of yourself / cheap punning ...' (As, 106).

[33] Belarusian poets follow the Petrarchan rather than Shakespearean sonnet. The former ends with two tercets after two quatrains (or an octet). Thus 'VAZ-111' may be seen as being the ending of a Belarusian sonnet.

of a car that was outworn before it was launched. Many of the poems in this cycle end with particularly striking tercets, as, for example, in 'VAZ-2108', a promising car that did not live up to expectations, as the poet summarizes in a witty conclusion:

> Пярэднепрывадным пацанскім стаў …
> Цяпер на іх глядзець — у сэрцы горка:
> Быў першы нах, а выйшаў першы блін.[34]

Yvanoŭ uses some very entertaining rhymes. In 'DUET' (As,134), for instance, he describes the attractiveness of a historic, ancient vehicle whose radiator's mastodon-like appearance reminds the poet of teeth, rhyming the word with orthodon(tist). 'GAZ-31105', a seven-line poem, depicts ironically a forty-year-old Volga car that has been tarted up, ending with three pithy lines:

> А колькі рознай моднае абвескі
> Дызайнэрамі зроблена было…
> На саракагодавае друхло.[35]

In 'ZIU-5' he imagines poets disporting themselves in a 1959 bus that looks like a torpedo of aluminium and steel; in 'AMO-715' a worker in a factory making heavy goods vehicles describes in a near-sonnet (three quatrains and a couplet) work on a production line that is as noisy as a waterfall, and the ubiquitous advertisements are no less rowdy, whilst the lorry itself sounds like a steam ship. If 'ZIS-102' had seemed a good vehicle for flirting, the rough off road vehicle 'LuAZ-969' seems rather less suitable when a white-pink lady (*panna*) is invited on board with a view to seduction: some of the rhymes are less than enticing, such as the lady's frightened groan (*spalochany stohn*) with the mouldy phaeton (*hnily faeton*) into which she is being lured.

The cycle 'Aŭtamabili SSR', like the life and work of Pasiukievič, is in a sense a project, and one that Yvanoŭ carries out with aplomb, though often in a low key, appropriate to the (for most people) uninspiring vehicles themselves. Both works, based on the Soviet past, show him to be a fluent and witty young poet.

Anochin

In addition to poetry, Kiryla Anochin is also interested in music and philosophy. The verses in his first book, *Aściarožna, drevy začyniajucca* (Be careful, the trees

---

34 'It became a juvenile front-wheel drive … / Now to look at them makes your heart sick: / It was fine at first and turned out a first curse' (As, 133). The reference to the well-known saying 'Pieršy blin komam' (The first pancaske always ends up in a lump' is too complex for a worthwhile explanation.

35 'And how many different fashionable additions / Had been made by the designers … / To the forty-year-old piece of rubbish' (As, 135).

are closing, 2013),[36] are written in free verse and are short, even minimalist. Some of these poems contain philosophical thoughts, others refer to his love life, and many display a wry sense of humour. Particularly successful is a series of haiku.

Untypical of Anochin's verse in terms of its relatively great length, but characteristic of the sense of light paradox, intimacy and humour found in many of his minimalist poems is the book's opening verse, 'na niebie niama viodraŭ …' (in heaven there are no buckets …):

на небе няма вёдраў
яно проста лье
як з вядра

і між намі не ноч
а проста цемна
як ноччу

і мы не адны
мы проста цэлае
як адно

пакуль не стала светла
пакуль не скончыўся дождж
і мы ляжым тут удваіх
давай спадзявацца
што нас ніхто не заб'е
мы проста будзем спаць
як забітыя (Adz, 3)[37]

Brevity, if anything, increases the power of Anochin's intimate poetry, giving it a sense of genuine urgency, as we see in the following two miniature poems:

заўтра
каб паспець сустрэцца
з табой
трэба прачнуцца
а лепшай гадзіне
хаця
і гэта запозна[38]

---

[36] 'The title is a simple play (by rearranging a few letters) on the words 'Aściarožna, dźviery začyniajucca' used on the Miensk underground. The English equivalent is 'Doors closing. Mind the doors'.

[37] 'in heaven there are no buckets / it just pours down / in buckets // and between us there is no night / but it is simply / dark as night // and we are not alone / we are simply together / as one // until it becomes light / until the rain stops / and the two of us are lying here together / let us hope / that nobody will kill us / we shall just simply sleep / the sleep of the dead' Numerical references preceded by Adz are to *Aściarožna, drevy začyniajucca*.

[38] tomorrow / in order to meet / you in time / I must wake up / at a better hour / although / even that is too late' (Adz, 5).

and

> хто калі не я
> каго
> калі не цябе[39]

The subjects of Anochin's humorous poems range from silence and Noah's ark to musicians in an orchestra pit. Silence is, by implication, an intrinsic element of such short poems, and 'padčas sieansu pytańniaŭ..' (during a question session …) suggests its place:

> падчас сеансу пытанняў
> лёгкія лунаюць вакол нас
> цяжкія падаюць мне ў лоб
> а тыя
> на якія я не магу адказаць
> віснуць у паветры
> ўтвараючы пятлю
> прызначаную
> для маўчання[40]

Loneliness is at the centre of the poem about Noah's flood:

> адзінота разліваецца па зямлі
> растуць хвалі новага
> сусветнага патопу
> сыходзячы пад ваду
> блаславляю ўсіх
> хто збудаваў свой каўчэг
> і знайшоў сабе пару[41]

There is, however, no such salvation for orchestral players in opera and other theatres:

> у гэтай яме
> ўсё сваё жыццё
> граў
> сумны аркестр
> таму што яму не хапіла нот
> выбрацца[42]

---

[39] 'who if not I / whom / if not you' (Adz, 13).

[40] 'during a question session / the easy ones soar around us / the hard ones fall on my forehead / but those / which I cannot answer / hang in the air / creating a noose / designed / for silence' (Adz, 18).

[41] 'loneliness is spreading over the earth / waves of a new / universal flood / are rising / as I sink under the water / I bless all those who have built themselves an ark / and have found themselves a partner' (Adz, 30).

[42] 'in this pit / all its life / there played / a melancholy orchestra / because it did not have enough notes / to get out of it' (Adz, 44).

Some of Anochin's poems, such as 'noč vypivaje …' (night drinks …) and 'na ŭvachodzie ŭ majo stanovišča …' (on entering my position …), are based on an image or conceit that produces a comic effect:

> ноч выпівае
> бутэльку белага святла
> і становіцца днём
> я выпіваю
> бутэльку чырвонага
> і ванітую[43]

and

> на ўваходзе ў маё становішча
> вытры аб мяне ногі
> я толькі што вымыў падлогу[44]

Epigrammatic philosophical points are made in several poems including 'usio syšlo na ništo …' (everything became nothing …) and 'zviestki …' (news …):

> усё сышло на ністо —
> і што было нічым
> стала ўсім[45]

and

> звесткі
> пра самых шчаслівых
> людзей
> да нас
> не дайшлі
> мы
> мусім дайсці
> да іх
> самі[46]

The book's title features in a little poem, 'zablukalym dziciom …' (like a lost child …) but with different punctuation which changes the tone from monitory to descriptive:

---

43 'night drinks / a bottle of white light / and becomes day / I drink / a bottle of red / and am sick' (Adz, 31).
44 'on entering my position / wipe your feet on me / I have just washed the floor' (Adz, 33).
45 'everything becomes nothing / and what was nothing / has become everything' (Adz, 41).
46 'news / about the happiest / people / have not / reached us / we/ must reach / them / ourselves' (Adz, 47).

заблуканым дзіцём
шукаючы выйсце
са свайго лядашчага
лесу
ўжо чую
як асцярожна
зачыняюцца дрэвы[47]

It might be expected that a miniaturist like Anochin would be attracted to the
Japanese form of haiku, once very popular amongst Belarusian writers.[48] In fact,
his cycle of ten poems in this form ring far more authentically, including the name
he gives the genre, than those of his older compatriots. Here are 'Chajku' (Haiku)
numbers four, six and eight:

Гнуцца дрэвы. Ім
нельга пайсці ні з ветрам,
ні супраць яго.[49]

Вярнулася на
дзень сонца. Паглядзець, як
мы тут без яго.[50]

Вясна. На дрэвах
лопнулі пупышкі ад
такога шчасця.[51]

The last poem in the book is entirely negative and, undoubtedly wrongheaded
(in the second half, at least):

няма
ні бога
ні зданяў
ні прыхадняў з космасу

нікому
мы
не патрэбны[52]

If the 'we' refers to mankind, it seems out of step with the ludic character of many
of the poems that precede it; if it refers to Belarusians, then it is utterly mistaken,
and if it refers to Belarusian writers, then it is disproved by, amongst other things,
Kiryla Anochin's own writing, His first book. *Aściarožna, drevy začyniajucca*, is

---

[47] 'like a lost child / looking for a way out / of my ancient / forest / I can already hear / how
carefully / the trees are closing' (Adz, 27).

[48] See, for example, Miraslaŭ Šajbak and Adam Hlobus (comps), *Choku bielaruskich paetaŭ*,
Miensk, 1996.

[49] 'The trees bend. They / can neither go with the wind / nor against it' (Adz, 36).

[50] 'The sun has returned / to the day. / To see how we are getting on without it' (Adz, 37).

[51] 'Spring. On the trees / the buds have burst from / such happiness' (Adz, 37).

[52] 'there is no / god, / nor ghosts, / nor visitors from other planets // we / are not needed / by
anybody' (Adz, 51).

a delightfully witty and thought provoking debut, completely unlike the work of any of his contemporaries.

Čajkoŭskaja

Volia Čajkoŭskaja, in addition to writing poetry, also records musical albums with her husband Jury Kruhlikoŭ whom she married in 2009, and by October 2012 they were on their fourth such collection: 'Mitrenhi' (Worries), as part of a project, MIATNA (PEPPERMINT). Her debut verse collection, with an introduction by Arciom Kavalieŭski, *Lupy* (Magnifying glasses, 2007)[53] contains some passionate love poems, reflections on writing and creativity, and many contrasts, for instance between sincerity and lies, and, particularly, originality and routine. Many of the poems refer to her soul, but for all her apparently happy marriage, the majority of her works are in a minor key. Her verse is mostly rhymed and rich in assonance.

To begin with the theme of creativity on a light, demotic note, in a humorous poem dedicated to Salvador Dali, 'Šedeŭr' (*Chef d'oeuvre*), the lyrical heroine seems to give birth to a masterpiece through her thigh, which has already seen much pain, and it is said to be no matter that the mother is a labourer. 'Novaje' (New) is a vigorous verse about creativity, laying emphasis on newness and originality, of which these are the last six lines:

Каб стварыць
   ад канца
   да пачатку
Па не складзеным шчэ
   парадку —
Н О В А Е. (Lup, 10)[54]

The opposite is bleak routine, as we read in 'Vy stali ...' (You have become ...):

Руціна!
Зацягне, як багна![55]

Čajkoŭskaja's living inspiration certainly comes from her native city:

Віцебск прарос мною!
Настойліва. Як пшанічнае зерне.
Мне Віцебск за пакуты нараджэння,
Відаць, яшчэ натхненне верне ... [56]

---

[53] An internet version of the book was published by kamunikat.org, in 2011 [accessed 23 October 2012].

[54] 'In order to create / from the end / to the beginning / By a yet unformed / order / something N E W' Numerical references preceded by Lup are to *Lupy*.

[55] 'Routine! / Will drag you down, like a bog!' (Lup, 30).

[56] 'Viciebsk has germinated with me! / Determinedly. Like a grain of corn. / It seems that for the torments of birth, / Viciebsk will also return my inspiration ...' (Lup, 22).

Also on this topic, there is a telling line in the poem 'Pryjdzi da mianie, nieviadomaje!..' (Come to me, unfamiliarity! ...): 'Пакутую ад звычаёвасці' (I am tormented by conventionality, Lup, 11).

One of the many poems about Čajkoŭskaja's soul is 'Maja duša — staraja safistka ...' (My soul is an old sophist ...):

Мая душа —
       старая сафістка,
Што хлуслівыя доказы
       калекцыянуе.
Мая душа —
       цыркавая артыстка,
Што скокнуць без страхоўкі
       спрабуе.
Мая душа —
       галубка...
             з падрэзанымі крыламі.
Мая душа —
       без вёслаў
             шлюпка...
З непатрэбнымі нікому
             сіламі...[57]

Many, but not all, of Čajkoŭskaja's love poems are sad, mainly because of separation from her husband-to-be, a good example of which is 'Adzinota' (Loneliness):

Адзінота

Мая адзінота —
       як банны ліст.
На душы павісла
       і трымаецца.
Сваёй адзіноце
       я танчу твіст.
І цела маё
       з ёй абдымаецца.

Я ўсё чакаю, калі ТЫ
Зоймеш месца адзіноты ...[58]

Another of the many poems dedicated or addressed to her husband is 'Ja pa śpinie ściany, što zlučyla ...' (I am on the other side of a wall that united ...), but by the

---

[57] 'My soul is an old sophist, / That collects mendacious arguments. / My soul is a circus artist, / That tries to leap without a safety net. / My soul is a dove with clipped wings. / My soul is a boat without oars ... / With strength that nobody needs ...' (Lup, 81).

[58] 'Loneliness // My loneliness is like a limpet / It hangs from my soul and remains fixed. / I dance the twist to my loneliness. / And my body embraces it. // I can't wait for YOU / to take the place of loneliness ...' (Lup, 51).

end of the verse the subject is more about Belarus than personal relations. Here are the last five lines:

Я душа — касмапаліт.
Без кала.
Без двара.
Без турмы.
Без айчыны.[59]

An unusual and sad love poem is 'pa mnie — liepš slota, čym maroz …' (In my opinion sleet is better than frost …). Here is the last of the three stanzas:

Па мне — лепш хоць на цябе
паглядзець
і больш ніколі цябе не ўбачыць,
чым сэрцу свайму дазваляць
халадзець
і ўласную смерць сасніць і прадбачыць.[60]

A final example of Čajkoŭskaja's love poetry, 'Dumak — kalaŭrot …' (The spinning wheel of my thoughts …) is slightly more cheerful, although the poet's apparent lack of confidence comes out even as she dreams about love. Here are the last four lines:

Мілага я сню …
рэдка.
То кахаю,
То люблю,
То губляю,
То лаўлю,
То пачуццямі
страляю метка.[61]

Kavalieŭski, in his somewhat whimsical introduction, compares the clarity of Čajkoŭskaja's vision to that of a child (Lup, 3–4), and in her verse there is something of the child in the uncompromising nature of her views, such as intense dislike of banality, clearly expressed in one couplet:

Адмахваюся ад банальнасцяў, як ад мух,
Як толькі пачую банальнасцяў дух.[62]

It is hard to overlook the expressions of melancholy or even despair found, for example, in two short poems, 'Ja nie čuju …' (I do not hear …) and 'Z kožnaj

---

[59] 'I am a cosmopolitan soul. / Without absolutely anything. / Without a home. / Without prison. / Without a fatherland' (Lup, 58).
[60] 'In my opinion it is better to look at you for at least one time / and then never see you again, / rather than allow my heart to grow cold / and to dream of and foresee my own death' (Lup, 57).
[61] ' I dream of my sweetheart rarely. / Now I make love to him, now I love him, / Now I lose him, now I catch him, / Now I shoot accurately with my feelings' (Lup, 73).
[62] 'I swat away banalities like flies, / As soon as I sense the spirit of banalities' (Lup, 11).

viasnoj …' (With each spring …). Though simple in form, they are crystal clear and strong in content:

> Я не чую —
> Я адчуваю.
> Я намацваю —
> Рукамі кранаю.
> Я па позірку
> Вызначаю
> Долю адчаю.[63]

and

> З кожнай вясной
> усё больш жыць хочацца
> І ўсё менш застаецца
> Часу.
> Ну што за злая заканамернасць …[64]

To end this brief survey of Volia Čajkoŭskaja's first book, here is a humorous poem to lighten the mood of some of the works quoted earlier, 'Źviesiŭ niechta leśvicu z nieba …' (Someone had let down a ladder from heaven …):

> Звесіў нехта лесвіцу з неба.
> Дзяўчынка падумала: <О! Клэба!> — І палезла.
> На неба палезла.
> Паблукала. Пашукала анёлаў там,
>   апосталаў, Бога.
> Не знайшла нікога.
> Назад знікла дарога.
>   Во нябога![65]

Čajkoŭskaja is a poet of imagination and ability, so that it must be hoped that her musical activities will not prevent her contributing further to Belarusian literature.

Kucharevič and Papoŭ

These two young poets, whose dates of birth are not known to the present writer, have collaborated in a humorous poetic 'double-bill' entitled 'Ščyra' (Sincerely)

---

[63] ' I do not hear / I feel / I touch with my hands. / I recognize / At a glance / My fate of despair' (Lup, 77).

[64] 'With each spring / I want to live more and more / And there is less and less / Time. / Well, what an evil pattern is that…' (Lup, 77).

[65] 'Someone had let down a ladder from heaven. / A little girl thought, "Oh! Fantastic!" — And climbed up. / She climbed up to heaven. / She wandered around. / She looked for angels there, the apostles, God. / She did not find anyone. / The way back had disappeared. / What a poor creature!' (Lup, 82).

and 'Nia ščyra' (Insincerely) in what appears to be a small-format joint debut publication of 2009).[66]

Śviatlana Kucharevič's poems are mainly about love and her lover, writing, and personified nature, especially trees. In 'Chaj mianie zahajdajuć chvali …' (Let the waves rock me …) she writes of the language that has come to her naturally:

> Маё цела ахутаюць словы
> Зразумелай нявучанай мовы. (Šč, 28)[67]

For her the Belarusian language appears to be closely related to the natural world, as we see in 'Vierš pra śnieh pieršy i śnieh apošni' (A poem about first snow and last snow), as is evident from the following three lines:

> Белыя дрэвы лепяць са словаў верш
> Белыя дрэвы страсаюць пушыстыя песьні
> Ціхія словы.[68]

The same may be said of 'Navošta vypaliŭ travu?..' (Why did you burn the grass? …) where her empathy is even more evident:

> Навошта выпаліў траву?
> А словы мовіць так балюча.
> І слова вымавіць баюся.
> Я лепей словы напішу:
> Навошта выпаліў душу?..[69]

Perhaps the strongest of Kucharevič's unpretentious but heartfelt verses is 'Vočy mohuć manić …' (Eyes can lie …):

> Вочы могуць маніць
> Словамі безважкімі й халоднымі
> Вусны могуць маніць
> Дакрананьнямі мяккімі
> Й пяшчотнымі
> Рукі могуць маніць
> Пацалункамі мармуровымі
> Па-за межамі раніцы
> Адбываецца вялікая гульня[70]

---

[66] In a description of this little book on the internet, the book is said (presumably by the editor, Žmicier Višnioŭ) to be 'not really poetry. It is not even prose': http://prastora.by/knihi/kucharevic-sviatlana-alies-papoŭ-ščyra-nia-ščyra [accessed 16 August.2014].

[67] 'My body is enveloped in words / of a language that I understand without having studied it' Numerical references preceded by Šč are to Ščyra.

[68] 'White trees fashion a poem from words / White trees shake down feathery songs / Quiet words' (Šč, 30–31).

[69] 'Why did you burn the grass? / But saying words is so painful. / And I am afraid to express a word. / I had better write the words: / Why did you burn my soul? …' (Šč, 34).

[70] 'Eyes can lie / With weightless and cold words / mouths can lie. With soft / and affectionate touches / Hands can lie / With marble kisses / Beyond the bounds of morning / A great game is taking place' (Šč, 16).

In other verses on nature and love she welcomes rain ('Dožǳyk' [A shower of rain, Šč, 5]) and feels that in autumn raindrops on window panes can produce both pictures and poems, as in 'Vosień piša karciny …' (Autumn paints pictures …, Šč, 6), whilst in 'Ja sluchala meliodyju …' (I listened to the melody …, Šč, 13) she finds that autumn rain with its unforgettable rhythm can be a phenomenon to emulate in her poetry. Another aspect of rain is that in another poem, 'Zdrada' (Betrayal), it caresses the poet, making her wonder whether it will make her lover jealous (Šč, 19–20). The latter, incidentally is now just a shadow, although she can remember all the details of this shadow: 'Ty — cień …' (You are a shadow …, Šč, 17–18).

This brief selection ends with a semi-nonsense 'Pajema' [*sic*] (Narrative poem) whose main interest, however, is that it also comes at the end of Papoŭ's verses, rendering it impossible to know which of them, if either, actually wrote it.

Kucharevič's early poems show a deeply romantic nature, and technique that should grow more sophisticated in time.

*

Aleś Papoŭ's 'insincere' verses are often humorous with sex rather than the romance of Kucharevič's seemingly more fervent 'sincere' poems. Brevity may be the soul of wit, but many of the few pieces representing him here are not only brief but decidedly laconic. 'krataŭ …' (of prison bars …) makes a change from the many Belarusian anguished 'political' poems, where *kraty* (prison bars) is regularly rhymed with *katy* (executioners). In Papoŭ's alliterative nonsense verse things are very different:

кратаў
краты
алігатар
не закратаны
ў кватэры
алігатар крочыў далей (Nia, 15)[71]

In 'Podych cioplaha dymu …' (The smell of warm smoke …) the poet offers thanks for the fact that a city, built for centuries, burned down overnight (Nia, 7). He seems similarly unconcerned in a girl and boy poem, 'Dziaŭčynka macaje chlopčyka …' (The girl fondles the boy …), that despite all the excitement, nothing happens because of the minus 20 degrees temperature outside (Nia, 6). 'U cioplych abdymkach …' (In warm embraces) an unpleasant sexual encounter appears to be between the lyrical hero and a prostitute:

---

[71] 'of bars / bars / alligator / not in a cage / in a flat / the alligator walked on further' Numerical references preceded by Nia are to *Nia ščyra*.

У цёплых абдымках
Бязглузда
Трапляю ў вусны
Фарбаваныя мылам
Агідна …
Вельмі нязвыкла
Гандляваць
Нерухомае целам.[72]

Slightly more ambitious is the last poem by Papoŭ before 'Pajema', 'Budujecca novy śviet …' (A new world is being built …); in it there will be needed a new philosophy and new sense of the meaning of life, self-identity and love. The last five lines give a disquieting idea of this transformation:

Далёка
Гатуюць
Законы каханьня
Стэрэатыпы адносін
Ды комплексы жыцьцякіраваньня.[73]

Papoŭ was clearly at a very early stage in 2009, but both he and Kucharevič have at least been allowed a debut volume, albeit a booklet, to themselves.

---

[72] 'In warm embraces / brainlessly / I land in lips / Painted with soap / Revolting … / It is very unfamiliar / To trade / a body for property' (Nia, 16).

[73] 'Far away / They are preparing / The laws of loving / the stereotypes of personal relations / And the complexes of controlling life' (Nia, 35).

CHAPTER 7

~

Performance Poetry

The heyday of performance poetry in Belarus was probably the period of Bum-Bam-Lit when much of that group's activities were public events and performances no less than the publishing of books. The two principal theorists of this time were Juraś Barysievič (b. 1966) and Žmicier Višnioŭ (b. 1973),[1] and an informative critical overview of the movement has been given by Hanna Kiślicyna.[2] Performance poetry still has a presence in the next generation and, although it is hard to assess only on the printed page, an example of this type of work is printed in a booklet from Višnioŭ's publishing house Halijafy, *Jana-Try-Jon* (She, three, he, 2010), with the additional bonus of detailed descriptions of some of the events where the book's authors made their performances. There are three poets, one of whom, Adam Šostak, is discussed later in a separate overview of his work. The other two are Juraś Lienski (b. 1985) and Voĺha Rahavaja (b. 1982). Also introduced in the booklet are Julija Zablockaja (b. 1986), a creator of performances and installations, and Vasiĺ Paŭlinyč (b. 1984), an artist.

Lienski

Juraś Lienski is represented by only nine verses, almost all of which seem more like intimate and melancholy love lyrics than performance poems.[3] Their principal themes are dreams and escape, aspects of love, and the sadness of his city. In 'Žbiehčy ŭ noč …' (To flee into the night …) escape from himself, a nameless madman, ends at dawn with his dream of taking refuge beneath a paper fabric (Jtj, 56–58).[4] Early elegiac moods, far from rare among writers of the

---

[1] For more information see McMillin, *Writing*, 855–67.
[2] Hanna Kiślicyna, *Novaja litaraturnaja situacyja: Žmiena kuĺturnaj paradyhmy*, Miensk, 2006, pp. 95–122.
[3] Neither of the two poems by Lienski whose performances are described ('Paema kachańnia i sieksuaĺnaha zmahańnia' [A poem of love and sexual striving, 2005] and 'Čakańnie' [Waiting, 2007]) appear in the part of the book containing the texts of verses cited here.
[4] Numerical references preceded by Jtj are to *Jana-Try-Jon*.

youngest generation, predominate in 'Hrukat abcasaŭ ...' (The clattering of heels ...), where the cold sounds surrounding the poetic hero mark the loss of his youth; after leaving his lover, his heart is buried in bloody furrows, as we read in the final lines:

> Змяінай атрутай
> тое юнацтва
> сышло ў пакоі
> Метра ...
>   Палітэну.
>
> Грукат абцасаў
> у начным калідоры.
>
> Сэрца схавалі
> ў крывавых разорах.[5]

In 'Śnieżań' (December) he writes of the sad city where loneliness hides, particularly due to the absence of his lover (Jtj, 60–61); in 'Kazać zhubiŭšy slovy ...' (To speak, having lost words ...) she is portrayed as his inspiration, allowing him to speak and write. In another verse, 'Śliozy tvaje ...' (Your tears ...), the sadness and delicate weeping of his lover, after apparent parting, is touching (Jtj, 58). The seasons play a role in many of Lienski's poems, and his verses about love are no exception. One such is a sad poem written from the lover's point of view, incorporating winter, spring and summer, each season accompanying her feelings. Here are the beginning and end:

> узімку збіраю ўраджай
> твайго пачуцця
>
> [...]
>
> улетку збіраю ўраджай
> майго расчаравання ...[6]

'Jon — taki sientymientaĺny čalaviek ...' (He is such a sentimental person ...) has an epigraph from Voĺha Hapiejeva, and describes obliquely the relationship between a man and a woman, although the former seems to be just a part of her indifferent dream, for she is also a sentimental person. (Jtj, 68, 71). Finally, may be mentioned another unusual love poem, 'Tvaje vočy ...' (Your eyes ...), of which this is the second half:

---

[5] Like snake's venom, / that youth / went away to the chambers / of the Metro ... / Politan. // The clattering of heels / in the night time corridor. // My heart was hidden / in bloody furrows' (Jtj, 66).

[6] 'in winter I gather the harvest / of your feeling // [...] // in summer I gather the harvest / of my disappointment' (Jtj, 72, 74).

І я зноўку шыю сабе адзенне
З тканіны тваёй пяшчоты
А потым павольна гайдаюся
Па хвалях тоненькіх нітак,
З якіх мы спялялі пачуцце …[7]

More evidence of Lienski's poetic potential will have to wait, but he is clearly a sensitive poet worth watching.

*

Rahavaja

Voĺha Rahavaja has ten poems in the booklet, one of which, 'Dvornik' (The caretaker), is also described as a performance made together with Šostak in 2005. In addition there are descriptions of four other events in which Rahavaja played a part: 'Miesiacovaja sanata' (Moonlight sonata, 2006, together with Lienski), 'Huĺnia' (A game, 2007), 'Kryly' (Wings, 2008, together with Lienski) and 'Prahrama "Zamknionаść. Kola"' (Programme 'Isolation. A circle), a show conceived by Rahavaja from a story of that name by Šostak.

The performance of 'Dvornik' apparently began with a depressed caretaker sweeping up dust in the auditorium, lamenting the meaningless of his life, constantly clearing up rubbish that immediately reappears. This was followed by Rahavaja reading her poem, which soon took the subject onto a metaphorical plane:

Дворнік

Падаруй мне прынамсі лісток
Да зімы. Да халодных завей.
З-за страху страціць адно
Забываем другое.
На месцы ссохлых пачуццяў
Заўсёды растуць другія.
ДРУГІЯ.
А гэты спаліць дворнік.
Дык можа, ты спрабуеш
Зрабіць гербарый?[8]

---

[7] 'I again sew myself clothes / From the fabric of your affection / And then I slowly rock / On the waves of the slender threads, / From which we wove our feelings …' (Jtj, 67).

[8] 'Give me at least a little leaf / Until winter. Until the cold snowstorms. / Because of the fear of losing one thing / we forget something else. / In the place of dried-up feelings, / there will always grow up others / OTHERS / And this one will be burned by the caretaker / But perhaps you will try to create a herbarium?' (Jtj, 78).

In many of the other poems in this short selection, the lyrical heroine is concerned by the impermanence of relationships, particularly with her beloved. In 'Dva poliusa' (Two poles) she emphasizes the difficulty of making decisions together, since someone always has to give way; she compares the dominance of white over black, though black is needed to make white stand out (something she demonstrates visually in the booklet), ending with a confession of confusion: 'Здаецца, я сябе не разумею' (It seems that I do not understand myself, Jtj, 76). In 'Adpuści' (Let me go) she suggests that silence is not a reproach, but that she longs to be almost invisible and free:

> Мне жыць прасцей дазволь амаль нябачна.
> Мне не хапае адзіноты.
> Адпусці …[9]

In 'Chto ty?' (Who are you?) the poet laments the loss of a departed lover, but still hopes to understand him, whilst in 'Ty pobač …' (You are alongside …) a third person seems to be also present, if only in thought. More complex is 'My idziom za tuman …' (We go beyond the mist …) in which she sets out with her lover in search of a dream, albeit by different paths. When they are brought together, however, it is in cold banality:

> А калісьці за марай ішлі …
> Рука нерухома, і позірк — наскрозь
> у нейкі пусты даляглад.
> Амаль бессэнсоўныя словы
> Пустэчу закрыць не змаглі.[10]

Comparable to this poem is 'Spadarožnik' (Fellow traveller), which depicts two trajectories at the end of which the lyrical heroine decides that her partner's path is not needed (Jtj, 86–87). In personal relations nothing seems simple. In another poem about attempts to ward off alienation, 'Nie zaraz. Kali-niebudź …' (Not immediately. Some time later …), the lyrical heroine describes her thoughts in a memorable image:

> І сінія думкі сцякаюць пад стол,
> Расплаўленыя парафінам …[11]

---

[9] 'Let me live more simply almost invisibly. / I do not have enough loneliness. / Let me go' (Jtj, 77).

Rahavaja's comment on loneliness is very different from the descriptions found in the work of many older poets. For more examples see: Arnold McMillin, 'Loneliness as a Topos in Contemporary Belarusian Literature', in Iryna Dubianetskaya, Arnold McMillin and Hienadź Sahanovič (eds), *Your Sun Shall Never Set Again, and Your Moon Shall Wane No More / Sonca tvajo nie zakocicca, i miesiac tvoj nie schavajecca*, Miensk, 2009, pp. 163–66.

[10] 'but once we followed a dream … / The hand was motionless, and the gaze — straight through me / to some empty horizon. / Almost meaningless words / could not close off the desert' (Jtj, 81).

[11] 'And my light blue thoughts run beneath the table, / melted by paraffin' (Jtj, 83).

Finally, in a complex poem, 'Siemantyka pačućcia' (The semantics of feeling), she again analyses her emotions, seemingly expecting at the end to be mocked by a fellow poet:

Семантыка пачуцця

Апазіцыя мар,
Прадчуванне сустрэчы
Паміж знакам і сэнсам.
Мы амаль што, амаль што дарэчы...

... Пераблытаны час,
транс-пазіцыяа танца
у разбітай сінтагме.
А ты — ты па-за кантэкстам
І будзеш смяяцца.[12]

Like Lienski, Rahavaja cannot be fairly judged by a handful of verses, but she too shows a lively poetic imagination.

Šostak

Adam Šostak has produced two enterprising books of verse, *Spatkańnie Nie* (A meeting? No, 2006) and *4.33* (2012). He is, moreover, a keen performance artist, and, according to Natalĺia Jakavienka who introduces his first book, a performer in life as well as in literature. In *Jana-Try-Jon* he was the author of a short history and rationale of the group's existence, and his name occurs several times earlier in this chapter. The descriptions of performances in the booklet, however, do not include any of Šostak's works published either there or in his two verse collections. The only poem not in the latter books is 'Pačućci' (Feelings), a performance in itself:

Пачуцці
(перформанс Юліі Заблоцкай)

Калі пырсне
апошняя мыльная бурбалка
застанецца
ПА-ЧУЦ-ЦЕ
і ніводнага слова не трэба больш

---

[12] 'The semantics of feeling // The opposition of dreams, The anticipation of a meeting / Between sign and meaning. / We are almost that, by the way almost that ... // ... A confused time, the trans-position of the dance / in a broken syntagma. / And you — you are beyond the context / and will laugh' (Jtj, 84).

For comparable feelings of alienation from 'the context' see Anatoĺ Ivaščanka, 'Pa-za kantestam', *Chaj tak*, pp. 18–19.

незнарок
збягаем туды дзе выключная
АД-СУТ-НАСЦЬ
словаў сэнсаў
і пачуцці на светлым прадвесні
і толькі пачуцці (Jtj, 88–89)[13]

Another notable performance poem, rich in sounds, from the 'Jana-try-jon' group
is 'Dyjahnaz: impuĺs kaktusa' (Diagnosis: impulse of the cactus, 2005–06). Here
are the closing lines:

… Мне магло так прысніцца —
падумаць толькі!
Не йначай: полірытмічна
Мы сядзім удваім на падлозе:

рэфлектарна-інэртнае сутонне.
Дрыжыкі-імпульсы згаслі.
… І цяпер меланхоліі млосна … (SN, 49)[14]

The main themes of *Spatkańnie Nie* are love, almost always linked to nature,
and creativity and inspiration, as well as history and memory. In addition there
are occasional poems on a variety of themes. Amongst the most striking love
lyrics may be mentioned 'Viasnovaja daroha' (A road in spring, 2004), in which
a young couple's feelings and intimacy are described as metaphorical and
allegorical, although by the end, when they part, they feel the breath of what
they have been through and a new sky; the road in spring has a special, private
meaning for the poet (SM, 30). Love in an unpromising environment is
described imaginatively in 'Vientkamiera No. 30' (Ventilation chamber No. 30,
2005) where the lovers find privacy in what seems like a thirtieth wonder of
the heavens, with flickering light reminiscent of an antediluvian projector,
whilst a grey crowd and closed windows can be seen though a gap in the metal
grating. The lyrical hero is reminded of his childhood by the distance and the
light:

---

[13] 'Feelings (a performance by Julija Zablockaja) // When the last soap bubble / bursts / there
remains / FEEL-INGS / and not a single word more is needed // inadvertently / we run to a
place where there is an exceptional / AB-SENSE / of the meanings of words / and there are
feelings at the bright eve of spring / and only feelings' (Jtj, 88–89).

[14] '… I could dream of it like that — / just think! / Exactly so: poly-rhythmically / The two of
us sit together on the floor: // the reflexively inert twilight. / The tremors and impulses have
died down. // … And now it is the nausea of melancholy …' Numerical references preceded
by SN are to *Spatkańnie Nie*.

дзяцінства
гуляе
ў маляваныя лялькі
па трыццатай камеры
венткамеры трыццатага дзіва
знойдзенага ў пошуках неба[15]

In 'biessistemnaść' (lack of system, 2005) even love suffers in a dysfunctional world: the hero, amidst domestic chaos, feels oppressed and suddenly crumpled by the lack of system in his lover's movements; here are the last lines:

а я незнарокам скамечаны
бессістэмнасцю тваіх рухаў
губляю паступова твае рукі
і шукаю цябе навобмацак

запісаў інтэрв'ю на дыктафон
буду апрацоўваць стужку папераю
а наперадзе — жудасны дом[16]

'Kropka Suśvietu' (A drop of the Universe, 2005–06), which is called a live broadcast, describes the rapid onset of love; the second and third stanzas followed by the last two lines will give an impression of the lyrical hero's happiness:

Ты размаўляла невядомымі мовамі,
Сыпала безліччу халдэйскіх гаворак.
Я закахаўся ў прамністыя вусны,
Нават не ўцяміўшы сэнсу прамоваў.

А над галовамі нашымі віўся
Прастрэлены куляй смяротнай штандар:
На ім чырванелі нязгасныя кроплі —
На ім быў адбітак усіх нашых мар.

[…]

… нас ахапіла каханне,
што хутчэйшае нават за сонечны бег…[17]

Šostak frequently alludes to writing, but there are few poems in this book devoted to inspiration and creativity as such. One exception is 'Paema

---

[15] 'childhood / plays / at painted dolls / through the third chamber / the ventilation chamber of the thirtieth wonder / discovered while searching for heaven' (SN, 48).

[16] 'but I am suddenly crumpled / by the lack of system in your movements / I gradually lose your hands / and I look for you gropingly // I wrote an interview on the Dictaphone / I shall create a paper version of the tape / but ahead is this awful house' (SN, 50).

[17] 'You spoke in unknown languages, / Scattered an endless quantity of Chaldee dialects. / I fell in love with your radiant lips, / Although I could not divine the meaning of what you said. // And above our heads there waved / A standard shot through by a fatal bullet: / On it unfading drops showed red / On it was a reflection of all our dreams. // […] // … we were seized by love, / which was rapider even than the speed of the sun …' (SN, 89).

Natchnieńnia' (Poem of Inspiration, 2004) in which a butterfly coming in at his window seems to arouse creative thoughts. Here is the third stanza:

> „„Я ўздыму свае рукі
> да аскепкаў Свабоды
> па-за межамі кратаў
> шэрых радкоў,
> па-за стосамі думак,
> па-за веліччу ночы
> і нахабнасцю творчай
> шчаслівай маёй ...[18]

Variety is a strong feature of *Spatkańnie Nie*. An interesting poem about history and memory is 'Bachčysarajskija sliozy (dylohija)' (The tears of Bakhchisarai [a dialogue], 2005). The first tear is romantically melancholy for the loss of the Crimean khanate, whilst the second is more prosaic:

> а праз дарогу ад ханскага палаца
> каля шашлычнай
> гаротнік склейваў
> аскепкі пашкоджаных грыўняў
>
> . . . .
>
> У сваёй зацёртай свядомасці[19]

The tragedy at the entrance to the Niamiha metro station in Miensk when crowds rushed from a nearby sports stadium to avoid a storm, killing in the crush many young people of Šostak's generation, is commemorated in a memorably touching poem with the date of the event as its title, '30.05.1999' (2000). It ends thus:

> Наш беларускі мікракатарсіс
> Мікраапакаліпсіс[20]

A broader tragedy is treated in an imaginatively impressionistic narrative poem about World War II, 'Kiniestatyka' (Kinaesthetics, 2005), which concludes that, just as laughter is a universal phenomenon, so are weeping and lament the same in any language. Finally may be mentioned 'Prastora-ziamlia' (The broad earth, 2001), a curious existential poem scattered with phrases in Church Slavonic and Latin (SN, 43–45).

Šostak's second book, *4.33*, which includes several of the best poems from *Spatkańnie Nie*, continues with increased sophistication many of the themes of

---

[18] '... I shall raise my arms / to the fragments of Freedom / behind the limits of prison bars / of grey lines. / behind the piles of thought, / behind the greatness of night / and my happy / creative effrontery ...' (SN, 18).

[19] 'and across the road from the Khan's palace / near a shashlik stall / a beggar was gluing together / fragments of damaged coins / ... / In his worn out consciousness' (SN, 32).

[20] 'Our Belarusian micro-catharsis / Micro-apocalypse' (SN, 58).

the earlier book. The title is derived from composer John Cage's famous silent piece, although at the end of the book this period of time is introduced again as a symbol of the lyrical hero's shyness.[21] Once more the dominating theme is romantic love, expressed in myriad inventive, occasionally bizarre, but always musical ways: in 'Vialikimi zrenkami …' (With large pupils …) he describes his lover's eyes, which reflect high principles and bring her into close touch with nature, although her individuality hides behind other names (4.33, 4–5).[22] In 'Paema dreva i ciabie' (Poem about a tree and you) beauty is revealed in their equally deep roots. Other love poems worth mentioning are 'apošni raz byŭ ščašlivy …' (the last time I was happy …), 'Viečarovymi pryciemkami …' (In evening half-light …), 'Zloviš moj pozirk …' (You catch my glance …) and 'tvoj soniečny bliask …' (your sun-like brilliance …). 'List' (A letter) is more curious: saying that he is his own worst enemy, the lyrical hero awaits a response to a letter, taking the opportunity to describe a fairytale land that has marvellous qualities unseen at home; he concludes by saying that a reply from her would elicit from him several replies at once (4.33, 9).

An example of the poet's good sense of humour is to be found in '+380',[23] an unrhymed poem about telephoning Admiral Nakhimov (of the Crimean War). His deserted street floats out of Sebastopol bay, part of the borders of broken empires:

> Адмірала Нахімава —
> далей невядомасць —
> мы дзесьці на межах
> зламаных імперыяў.
> На вуліцы,
> Адмірала Нахімава
> Нікога няма …
> На вуліцы, што выплывае
> з бухты Севастапаля …
>
> Набіраю табе
> ў міжнародным фармаце:
>
> плюс трыста восемдзесят
>
> плюстрыставосемдзесят[24]

---

[21] Private communication from the author.

[22] Numerical references preceded by 4.33 are to 4.33.

[23] The title is the international telephone code of Ukraine.

[24] '+380 // Of Admiral Nakhimov — / nothing much is known now — / we are somewhere on the borders / of broken empires. / On Admiral Nakhimov street / there is nobody … / On the street that is floating out / into Sebastopol bay … // I dial your number / in the international format: // plus three hundred and eighty // plusthreehundredandeighty' (4.33, 23).

This poem acquired unplanned but extensive echoes in the Ukrainian and Crimean conflicts of 2014–15.

Several other poems make play with numbers and enjoy the deliberate confusion
of sound and meaning. It is not possible to cover the wide thematic range of
Šostak's verse, which is characterized by extensive cultural and historical
references. As a final example, here is the last stanza from a poem that is at one
level about Dadaism, 'daDAtak dadaIZM':

> Дадатак — стратасвера
> усіх сферычных сфераў!
> Дадатак? Ён et cetera і сімвалізм быцця!
> Ён Да-да-да-да-ІЗ-мус,
> Да-да-да-да-да-ЮН-чык;
> і ты-ры-БЫР да-Да-да,
> і вечная да-Да!!![25]

As well as being a talented performer, Adam Šostak clearly has a future as a
very modern poet of rich imagination, considerable technique and broad cultural
background.

---

[25] 4.33, 59–60. Such linguistic play on several words, meaning, inter al., 'yes', 'addition' and
DADA, is impossible to translate satisfactorily.

CHAPTER 8

~

Writers and Poetic Inspiration

About half the young poets in this book devote imaginative, even bizarre, poems to the process of writing and to the problems and delights of poetic inspiration. It is perhaps a natural theme for youthful writers who are finding their way at the start of their careers (as, indeed, is love — which is too nearly universal to form a separate chapter). Not all the poets who write about their craft will necessarily become mature poets, but their early introspection is natural rather than egotistic, and a normal part of the literary process.

Malachoŭski

Rahnied Malachoŭski is a photographer and composer of music, as well as poet. His first two books of verse appeared in 2005, *Bieražnica* (Lake goddess), and 2012, *U dzionnaj mituśni* (In the turmoil of everyday life). His restrained, formally traditional verse reveals a distinctive individual voice, and his work has been translated into Russian and Bulgarian.

The lake goddess in the title of the first collection is the name of a mythical young girl dressed in white, who, by tradition, preserves the spiritual values of Belarus, and there is a poem about such maidens in Malachoŭski's second book: 'kazačny čovien plyvie' (a magical boat sails …, Udm, 21).[1] Many of the verses in *Bieražnica* are about the poet's feelings, inspiration and the impulse to write, as well as writing itself. His amatory lyrics are unconventional and often reflect frustration and sadness. Other recurrent themes are loneliness, tears, despair and fate, whilst questions of morality are also prominent in several poems. The greater part of Malachoŭski's poems keep to regular rhyme schemes, and where he departs into blank verse, for instance in 'Sčaście' (Happiness, B, 35),[2] he is sometimes less successful.

The first poem of *Bieražnica* 'Ahoń na daloni' (Fire in one's palm), reflects on time wasted in the bosom of nature, and the poet awaits nightfall, which is wiser

---

[1] Numerical references preceded by Udm are to *U dzionnaj mituśni*.
[2] Numerical references preceded by B are to *Bieražnica*.

than he and more generous than the light. The stars can reduce to ashes the shadow of the devil, and he hopes the skies will help his writing. As dawn comes, the fire in his palm is reduced to ashes that must be scattered. The third stanza eloquently expresses his doubts and expectations:

Ці уратуе неба ад нікчемных,
Бяздумных і сухіх калекаў-слоў?
Імкнуся ў свет пачуццяў узаемных,
Ды толькі прачынаюся ізноў.[3]

In 'Viečar' (Evening), at a time of peace and relaxation, the poet's heart is freed from its problems:

Сэрца вызваляецца ад крохкіх
Хваляванняў і нясмелых слоў.[4]

The present time may not be a propitious one for poets, judging by 'Moj vierš' (My poetry), which explains the impermanence of poetry philosophically, though the pain seems real enough in the last line: 'Мой верш — мой боль зялёнага жыцця' (My poem is my pain of a green life, B, 7); in a neat little verse 'Paet i kat' (Poet and executioner) the poet distinguishes between two types of pain, emphasizing that of the poet:

Боль, выліты праз слёзы, — проста плач,
А словам выказаны боль — паэзія.[5]

The mood of some other verses about poetry is far more peaceful. In 'Paezija' (Poetry, B, 22), for instance, he calls for gentle but truthful writing, declaring that there is no need for a mask. In 'Duša paeta' (The soul of a poet, B, 11), he writes of the young poet's soul singing like a lark high in the sky, although his inspiration often seems to come to him at night, as we learn from 'Spoviedź arkušu' (Confession of a sheet of paper):

Ноч мне дыктуе:
—Пішы
Таемную споведзь душы.[6]

Love in Malachoŭski's poetry seems mostly unhappy and elusive, particularly in his second book. From *Bieražnica* 'Pieśnia' (Song, B, 8) is an appropriately melodious poem about love rather than a love poem as such, whilst in 'Mroja'

---

[3] 'Will the heavens save me from worthless, / Unthinking and dry cripple-words? / I rush to the light of mutual feelings, / But only wake up again' (B, 5).
[4] 'My heart is freed from frail / Worrying and timid words' (B, 7).
[5] 'Pain poured out through tears is only weeping, / But pain expressed in words is poetry' (B, 43).
[6] 'Night dictates to me: / "Write / The secret confession of your soul"' (B, 10).

(Daydream) the poet imagines living in a happy loving relationship, as may be seen in the following three lines:

> Душу каханнем выдуманным грэць?
>
> [...]
>
> Так хочацца, як у чароўным сне
> Шчасліва, да бясконцасці кахаць.[7]

There is far less romance, however, in 'Svaboda' (Freedom); indeed, there is positive relief when the torments of love are escaped:

> А я стаміўся быць з табой,
> Пакутаваць. І болей
> <Кахання> слоў не пажадаю чуць я.[8]

More mildly in 'Čamu' (Why, B, 59), the poet, though clearly still in love, finds that his heart longs for solitude (прагне адзіноты).

The future and fate of Belarus figure in several poems. Nature is shown as part of the country's purification when the constant sun appears at the end of 'Navaĺnica' (Thunderstorm), but not before, in the second stanza, we have been given a devastating picture of the people who are in urgent need of purification:

> Жахнуўся і хаваецца нядбайны грэшны люд
> Уласнаручна створанага пекла.
> Няхай прырода-матухна бяздумства змые бруд,
> І сонца шэрасць промнямі рассекла.[9]

On the whole, however, the emphasis is on the resilience of the people's will and the younger generation's role in national survival, as emerges from 'Adradžeńnie' (Renaissance), of which these are the first and last lines:

> Нам не знікнуць бясследна ў паветры
>
> [...]
>
> І не быць нам бяздушша ахвярай'.[10]

---

[7] 'To warm my soul with imaginary love [...] I so wish, as in an enchanted dream, / To love happily and eternally' (B, 57).

[8] 'But I am tired of being with you. / Of suffering torments. And more / Words of "love" I don't want to hear' (B, 52).

[9] 'In terror the feckless, sinful people hides in / The hell of their own making. / Let Mother Nature wash away the filth of improvidence, / And the sun with its rays cut the greyness apart' (B, 20).

[10] 'We shall not disappear without trace in the wind [...] And we shall not become a sacrifice to callousness' (B, 28).

The last poem of *Bieražnica* gives a clear message concerning the duty of Malachoŭski's own generation to prove to the world that Belarus is still alive: 'Nie pamiorli my' (We have not died), of which these are the last two lines:

Сябе спазнаўшы, наша пакаленне
Дакажа свету, што не ўмёрлі мы.[11]

The last two lines of an untitled poem, 'Pačni žyćcio sapraŭdnae spačatku ...' (Begin again with a real life ...) express similar sentiments but more closely related to the poet's individual duty:

Я проста чалавекам быць жадаю
Іначай нельга — час прыспеў такі[12]

In contrast to the sentiments in the above poems, some verses are pessimistic on a personal level. 'Nie moj dzień' (Not my day), for instance, is unrelievedly gloomy:

Не мой дзень

Я навучыўся бачыць гэты дзень,
Сатканы з мітусні, спакус і дыму.
Паволі гасне велічны прамень.
Парыў нянавісці на свет нахлынуў.

І я стаміўся бачыць цьмяным дзень.
Усё без сэнсу, зрэдку — безнадзейна.
За мною сочыць, быццам шэры цень,
Халодны позірк шчасця ліхадзейны.[13]

All personal gloom and happiness pale beside a national disaster like Chernobyl, a subject tackled by many poets and prose writers of older generations. Malachoŭski's moving poem, 'Śliozy žaloby' (Tears of pity), concentrates on the victims and survivors of the catastrophe, on the great loss to Belarus. Two lines from the middle achieve particular pathos, both by the use of plants known for their soothing qualities, and the phrase 'melody of life':

Тужлівы плач рамонкаў невыносны
Узнёс на крыж мелодыю жыцця[14]

---

[11] 'Having discovered itself, our generation / Will prove to the world that we have not died' (B, 73).
[12] 'I simply want to be a man / anything else is impossible — the right time has come' (B, 60).
[13] 'Not my day // I have learnt to see this day, / Woven from turmoil, temptation and smoke. / Slowly a majestic ray of sunlight dies. / A surge of hate has burst over the earth. // And I am tired of seeing the day as dark, / Everything without meaning, sometimes without hope. / I am followed, like a grey shadow, / By the cold and evil gaze of happiness' (B, 31).
[14] 'The grieving wail of the camomile plants / Crucified the melody of life' (B, 47).

There is a strong moral tendency evident in *Bieražnica*, whether it concern specific topics like abusive sex in 'Hrech' (Sin, B, 53) or drinking and smoking in '"Kazka"' ('A fairy story', B, 56), with encouragement to change old habits. More abstractly in 'Praz horan' (Through a forge, B, 72) the poet creates a powerful image of evil being smelted down to produce a statue to Good. Finally, mention may be made of 'Apošniaje imhnieńnie' (The last moment), a rather bleak poem of long lines in couplets, which ends with two eloquent images:

> На чорны крыж быцця прыкута безнадзейнасць,
> Навокал свет застыў, адбыўшы сваю дзейнасць,
> Па струнах вечнасці імгненне смыкам водзіць.
> Жывая радасць успамінаў карагодзіць.[15]

*

Rahnied Malachoŭski's second book, *U dzionnaj mituśni*, is rather different from his first, although some of his earlier themes are returned to in different forms. The book comprises short impressionistic poems (many of about half a dozen lines, and all published earlier in various periodicals) that reflect the poet's intimate thoughts on various subjects as he lives through the turmoil of everyday life, as the title suggests.[16] One theme familiar from *Bieražnica* (notably in 'Mroja', B, 57) is the difficulty of stable, fulfilling love, which often seems elusive to the poetic hero. In 'kupalskim viečaram …' (on the evening of Kupalle …, Udm, 3), for instance, the figure of a woman, like the traditional fern flower (папараць-кветка), is endlessly approaching, but always out of reach. In 'niaspraŭdžanaj nadziejaj …' (like unjustified hope …, Udm, 5) he longs for contact when she stands at a crossroads, and in 'moj cień …' (my shadow, Udm, 46) he refers to her indifferent eyes, but there is undoubtedly more hope in her remote gaze, which he imagines in the current of a river in another verse, 'u pramieńni …' (in the ray …). In 'zvykajusia z dumkami …' (I grow accustomed to thoughts …, Udm, 35) he again (as in 'Mroja') writes of imaginary love, although it is, even so, hard to part with. By comparison the memory of first love in 'zakinuty pirs' (the abandoned pier, Udm, 12) is elegiac rather than tragic in its image of rotting planks as the ageing witness of the earliest steps of love. Another memorable picture is that of the time after sexual intimacy in 'soniečny zajčyk …' (a spot of sunlight …):

---

[15] 'Hopelessness has been nailed to the black cross of existence, / All around, the world has grown cold after performing its activity, / Over the strings of eternity, a moment draws its bow, / The living joy of memories dances' (B, 61–62).

[16] The form of these reflections falls between electronic tweets and the haikus that were so popular in Belarus of the 1990s.

сонечны зайчык
апякае ранішнімі
здрадніцкімі пацалункамі
тлее асалода
на пажарышчы
нашае жарсці[17]

Other themes in this book include the poet's feelings and personal situation, his family, and, notably, a pessimistic view of the future of the world, including Belarus. The eponymous poem, 'u dzionnaj mituśni …' (in the turmoil of everyday life), compares the hectic business of life to the peace of the natural world, as the poet, late for a meeting, sees a leaf calmly resting on a bench. Nature is more active in 'Na padvakońni kaktusy …' (Cactuses on the window-sill …):

на падваконні кактусы
ці то жывуць
ці то паміраюць
спрабуюць укалоць
маё раўнадушша
для іх я згустак мітусні[18]

The poet himself is always hoping for change, as we read in 'adnastajnyja sny …' (monotonous dreams …, Udm, 15). It is not, however, that Malachoŭski feels himself in prison, despite the imaginative 'źlieva i sprava …' (to left and right, Udm, 13), in which a prison guard is asked what the cloud beyond the barbed wire is dreaming of.

The fate of the wider world also occupies the poet's thoughts in 'planieta hubliaje …' (the planet is losing …, Udm, 42) and 'atamnaja enierhija …' (atomic energy …, Udm, 42), while in 'usio minie …' (everything passes …, Udm, 39) all that is left to quench mankind's thirst is boiling lava from the breasts of the volcano which is our life. Another strong, albeit enigmatic image is found in 'popiel piakučy …' (burning ash …) where the narrower focus appears to be on the pitiful state of Belarus:

попел пякучы
кладзецца на твар
надзея сагрэцца
радзімае
амаль безнадзейнае
цяпельца[19]

---

[17] 'a spot of sunlight / warms with its morning / treacherous kisses / the sweetness smoulders / on the great fire / of our passion' (Udm, 26).

[18] 'on the window-sill the cactuses / now live / now die / they try to prick / my indifference / for them I am a bundle of turmoil' (Udm, 59).

[19] 'burning ash / settles on my face / the hope of being warmed / of our native / almost hopeless / little bonfire' (Udm, 43).

The last thematic cluster of these miniatures concerns family relations. Personified nature forms the first family in 'holyja drevy-blizniaty ...' (bare twin trees ...):

голыя дрэвы-блізняты
галінамі тонкімі
з ветрам гуляюць
пад пільным наглядам
восені-маці[20]

In another miniature verse, 'nad dziciačaj pliacoŭkaj ...' (above the playground ..., Udm, 51), the sun waits to give back to children their confiscated childhood.[21] Two other verses touch on the extremes of human life: 'duša dziciaci....' (the soul of a child ..., Udm, 23) imagines a child when he is little more than a twinkle in adults' eyes; in 'iržavieje zaščapka ...' (the hook is rusting ..., Udm, 45) the broken-down hut of his grandfather's house reminds the poet that something important has gone from this 'overgrown earth'.

Whilst the above examples are far from the only themes explored in these short poems, they give some idea of the range of the poet's concerns, and show his skill in expressing strong thoughts in a few words.

Rahnied Malachoŭski has a distinct poetic voice that is particularly evident in *Bieražnica*, but also in the short philosophical miniatures of his second book.

Pačkoŭskaja

Vijalieta Pačkoŭskaja, in addition to her original poetry, also translates from Polish. The main themes in her first book, *Arechapadzieńnie* (The falling of nuts, 2012), are young capricious love, writing, childhood and the seasons; her urban poems are mostly about foreign cities. Pačkoŭskaja makes much use of unpunctuated stream of consciousness with infrequent rhyme, although with considerable assonance and musicality, as well as some rich imagery, often illuminated by demonstrations of a bizarre imagination.

In the opening poem, 'tvaje vusny — jak komin nad chataj majoj babuli ...' (your lips are like the chimney over my granny's house ...) she describes her partner, beginning with the lips, and going on to anticipate the future when he may eventually give up smoking and begin eating soup. The strange and unflattering comparisons to which he is subjected seem to be offset by acknowledgment of an exceptional inner light. Here are the opening lines:

---

[20] 'bare twin trees / with their slender branches / play with the wind / under the careful gaze of Mother Autumn' (Udm, 50).
[21] This is a transparent reference to the excellent verse collection of Vika Trenas, *Cud kanfiskavanaha dziacinstva*, Minsk, Lohvinaŭ, 2005.

твае вусны — як комін над хатай маёй бабулі
толькі паліш часцей, чым яна ў печы
толькі вусны — як слімак на старой слівіне
пяшчотныя і выкшталцоныя
валасы як халодныя макароніны
звіваюцца долу, падаюць у міску
ты некалі будзеш з залысінай
як мой дзед, ты й зараз да яго падобны:
стары грыб — худыя ногі, цыгарэта ў зубах
і выключны ўнутраны свет
толькі што не храпеш, але гэта
прыйдзе з часам … (Ar, 3)[22]

An indifference to age is also found in the next poem, 'kab zapliuščyć vočy …' (in order to close one's eyes tight …), where the romantic mood is dispelled not by the lack of verbal communication but by details such as her bedfellow's attention to her breathing, socks on the floor and teeth on a bedside table. The ending, however, seems to be joyful:

мы з табой катаемся на санках
да самага-самага ранку[23]

Distinctly bizarre is 'architektura tvaich kaściej …' (the architecture of your bones …), where, instead of a rib, her lover has an exit on his right side from which, in a crystal clear wind, tea, sugar and a runny nose come out in turn (Ar, 7). Also weird is 'ja chaciela b uhnać tramvaj …' (I should like to hijack a tram …), a fantasy in which she dreams of chasing her man in a tram to America, where trams come together, smoking and drinking (and perhaps making little trams) (Ar, 10).

Writing itself takes an inventive but strange form in 'Vierš pra kambajn' (Poem about a combine harvester):

Верш пра камбайн

Я — машына
па вытворчасці метафар
Я — аматар
у справе тонкай лірыкі
калі крылатыя вампірыкі
п'юць маю бензінавую кроў

---

[22] 'your lips are like the chimney over my granny's house / only you smoke more often than it does through the stove / your lips are like a snail on an old plum tree / warming and refined / your hair is like cold macaroni / curling downwards into a bowl / sometime you will go bald / like my granddad, you look like him now: an old fogey with skinny legs and a cigarette in his teeth / and an exceptional inner light / the only thing is that you do not snore yet, but that / will come with time…' Numerical references preceded by Ar are to *Arechapadzieńnie*.
[23] 'you and I ride on sledges / right until the very break of day' (Ar, 4–5).

ну, будзь здароў!
і плясь па твары
Я напішу пад вашыя штандары
транспаранты
матам —
з багаццем мастацкіх сродкаў
у сваім зародку
і хай хто скажа
што я камбайн
для збору эпітэтаў[24]

The last poem in the book, 'huliajusia ŭ paeziju …' (I play at poetry …), contains a more conventional view of writing that is potentially relevant to others who have ideas in the night:

гуляюся ў паэзію:
алоўкамі на аркушах
што трапляюць пад руку
пішу ў цемры вершы
а раніцай
якой так цярпліва чакала
дзіўлюся:
няўжо гэта і ёсць тое
што ўначы было ТЫМ?[25]

Finally on writing may be noted an interesting poem, '… pašyj mnie, maci, novyja laty …' (… sew for me, mummy, new patches …). After a series of requests, she apologizes to her mother for muddling the feet in her poems and breaking the rhythm; she has asked for too much, but at the end of the poem her desire for creative freedom is declared to be essential. Here are the final lines:

даруй мне, маці, што зблытаў стопы,
парушыў рытмы, прасіў замнога.
мне трэба воля вышэйшае спробы,
таму для сэрца адна дарога.

… пашый мне, маці, новае сэрца.[26]

---

[24] 'Poem about a combine harvester // I am a machine / for creating metaphors / I am an amateur / in the field of delicate lyrics / when little winged vampires / drink my petroleum blood / well, Gesundheit! / and a slap on the face / I shall write your standards / banners / with four-letter words — / with riches of artistic means / from birth / and let anyone say / that I am a combine harvester / for reaping epithets' (Ar, 22).

[25] 'I play at poetry: / with pencils on pieces of paper / that come to hand / I write poems in the dark / and in the morning / which I have waited for so patiently / I am amazed: / is this really the same thing / that in the night was THAT?' (Ar, 34).

[26] 'forgive me, mother, that I have muddled the feet, / have broken the rhythms, asked for too much. / I need freedom of the highest quality / that is why there is only one road for the heart. // sew for me, mother, another heart' (Ar, 31).

The book's title poem, 'Arechapadzieńnie' (The falling of nuts) is rather more conventional: a lively description of the poet's growth from a tomboy to mature woman (Ar, 33).

Pačkoŭskaja's poems about foreign cities are not without interest. Paris is the setting of 'Śmierć Dzieda Maroza' (The death of Father Christmas), a rather pathetic poem, despite its parodic epigraph from Nietzsche ('Father Christmas is dead') in which the eponymous hero is mugged and ignored by everyone on the wintry street (Ar, 29–30). Berlin is represented in 'A liepšym byŭ toj …' (And the best one was he …) by a vividly impressionistic picture of loneliness at a seedy pub, where an immigrant whose visa is coming to an end plays a fruit machine and slips a spoon into his pocket, 'like the finger of a saint', as a keepsake (Ar, 16–17). In Holland it is a coffee shop that reveals various wonders in 'a ŭ Halandyi … a ŭ Halandyi charašo …' (but in Holland … but in Holland things are good …). Here are the last four lines of this short poem:

там можна карміць галубоў і паіць галубых
там можна смяяцца і біць гапату пад дых
а ў Галандыі… так, там так харашо!
Колькі ўсяго ўбачыць, зайшоўшы ў кафэ-шоп!..[27]

Two poems about the changes of season in Belarus are worth mentioning, firstly a vivid account of the coming of frosts, although the mention of a shortage of tea seems mainly driven by rhyme:

Маразы

акуляры надзелі лужыны
падабрэлі сям-там батарэі
напужаныя першай сцюжаю
пажаўцелі лісты, захварэлі
і гарбаты на вечар мала
і на пенсію парасон
уцякаю пад пакрывала
ад пакроўскіх маразоў[28]

Another seasonal poem, this time about the first signs of spring, 'pasypliu svoj holaŭ śnieham …' (I shall sprinkle snow on my head …), is very characteristic of Pačkoŭskaja, and a suitable poem to end this survey of her work:

---

[27] 'there you can give food to pigeons and drink to gays / there you can laugh and hit hip-hop music in the stomach / but in Holland … yes, there it is so good! / you can see so much of everything, having gone into a coffee shop …' (Ar, 21).
[28] 'Frosts // the puddles have put on spectacles / have captured radiators here and there / alarmed by the first bitter chill / the leaves turned yellow and fell sick / and there was not much tea for the evening / and the umbrella was pensioned off / I dive under the covers / to escape the frosts of the Feast of the Protection' (Ar, 14).

пасыплю свой голаў снегам
апошнім снегам, сабраным па горадзе
вось і вясна
а я не хачу, не маю права на яе
толькі перасоўвацца моўчкі па вуліцах
змяняць хранатоп сваіх думак
у межах мінулага тыдня
ты забудзешся? Не
ты дакладна не забудзешся
ты проста станеш
расчыненым акном
сумнай усмешкай у метро
пупышкай на каштане
што дачакаецца вясны
на якую я згубіла права
на якую мы згубілі ўсякае права[29]

Vijalieta Pačkoŭskaja's first book of verse is consistently entertaining, occasionally very surprising (not least in the poems about writing itself), and without any feeling of routine, therefore never boring. Her future development will be anticipated with interest.

Vieliet

Ciemryk Vieliet is an unusual poet who creates vivid, complex pictures of the life around him, with particular attention to the seasons and birds. Death and departure are strong themes, as is his consistently deprecating attitude towards himself. His first book, *Most* (The bridge, 2007), is a slim but striking collection. Apart from the originality of the poems, it is an unusual book in the occasional use of bold type, capitals, a brief glossary of words he feels may be unfamiliar to readers, and explanatory notes; the titles of poems are all given in brackets. The content is hardly less unusual: the first poem is an ironically humorous introduction about physical and metaphorical bridges, including warm thanks to fellow-poet Vika Trenas who helped to bring the book to fulfilment.

Vieliet has much to say about his own writing, usually enlivened by striking imagery: 'mineraĺnaść žyćcia i źmiainyja ruchi apalaj listoty ...' (the mineral nature of life and snake-like movements of the fallen leaves ...), for instance, ends with two enigmatic lines about his first steps:

---

[29] 'I shall sprinkle snow on my head / the last snow collected from around the city / here is spring / but I do not want it, I have no right to it / just to move around the streets silently / and change the chronotope of my thoughts / in the boundaries of last week / will you be forgotten? No / you certainly will not be forgotten / you will simply become / an open window / a sad smile on the metro / a chestnut bud / which will wait until spring / to which I have lost the right / to which we have lost any right' (Ar, 15).

я на прыступках лесьвіцы але павіснуў
на Парэнчах колеры трыюмфальнага зла (M, 5)[30]

Hardly less enigmatic is 'majo paŭdniovaje mnostva' (my southern multitude) which ends thus:

мае скалечаныя вершы ніколі ня стануць прыкладам вялікага красамоўства
проста сёньня на вуліцы сьнег і першы
ліст дасланы табе маё паўднёвае мноства[31]

In 'mnie tak pryjemna niščyć biez patreby čas …' (I so enjoy wasting time for no reason …) he writes of his worn-out (*zmulieny*) words and punctuation marks (M, 21), and he reveals other problems and a source of inspiration (from bridges) in 'palymniejuć na ŭzbolatku ŭzdychami vokny damoŭ …' (the windows of houses on the edge of a lake burn with sighs …), for instance, in the following rather long but characteristic passage from the end of the poem:

мне цяжка разгарнуць увесь талент сказа:
ён тхне, цяжарнай цёткаю
вісіць на языку,
ўпіваецца ў розум і мысленьне адразу
спыняе і бразгае дзьвярыма
нібы ўсё прайшло
на бляклым ад пустэчы скразьняку.

а вось напрыклад:
учора я йшоў уздоўж сьмярдзючае ракі
маёй прыватнае сталіцы,
ня мог спыніцца, ня мог стаміцца
ад словаўтварэньняў,
што мне падказвалі масты.[32]

Vieliet appears to feel himself alone in his feelings and talent, as we can read in two lines from the fifth poem in a cycle entitled 'častki' (parts), 'ja viečna vieru ŭ abrydlaść času …' (I constantly believe in the hatefulness of the times …):

мой малады ўзрост і адчуваньне роднай глебы,
і верша, мовы, што сталі ўпоперак усіх але?![33]

---

[30] 'I am at the bottom rungs of the steps but have hung / on the Rails the colours of triumphal evil' Numerical references preceded by M are to *Most*.
[31] 'my crippled poems will never become an example of great eloquence / it is just that today there is snow on the street and my first / letter is sent to you my southern multitude' (M, 12).
[32] 'it is hard for me to unfold all the talent of the sentence: / it gives off the feeling of a pregnant old woman / it hangs on the tongue, / it bites into reason and thinking immediately / it holds and bangs the door / as if everything were over/ on the wan draught from the emptiness. // And now, for example: / yesterday I was going along the stinking river of my private capital, / I could not stop, I could not feel tired / of the word formations, / which the bridges suggested to me' (M, 39–40).
[33] 'my young age and feeling for my native soil, / and poetry, language, which have defied everyone but?!' (M, 47).

In another poem, with an epigraph from Hugo von Hofmannsthal, he suggests that poets are hated before they die, although some people like to see them humiliated in a cage. Here is the first stanza:

паэта павінны ўсе патроху ненавідзець
жадаць ягонай сьмерці як лепшае пары
астатнія хай любяць глядзець як ён у клетцы
забіўшыся ў кут ляпеча слова нагамі дагары[34]

For all his talent as a poet, Vieliet seems to suffer from low self-esteem, as may be seen clearly in the last six lines of a poem 'chacieй by srać na hety novy hod ...' (I should like to shit on this new year ...), where the lyrical hero wishes to hide himself and his rags under the fine blankets that rush by:

хавай-хавай пад імі ўласнае душы рызьзё
і прыкры сполах на бязглуздых шчасьця ловах.

сябе я ненавіджу, і гэта дрэнны знак,
усё працягнецца яшчэ на колькі год,
ты будзеш быццам мёртвы грак,
да жэрдкі прывязаны, умерзлай у шызы лёд.[35]

Two lines from 'ja žyvu — heta doždž za vaknom ...' (I am alive — it is rain beyond the window ...) confirm the impression of self-loathing:

я маўчу і гляджу на сябе:
на вырадзкія рысы і плямы хлусьні...[36]

It would be misleading to suggest that all of this poet's work is introspective or, at least, concerned with himself. In the sixth poem of the 'častki' cycle, for instance, Vieliet's distress is given a broader context: 'як мы стаялі, так і стаім, бы гавяда' (as we stood, so we stand, like cattle, M, 48). In the seventh poem he presents his apprehension about the future of Belarus in an unusual form:

час бліжэй і бліжэй мяжуе са сьмерцю,
а пад скурай маёй беларусь
кіпцюры выпускае нясьмела.[37]

Vieliet's contribution to the volume of poems and songs from the repressed protests after the 2005 elections, *Plošča*, was 'A praz turmy zimy prarastaje viasna ...' (And through the prisons of winter spring breaks through ...), in which

---

[34] 'everybody should hate the poet a little / wish for his death as the best time / let the rest enjoy looking at him in a cage / squashed in a corner muttering something with his legs in the air' (M, 41).

[35] 'hide, hide under them the rags of your own soul / and the foul fear in the brainless hunt for happiness. // I hate myself, and that is a bad sign, / it has been going on for many years, / you will be like a dead rook / tied to a stake, frozen with grey-blue ice' (M, 36),

[36] 'I fall silent and look at myself: / at my degenerate features and the stains of lying...' (M, 32).

[37] 'time moves closer and closer to death, / and under my skin Belarus / cautiously shows its claws' (M, 49).

he wakes up wishing he was in Lithuania where, nonetheless, Belarusian identity is strong:

> Я прачынаўся, а за межкамі ложку Літва —
> Край мой, зьмерлы ў руінах антычнага сьнегу.
> Чуеш?
> Якою ракою яна адплыла
> Ў тіхі край, дзе брыняе крывёю сьцяг белы.[38]

In the already mentioned 'ja žyvu — heta doždž za vaknom …' the theme of departure recurs in the last stanza:

> пенку хмараў ірве птушкі крыло
> над курганамі сьвет пралівaецца
> не глядзі ў іхні бок — там усё адплыло,
> толькі кветкай зламанай матляецца…[39]

Compared with other poets of his age, Vieliet seems very reticent about his *vie intime* and when he does mention a presumed beloved, as in a poem with an eloquent first line, 'tvoj vobraz zhniŭ u pamiaci majoj …' (your image has grown mouldy in my memory …) he seems by the end nostalgic for a voice, but not before declaring himself totally evil: 'я адно зло, пустое зло' (I am only evil, empty evil):

> вісеў у цямрэчы голас твой,
> але маўчаў, я ўсё адно маўчаў,
> і кожны вір ракі шалёнай і сівой
> мне лінію цябе бязьлітасна, ціхенька нагадаў.[40]

Clearly this poet, like many others, dislikes the city and resents its destruction of the countryside, as may be seen from 'bruku na ziamli bоĺš, čym ptušak u niebe …' (there are more roads on earth, than birds in the sky …), of which this is the first stanza:

> бруку на зямлі больш, чым птушак у небе,
> а часам здаецца, што асфальту больш, чым жывое вады,
> і тое, што наступны патоп адвечны
> будзе створаны з чалавечай крыві.[41]

---

[38] 'I was waking up, and beyond the bounds of my bed was Lithuania — / My country, dead in the ruins of ancient snow. / Do you hear? / By which river did it float away / Into a quiet country where the white standard bursts out with blood': *Vieršy j pieśni Ploščy*, Miensk, 2006, p. 15.

[39] 'the wing of a bird tears the foam of clouds / light pours over the burial mounds / do not look in their direction — there everything has floated away, / only waving like a broken flower …' (M, 33).

[40] 'your voice hung in the dark, / but I was silent, I continued to be silent, / and every whirlpool of the crazy, grey river /reminded me of your contour quietly and mercilessly' (M, 54).

[41] 'there are more roads on earth than birds in the sky, / and at times it seems that there is more asphalt than living water, / and that the next immemorial flood / will be made of human blood' (M, 25).

Although Vieliet clearly has affection for the natural world he does not romanticize it; for example, in 'i ŭdzień, i ŭnačy niamaja kinastužka nieba ...' (both by day and night there is a silent film still of the sky ...) birds are said to stick to clouds like shit (M, 44). Most of the references to nature concern the death or passing of seasons, in other words, accord with the generally depressed mood of the other poems.

The last poem in *Most*, printed like the first in bold, describes a spider descending from the ceiling into the poet's open mouth and making a web while he sleeps; but seemingly of more relevance to his work as a whole is a poem about last things; 'apošni' (the last) ends with a final echo over reaped fields, which he compares to the last line of a poem:

> застаецца апошняе рэха над пожняю
> як апошні радок
> кропка
> куля
> канец[42]

For all the gloom of Ciemryk Vieliet's verse, he shows himself an imaginative and gifted poet, especially in his striking imagery. It must be hoped that this is not the end, but the beginning of a poetic career.

Makarevič

Kaciaryna Makarevič's first collection, *Soĺ i niespakoj* (Salt and disquiet, 2012), was introduced by Arciom Kavalieŭski (b. 1979) with a sequence of headings and questions ostensibly referring to aspects of her work. The main themes in this slim debut volume include alcohol, illness, the sea, and love (although the references to her lover are often obscure or deliberately opaque). There are several references to kaleidoscopes in Makarevič's verse, and it does at times create the feeling of such a toy or perhaps a mosaic in its quickly changing themes and moods, A lively sense of fantasy is rarely far away. The book's first poem, 'navošta spadziavacca na nieviadomaść ...' (why put your hopes on the unknown ..., 2010), consists of a series of questions without answers, where the memorable ninth and tenth lines paint an unattractive picture of her own writing:

> выпускаць з запясцяў гнілыя вершы
> самаробныя пачуцці ды бязважкія пытанні (Sin, 5)[43]

Also related to writing is 'dzie kropka ...' (where there is a full stop ..., 2009), which examines what she regards as the negative role of this punctuation mark:

---

[42] 'there remains a final echo over reaped fields / like the last line / a full stop / a bullet / the end' (M, 8).

[43] ' to release from my wrist mouldy poems / homemade feelings and insignificant questions' Numerical references preceded by Sin are to *Soĺ i niespakoj*.

дзе кропка
там заканчваецца імклівасць
пасля кропкі няма волі
кропка спыняе
скарачае развагі да першага гука

сядзі і дадумвай
свае вяснучатыя думкі
на твары ў вечнасці[44]

In another poem, 'horš za malako z miodam moža być tolki …' (the only thing worse than milk and honey …, 2010), the topic of drinking milk seems to pass seamlessly into questions of punctuation:

горш за малако з мёдам можа быць толькі
твая адсутнасць у маіх думках

каму дзякаваць невядома
але я не п'ю малака ўвогуле
не стаўлю кропак і асцярожна выбіраю
іншыя знакі прыпынку

на пунктуацыю ў гэтае лета
зыбкае вострае і невыносна лёгкае
я забылася

у млыне памяці паступова становіцца пылам
зерне халодных павек і заблытаных літар[45]

Two other poems concern illness directly. In the first, with a title that curiously echoes the themes above, 'Znaki prypynku' (Punctuation marks), she repeatedly asserts that she is not ill. Here are the first five lines of this mosaic-like poem:

Няправільна складзеная мазаіка.
Боль толькі ў самых кончыках пальцаў.
Прасіць, абавязкова як пазыкі, смерці …
Не, не аддам.
І вінаватай сябе не лічу.[46]

---

44 'where there is a full stop / there ends headlong progress / after a full stop there is no will power / a full stop restrains / cuts short reflections until the first sound // sit and think through / your freckled thoughts / on the face of eternity' (Sin, 28).
45 'the only thing worse than milk and honey / is your absence in my thoughts // I do not know who to thank / but I do not drink milk at all / I do not put in full stops and I choose carefully / other punctuation marks // about punctuation this summer / rippling sharp and unbearably light / I forgot // in the mill of my memory gradually turns to dust / the grain of eternally cold and muddled letters' (Sin, 31).
46 ' An incorrectly laid-out mosaic. / The pain is only at the very ends of my fingers. / To request, definitely as a loan, death … / No, I shall not surrender. / And I do not consider myself to blame' (Sin, 20).

The second poem, 'liačusia …' (I am healing myself …, 2009), speaks, with some humour, of physical and intellectual cures, only specifying the actual illness at the very end:

> лячуся
> запарваю ліпавыя кветкі
> і адрасаваныя мне словы
> сабраныя з тваіх вуснаў
> і прылежна засушаныя
> па ўсіх правілах
> беларускай граматыкі
> ачуньваю і падбіраю канчатак
> для гэтай хваробы:
> стомленасць пачуцця
> ці
> стомленасць пачуццём[47]

The poem from which the book's title derives is 'Mora?' (The sea?, 2011); it repeats the title at the end, and depicts the sea as a pagan entity that lures people away from their chosen faith, although it does not lead to happiness, but, amongst other things, to salt and disquiet, for all its lustful whispering and empty promises (Sin, 12). The rich imagination of this poem is also found in 'pytaĺnikami lichtaroŭ…' (with the question marks of lights…, 2011), of which these are the first three and last lines:

> пытальнікамі ліхтароў
> штрыхкодамі кніжак
> падплывае восень
>
> […]
>
> выратавальны круг лета быў бракаваны[48]

In another poem, 'cyhanskija dzieci …' (gypsy children …, 2011), eyes are compared to the face of a broken watch:

> вочы застылі
> зламаным гадзіннікам[49]

Makarevič's poems about love contain some memorable images; 'zabudźsia na heta …' (forget it …, 2010), for instance, of which these are the last lines:

---

[47] ' I am healing myself / I steam lime flowers / and words addressed to me / collected from your lips / and diligently dried / according to all the rules / of Belarusian grammar / I recover and choose an ending / for this illness: // tiredness of feeling / or / tiredness through feeling' (Sin, 24).

[48] 'with the question marks of lights / with the bar codes of books / autumn sails in // […] // summer's lifebelt was defective' (Sin, 17–18).

[49] 'the eyes froze / like a broken watch' (Sin, 9).

і калейдаскоп цыгарэтнага дыму
не будзе складвацца ў рэзкі профіль
з мяккасцю вачэй пры ўсмешцы[50]

A memorably unconventional love poem is 'sustrečy ŭ mietro' (meetings in the metro, 2009):

сустрэчы ў метро
непадобныя да іншых
дрэнны зрок
не пазбавіць магчымасці
спыніць час
як высахлае рэчышча
без цябе баляць вены
я разумею гэта
калі спускаюся ў паветра
колеру тваіх валасоў
і хуткасць мрояў
больш за хуткасць цягніка
які вязе нас
да прыпынку "сустрэча"
ты едзеш у маіх думках
а лічыш што ў вагоне[51]

Set in more natural surroundings is 'natatki pad bokam u mora' (notes from beside the sea, 2010). Here is the first note:

думкі
застылыя пенай
на кончыках хваляў
застаюцца нявыказанымі
белымі
салёнымі
такімі ж
як і ты[52]

A last example of Makarevič's unusual love lyrics, and, indeed of her poetry as a whole in *Sol i niespakoj*, is 'nie treba hliadzieć u tvaje vočy kab zdahadacca ...'

---

[50] 'and the kaleidoscope of cigarette smoke / will not set in sharp profile / with the softness of smiling eyes' (Sin, 14).
[51] 'meetings in the metro / are unlike any others / bad eyesight / does not remove the possibility / of stopping time / like a dried up river bed / without you my veins hurt / I understand that / when I descend into air / the colour of your hair / and the speed of daydreams / is quicker than the speed of the train / which is taking us / to the "meeting" station / you travel in my thoughts / and you think you are in the carriage' (Sin, 23).
[52] 'thoughts / frozen like foam / on the tips of waves / remain unspoken / white / salty / just like / you' (Sin, 32).

(there is no need to look into your eyes to guess ..., 2010), of which these are the last five lines:

> падзяляю толькі на простае і складанае
> не зважаючы што ты разумееш усе варыянты
>
> мне б хацелася сядзець на якім-небудзь радку
> рэалістычнага рамана а ў выніку
> я толькі алюзія на саму сябе[53]

Kaciaryna Makarevič is far from least amongst her generation's young poets, and her first slender collection shows real talent.

Julija Novik

Julija Novik is an impressionistic poet with a somewhat fantastic and bleak imagination; her short dark verses pay particular attention to sadness, loneliness, death and decay. Not all her love poems, however, are gloomy or filled with pain. A particularly frequent theme is sleep and waking. In addition to Belarusian poems she also writes French verse, but her first book, *Sonca za terykonami* (Sun behind heaps of waste, 2007), contains only poems in Belarusian.

Novik brings to the topic of writing some unusual ideas and interesting images. In 'Napišy' (Write), for instance, it is suggested that poetry is connected with pain and anger and that only by writing for yourself alone can you communicate with others:

> Напішы
>
> Напішы для сябе адной
> Толькі так, каб было відаць,
> Як успыхнуў радкамі боль,
> Як ад гневу радкі гараць.
>
> Напішы для сябе адной —
> Атрымаецца як для ўсіх —
> Тых, хто сэрцам жывым даўно
> Замяняе і зрок, і слых. (Szt, 8)[54]

An even bleaker poem is 'Radok vyrastae z ciemry ...' (A line grows from the darkness ...) of which these are the first two stanzas:

---

[53] 'I only divide into simple and complex / paying no attention to the fact that you understand all the variants // I should like to sit on some line or other / of a realist novel and as a result / I would be only an allusion to myself' (Sin, 37).

[54] Write // Write for yourself alone / Only thus can you see / How pain flares up from the lines, How the lines burn with anger. // Write for yourself alone — / It will turn out to be for everyone — / Those whose living hearts have long since / Been replaced by sight and hearing' Numerical references preceded by Szt are to *Sonca za terykonami*.

Радок вырастае з цемры,
Нібыта яму наканавана
Нарадзіцца ў пекле,
Але не ў сэрцы.

Цемра паўзе ў радкі.
Можа, таму яны
Сонныя і бязважкія.[55]

The poet's lyrical heroine appears concerned about lack of (self-) belief, as is clear from 'Smutkuje cicha …' (I feel quietly sad …):

Смуткуе ціха
Шматок паперы:
Хоць ёсць натхненне,
Бракуе веры.[56]

In '"Apošni hieroj"' ('The last hero') we read that it is not heroes but the more heroic ghosts of poems that fly into the fire:

Ды пакуль ляцяць
На агонь не героі,
А прывіды вершаў.[57]

Her poems seem, to say the least, vulnerable although the first line of a short untitled verse defuses anything serious; for all the gloom of some of the poems Julija Novik has a good sense of humour:

Пішу па вадзе —
Хай чытаюць
Нахабныя чайкі
Мой верш.[58]

Having written, in 'Kažuć …' (They say …, Szt, 36), about avoiding repetition in a world where 'everything has already been said' she turns to the comic caricature of a discontented writer in 'Paet adnaho vierša …' (A poet of only one verse …):

Паэт аднаго верша
Пісаў макулатурныя раманы,
Не мог ніяк змірыцца з лёсам
Паэта аднаго верша.[59]

---

[55] 'A line grows from the darknesss, / As if it were destined / To be born in hell, / But not in the heart. // Darkness crawls into the lines. / Perhaps for that reason they are / Sleepy and weightless' (Szt, 54).

[56] 'A piece of paper / Is quietly sad: / Although there is inspiration, / There is a lack of belief' (Szt, 40). A comparable theme is featured in 'Žviniać kapiažy …' (Drops of water ring out …, Szt, 50).

[57] ' And for the time being fly / Into the fire not heroes / But ghosts of poems' (Szt, 26).

[58] 'I write on water — / Let brazen seagulls / Read / My poem' (Szt, 39).

[59] 'A poet of only one verse / Wrote pulp novels, / He could in no way reconcile himself to the fate / Of a poet of only one verse' (Szt, 40).

In 'VTT' the image of a lost photograph of the lyrical heroine's beloved will haunt her for ever until she writes out in verse everything she remembers about him. Her description of the image is humorous rather than tragic. Here are the last lines of the poem:

> Выраз твайго твару — ВТТ — скарочана —
> Дэфіцытны тавар,
> Нешта з надпісам: <Не кантаваць>.
> ВТТ будзе праследаваць мяне,
> Пакуль я не выпішу ў вершах
> Усё, што помню пра цябе.[60]

'VTT' comes in the last section of the book, entitled 'Вымяраецца ўсё табой' (Everything is measured against you), which contains the majority of the love poems, many of which are tinged with doubt, but not the grey and other dark colours that are widespread elsewhere in Julija Novik's first book. Particularly successful is an acrostic poem reading 'Kachańnia śviatlo' (Light of love), which combines sophisticated form with apparently spontaneous passion:

> Акраверш
>
> Краіна мар маіх і сноў,
> Адкрый кахання таямніцы.
> Хачу тваёй улады зноў,
> Ад шчасця звонкага стаміцца.
> Надзею шчыра дорыш мне,
> Народжаную светлым раннем.
> Я верую, што сум міне.
>
> Салодкіх прагну я прызнанняў,
> Віном усмешак захмялець,
> Як першы раз, чакаць спаткання.
> Табою жыць увысь ляцець,
> Любіць, не шкадаваць кахання.
> О! Каб збываліся жаданні …[61]

The lyrical heroine's love life seems filled with doubts and potential disappointments, for her relationships are depicted as very uneven, although there is sometimes a final note of hope. In 'Čakańnie' (Waiting) this familiar

---

[60] 'The expression of your face — EYF — in short — / Is a commodity in short supply, / Something marked 'Keep upright'. / EYF will haunt me / Until I write out in verse / Everything that I remember about you' (Szt, 87).

[61] 'Acrostic // Land of my reveries and dreams, / Reveal the secrets of love. / I want to be in your power again, / To become wearied by clear happiness. / You sincerely give me hope, / Born of bright morning. / I believe that my melancholy will pass. // I long for sweet confessions, / To be intoxicated by the wine of smiles, / Like the first time, to await a meeting, / To live with you, to soar on high, / To love, not sparing love-making. / Oh! Let my wishes come true …' (Szt, 84).

aspect of young love becomes more and more intense until the resigned last two lines:

> А я не чакаю ўжо даўно,
> Бо твой матылёк мне разбіў акно.[62]

The first two lines of a short untitled verse express vividly her uncertainty:

> Твая душа мне ўсміхнулася
> Ці толькі падалося?[63]

Her relations with her lover are nothing if not fragile, as we read in 'Siarod dnia ciabie spyniu …' (In the middle of the day I shall stop you …):

> Сярод дня цябе спыню,
> Зазірну табе я ў вочы,
> Бо баюся, як агню,
> Думак злых сваіх дзявочых.
>
> А ў вачах тваіх знайду
> Сто адзін сакрэт, на згубу.
> Пашаптаць бы на ваду,
> Каб з табой застацца, любы.[64]

No less destruction, though without drama, is found in the bleak but comic image in this two-line verse:

> Горкі шакалад тваіх слоў
> Без абгорткі сапсаваўся.[65]

Julija Novik's lyrical heroine describes her house as 'a little island of sadness' (Мой дом астравок тугі)[66] and in 'Nie ŭ darohach zablytacca …' (Not to get lost when travelling …) her inner being is crippled:

> А нутро пакалечана,
> А душа пакамечана.[67]

In the last two lines of 'Moj kryž — nie pačuć adkazu …' (My cross is not to hear a reply …) she writes graphically of her pain and weeping:

> Мой боль умацуе сілы
> Каб праз сон пранесці свой плач.[68]

---

[62] 'But I have long since stopped waiting, / For your butterfly has smashed my window' (Szt, 82).

[63] 'Your soul smiled at me / Or is that only how it seemed?' (Szt, 81).

[64] 'In the middle of the day I shall stop you, / I shall look into your eyes, / For I fear like fire / My wicked girlish thoughts. // And in your eyes I shall find / A hundred and one secrets leading to ruin. / I should like to whisper on the water, / In order to remain with you, my beloved' (Zst, 88).

[65] 'The bitter chocolate of your words / without its wrapper was spoiled' (Szt, 80).

[66] 'Paślia śviata zdymajuć ściahi …' (After the holidays they take down the flags, Szt, 42).

[67] 'But my inner being is crippled, / But my soul is crushed' (Szt, 10).

[68] 'My pain increases in strength /To bear my weeping through sleep' (Szt,48).

Her 'thoughts perish in "a universal spider's web"' (А думкі гінуць у 'сусветнай павуціне')[69] and 'life suddenly becomes sleet' (Як жыццё раптам робіцца слотай).[70]

Life, however, must go on, and several poems express if not optimism then resolution: 'But life must be lived' (Ды трэба жыць)[71], and particularly in the present rather than the future, when it will be too late,[72] although she is disappointed at the way people seem to be separate and even hide from each other: 'Ты з узімі, і ўсё ж ты адзін' (You are with everyone, and all the same you are alone. Szt, 19); in 'Parasony' (Umbrellas) people hide their faces under these objects, even though there is not a cloud in the sky (Szt, 56).

On a brighter note may be mentioned an excellent verse about a poet who since his early death has inspired Soviet, émigré and post-Soviet poets alike: 'Maksimu Bahdanoviču' (To Maksim Bahdanvovič, Szt, 74), whose star[73] she calls 'Душа Эпохі' (the Soul of the Epoch, Szt, 74). Life does, indeed, seem to have been easier in earlier days, or at least that is the impression given by 'U vioscy' (In the village) where any feelings of loneliness or melancholy are dispelled by her grandmother as we read in the last lines of the poem:

> Адчужданасць і прыспешанасць,
> Аднолькавасць будняў сляпых
> Знікаюць пад зоркамі свежымі
> Бабулі вачэй маладых.[74]

Julija Novik's first book reveals considerable talent and perhaps a bleak outlook on life. It remains to be seen whether the latter changes or intensifies in her later work.

Nilava

Working in the Homiel media, Taćciana Nilava writes in both Russian and Belarusian. Her début collection of Belarusian verse, *Hotyka tonkich padmanaŭ* (The Gothic of subtle deceptions, 2008) has an introduction by Iryna Šaŭliakova, and it is on this book that what follows is based. The elements of the intriguing title are found in some of the poems, but do not seem to be central; the main theme of the book, as with so many young women (and not only women) poets,

---

[69] 'Jak Mliečnym šliacham spakusilasia Ziamlia …' (When the Earth was seduced by the Milky Way …, Szt, 12).

[70] 'Niezajdrosnaja, liudzi, uciecha …' (It is an unenviable entertainment, people …, Szt, 45).

[71] 'Niervy patonuć adnojču ŭ vinie' (One fine day my nerves will drown in wine, Szt, 16).

[72] See 'Potym' (Later, Szt, 27).

[73] The reference is to Bahdanovič's celebrated 'Ramans' (Romance, 1912).

[74] 'Alienation and haste, / The uniformity of blind ordinary days / Disappear under the piercing fresh / Young eyes of my granny' (Szt, 72).

is love. The collection, however, is not confined to youthful joys and torments, but also contains many poems that respond to history, society, religion, writing and patriotic feelings. Her excursions into macaronic words and phrases meet with mixed success, as does her sometimes intensive use of repetition. On the other hand, at best her imagery is strong and at times very original.

Beginning with the amatory lyrics, the book opens with several poems like 'Pakryšany dzień …' (The fragmented day …), 'Ja chacieǔ calavać …' (I wanted to kiss …), 'Prosta hliadzi na mianie …' (Simply look at me …) and 'Kab toĺki viedaǔ ty …' (If you only knew …), the last being a less usual love poem of regret and demand, verging, perhaps, on the Gothic:

> Каб толькі ведаў ты
> гора ўзарванае цішы …
> Каб толькі бачыў ты
> горад старое памяці …
> Каб толькі прадбачыў ты
> здань маю апраметную —
> ты змяніў бы ход часу,
> ты звясціў бы нябёсы
> пра адсутнасць … жыцця. (Htp, 28)[75]

There are also faintly Gothic elements in 'Ja nie tvoj fanat …' (I am not fanatical about you …) where the lyrical heroine sees unbridled dreams of her lover, describing her inner self as a broken tuning fork (Htp, 46). Quite differently, 'Voś tak …' (Here's how it is …) imagines torturing a humiliated partner, to whom she is a merciless executioner:

> Вось так:
> згвалчу — і не ўбачу,
> як ён, бы малое дзіця,
> нахіліўшы галоўку,
> жаласна так плача.
> І вось я — кат.[76]

Also with unmistakable Gothic elements is 'Ja chaču abniać dzicia, kab adčuć …' (I want to embrace a child in order to feel …), where the heroine wishes to find out whether she is more genuine or helpless than a child; and, moreover, what is better — stamping on cracked ground or on patched hearts (Htp, 64).

---

[75] 'If only you knew / the grief of harshly broken silence … / If only you knew / the city of ancient memory. / If only you had foreseen / my ghost from the underworld — / you would have changed the course of time / you would have informed the heavens / of the absence … of life' Numerical references preceded by Htp are to *Hotyka tonkich padmanaǔ*.
[76] 'Here's how it is: / I shall defile him — and not see / how he, like a little child, / bends his head, / and weeps so piteously. / And now I am an executioner' (Htp, 66).

In 'Ciela ŭ lipavym aliei …'(My body is in a path lined with lime trees …) a room after love-making is described with many repeated words and phrases that do not, however, appear to achieve any specific effect (Htp, 16). Finally worthy of mention is 'Ja vykryŭliaju prastoru — …' (I straighten out space …) in which her man's getting dressed is connected with deception; clothes are described as a closed circle, and sets of three adjectives are used for the description — one of Nilava's favoured devices (Htp, 76). A poem in seven parts, 'Dziońnik' (Diary) contains a mixture of threats and affection. Day 1 begins, 'Вы —мне. Я не Вам' (You are to me. I am not to you) and Day 6 reverses the relationship to 'Я — Вам. Вы не мне' (I am to you. You are not to me, Htp, 70–71). The heroine's conflicted emotions emerge clearly from the first two lines of Day 5:

> Я лаюся матам на Вас,
> каб назаўтра на Вас маліцца[77]

Nilava's poems contain relatively little about writing as such, but in 'Ja stračvaju dar movy …' (I am losing the gift of speech …) this does not seem to matter very much, happening to her in a cultural revolution, although it is not clear what this revolution is:

> Я страчваю дар мовы,
> таму што лепей жывіцца моўчкі
> высокім небам і глыбокай зямлёй.
>
> Я страчваю дар мовы:
> яна перашкаджае мне дыхаць,
> перашкаджае мне думаць
> і гаварыць перашкаджае.
>
> Гэта спачатку было слова.
> Гэта спачатку быў хаос.
> А цяпер у нас —
>   культурная рэвалюцыя.[78]

In 'Asadkaj …' (With a pencil …) writing appears to be a confession of love and its difficulties (Htp, 39). A comparable poem is 'a ciapier u finaĺnym tury …' (and now in the last round …) she attempts to paint a picture of her beloved in order to discover his universe, but at the end he is suddenly overcome by embarrassment at this examination; typical of the intrusion of banal reality into poetry is a mobile phone that rings during the session (Htp, 78). Another poem,

---

[77] 'I swear at you black and blue, / in order to worship you the next day' (Htp, 71).
[78] 'I am losing the gift of speech /because it is better to nourish oneself silently / from the lofty sky and the deep earth. // I am losing the gift of speech: / it hinders my breathing, / it hinders my thinking / and hinders my speaking. / In the beginning was the word. / In the beginning was chaos. / And now we have — / a cultural revolution' (Htp, 50).

'Ty dalioka, bo tak liahčej …' (You are far away, for that is easier …) ends with the casual and potentially dismissive, 'да пабачэння' (See you, Htp, 24).

One of the best poems in the book is the unambiguous 'Kupala', devoted to one of Belarus's greatest poets (Janka Kupala, 1882–1947) who is presented as an inspired, lonely romantic, striving for the country in which he believed. Here is the last stanza:

Купала —
кувае зязюля ў ліпені клейкім,
палае каханнем дзяўчына,
шуміць аер.
Купала — глядзіць на неба,
загадкавы нейкі —
Купала — прарок Айчыны,
ў якую верыў.[79]

Two of Nilava's own poems about her Fatherland are quirky rather than pious. In 'Proza žyćcia …' (The prose of life …) she, for instance, writes of the pain of her country and of drinking rather than dying for it:

Проза жыцця.
Эрозія… Розглас.
Стоп! Адпачынак.
Я — частка болю твайго,
Айчына.

Шкло там знутры —
а раптам патрапіць у сэрца?
Хочацца піць … не памерці —
з тваёй прычыны,
Айчына.[80]

In another poem, 'Viecier mknie …' (The wind presses …) the wind brings the drunken smell of her great Native Land and she seeks a broth to cure both of them on the morning after (Htp, 47).

A few potentially Gothic elements have already been mentioned. Perhaps there is an element of subtle deception not only in 'Dzionnik' but also in 'Taktyĺna …' (Tactile …):

---

[79] 'Kupala — / a cuckoo calls in sticky July / a girl burns with love, / the sound of sweet flags is heard. / Kupala looks at the sky, / somehow mysterious, / Kupala is the prophet of our Fatherland / in which he believed' (Htp, 49).
[80] 'The prose of life. / Erosion … disharmony. / Stop! A rest. / I am a part of your pain, my Fatherland. // There is glass inside / and what if it suddenly enters my heart? / I want to drink … not to die — / on your account, / my Fatherland' (Htp, 43).

Тактыльна,
тактоўна
і па-за натоўпам —
сустрэцца.
Скарыцца рэакцыі
і аперцэпцыі —
цынік!

Дарэчы,
нядрэнны вынік.[81]

The last poem in the book, 'Jak paćućcio realnasci ...' (As a feeling of reality ...),
is neither Gothic nor deceitful, bringing a note of calm domesticity after the
earlier passions:

Як пачуццё рэальнасці,
рэальнасць — пачуццё.
ні больш ні менш.
У кожнага — былое.
І нам ніколі
не прыдумаць лепш
за сонечную раніцу ў пакоі.[82]

Taćciana Nilava's poems vary in both quality and content, but it is certainly to
be hoped that her creative energies will in future be devoted to Belarusian rather
than Russian literature.

---

[81] 'Tactile, / tactful / from behind a crowd / to meet. / To make use of reactions / and
perceptions — cynic! // By the way, not a bad outcome' (Htp, 68).
[82] 'As a feeling of reality / reality is a feeling, / neither more nor less. / Each of us has a past. /
And we shall never / think of anything better / than a sunny morning in our room' (Htp, 81).

EPILOGUE

Just over a century ago the great poet Aleś Harun included a telling phrase in his emblematic poem 'Liudziam' (To People): 'сам народ - пясняр' (the nation is a bard), words that anticipate the continuing prevalence of poetry over other genres in Belarusian literature.

It has been a pleasure to review in this book the earliest poetic works of representatives of the youngest generation of Belarusian writers.

The future cannot easily be foreseen, although one of these poets, perhaps unconsciously echoing T. S. Eliot, has suggested that our end is our beginning. In the case of this variegated group, however, the beginning is all that can be judged at present. In the words of the 17th-century poet Sir John Denham:

> Youth, what man's age is like to be doth show
> We may our ends by our beginnings know.

Undoubtedly, most of these poets will develop their craft and continue to produce interesting books, in some cases of prose and drama as well as, or instead of, verse. The case for optimism is expressed well in the following lines.

> Сябе пазнаўшы, наша пакаленне
> Дакажа свету, што не умёрлі мы.[1]

Quite certain is that with its wide range of talent, courageous spirit and broad thematic interests this generation of Belarusian poets is very much alive.

Long live Belarus!

---

[1] 'Having discovered itself, our generation / Will prove to the world that we have not died': Rahnied Malachoŭski, *Bieražnica*, Miensk, 2005, p. 73.

BIBLIOGRAPHY

ALEKSIEVICH, SVETLANA, *Vremia sekond khend* (Moscow: Vremia, 2013)
——, *Čas second-hand: Kaniec čyrvonaha čalavieka* (Minsk: Lohvinaŭ, 2013)
ANOCHIN, KIRYLA, *Aściarožna, drevy začyniajucca* (Minsk: Knihazbor, 2013)
AŬČYŃNIKAVA, HANNA, *Ad začynienaj bramy* (Harodnia: Haradzienskaja biblijateka, 2011)
BAJAROVIČ, ŽMICIER, *Šali* (Minsk: Halijafy, 2012)
BARADZINA, MARYJA, *Vyšej za paŭnočny viecier* (Minsk: Lohvinaŭ, 2006)
BARANOŬSKI, ALEŚ, *Čujnaje akno* (Minsk: Knihazbor, 2008)
——, *Viaśliar* (Minsk: Knihazbor, 2010)
——, *Tvorčaja samabytnaść Niny Škliaravaj* (Minsk: Kaŭčeh, 2010)
——, *Dyjamientavy nimb dlia anhiola* (Minsk: Charviest, 2013)
BAROŬSKI, ANATOĹ (ed.), *Palac. Litaraturny aĺmanach. Homiel. 2013* (Minsk: Knihazbor, 2014)
BARTAŠ, HIEORHIJ, 'Demahahičnyja pryjomy ŭ artykulie M. Južyka "Technalohij paetyčnaha vyčuvaniia"', *Teksty*, 4 (2013), 318–27
BORTNOWSKA, KATARZYNA, *Białoruski postmodernizm: Liryka "pokolenia Bum-Bam-Litu"* (Warsaw: Wydawnictwa Uniwersytetu Warszawskiego, 2009)
BRYĹ, ANTON, *Nie ŭpaŭ žolud* (Minsk: Lohvinaŭ, 2011)
——, *Jan Jalmužna* (Minsk: Knihazbor, 2014)
ČAJKOŬSKAJA, VOLIA, *Lupy* (Viciebsk: Dyjaloh, 2007)
ČUMAKOVA, HANNA, *Moj aniol pryśniŭ mianie* (Minsk: Čatyry čverci, 2012)
FILON, NADZIEJA, *Kropli śviatla* (Minsk: Bielaruski Dom druku, 2012)
HLUCHOŬSKAJA, KACIARYNA, *Kali drevy rastuć z halavy* (Minsk: Halijafy, 2013)
HOLUB, JU (ed.), *Novy zamak: Litaraturny aĺmanach. Hrodna, 1 MMXIII* (Minsk: Knihazbor, 2013)
IVAŠČANKA, ANATOĹ, *Vieršnick* (Miensk: Biellitfond, 2006)
——, *Chaj tak* (Minsk: Halijafy, 2013)
JEMIAĹJANAŬ-ŠYLOVIČ, ALEŚ, *Parasoniečnaść* (Minsk: Knihazbor, 2013)
JUŽYK, MICHAŚ, 'Technalohija paetyčnaha vyčuvaniia. Artykul pra sučasnuju paeziju', *Teksty*, 2 (2012), 141–64
KACIURHINA, ANASTASIJA, *Pad vietraziem ranku* (Minsk: Knihazbor, 2011)
——— *Parason* (Minsk: Kovcheg, 2011)
KALIADKA, S. U., *Bielaruskaja sučasnaja žanočaja paezija: Mastackija kancepcyi 'žanočača ščaścia'* (Minsk: Bielaruskaja navuka, 2010)
KARŁOWICZ, JAN, *Podania i bajki ludowe zebrane na Litwie staraniem Jana Karłowicza* (Cracow: Drukarnia Uniwersytetu Jagiellońskiego, 1887)
KOŬHAN, SIARHIEJ, *Pieršyja kroki: Zryfmavanyja dumki pra minulaje i sučasnaje*, (Minsk: Lohvinaŭ / St Petersburg, Nevskii Prostor, 2002)
KIŚLICYNA, HANNA, *Novaja litaraturnaja situacyja: Žmiena kuĺturnaj paradyhmy* (Minsk: Lohvinaŭ, 2006)
KUCHAREVIČ, ŚVIATLANA, *Ščyra* and ALEŚ PAPOŬ, *Nia ščyra* (Minsk: Halijafy, 2009)

KUDASAVA, NASTA, *Liście maich ruk* (Minsk: Lohvinaŭ, 2006)
——, *Ryby* (Minsk: Charviest, 2013)
KULIKOŬ, IHAR, *Pavarot na mora* (Miensk, n.p., 2011)
——, *Svamova* (Minsk: Medisont, 2013)
KUŹMIENKA, ŽMITROK, *Pakuĺ žyvu, spadziajusia ...* (Minsk: Halijafy, 2012)
LIENSKI, JURAŚ, *Jana-try-jon* (Minsk: Halijafy, 2010), 56–74
MCMILLIN, ARNOLD, 'Loneliness as a Topos in Contemporary Belarusian Literature',
    in Dubianieckaja, McMillin and Sahanovič (eds), *Sonca tvajo nie zakocicca, i
    miesiac tvoj nie schavajecca*, Miensk, 2009, 163–66
——, *Writing in a Cold Climate: Belarusian Literature from the 1970s to the Present
    Day* (London: Maney publishing for the Modern Humanities Research
    Association, 2010)
——, '"Where Are You, Kastuś Kalinoŭski?": Overt and Covert References to
    Kalinoŭski and His Fate in the Work of Young Belarusian Poets"', *Studia
    bialorutenistyczyne*, 8, 2014, 107–16
MAKAREVIČ, KACIARYNA, *Soĺ i niespakoj* (Minsk: Halijafy, 2012)
MALACHOŬSJI, RAHNIED, *Bieražnica* (Minsk: Mastackaja litaratura, 2005)
——, *U dzionnaj mituśni* (Minsk: Maladaja paezija Bielarusi, 2012)
MANCEVIČ, NASTA, *Ptuški* (Minsk: Lohvinaŭ, 2012)
MARCINOVIČ, VIKTAR, *Mova* (2nd edition: Minsk: Knihazbor, 2014)
MARTYSIEVIČ, MARYJA, *Cmoki liatuć na nierast* (Minsk: Lohvinaŭ, 2008)
——, *Ambasada* (Minsk: Knihazbor, 2011)
NIADBAJ, TAĆCIANA, *Sireny śpiavajuć džaz* (Warsaw: Polackija labirynty, 2014)
NIATBAJ, TAĆCIANA, 'Žyćcio praciahvajecca ...', *Termapily*, 16, 2012, 159–67
NIETBAJEVA, TAĆCIANA, *Čalaviek i historyja ŭ bielaruskich miascovych chronikach
    XVII–XVIII stst* (Miensk: Bielaruski knihazbor, 2012)
NILAVA, TAĆCIANA, *Hotyka tonkich padmanaŭ* (Minsk: Halijafy, 2008)
NOVIK, HANNA, *Sumioty ahniu* (Minsk: Kovcheg, 2010)
NOVIK, JULIJA, *Sonca za terykonami* (Minsk: Mastackaja litaratura, 2007)
PAČKOŬSKAJA, VIJALIETA, *Arechapadzieńnie* (Minsk: Lohvinaŭ, 2012)
PAŠKIEVIČ, ALEŚ, *Sim pobediši* (Minsk: Knihazbor, 2012)
PLIAN, ŽMICIER, *Taksydermičny praktykum* (Miensk: Lohvinaŭ, 2004)
PRYLUCKI, SIARHIEJ, *Dzievianostyja forever* (Minsk: Medisont, 2008)
PŠANIČNY, JARYLA, *Piščavyja liški* (Minsk: Halijafy, 2011)
RAHAVAJA, VOĹHA, *Jana-try-jon* (Minsk: Halijafy, 2010), 75–87
Repartaž ź miesca padziejaŭ: Vieršy j pieśni Ploščy (Miensk: n.p., 2006)
RYŽKOŬ, VITAĹ, *Dźviery, zamknionyja na kliučy* (Minsk: Lohvinaŭ, 2010)
SIAMAŠKA, VIKTAR, *ReRa* (Minsk: Halijafy, 2011)
——, *Habitacyja* (Minsk: Halijafy, 2013)
SIDORKA, NAŚCIA, *Pialiostki* (Brest: Aĺternativa, 2013)
SIVIEC, TAĆCIANA, *Lipieńskaja navaĺnica* (Minsk, Mastackaja litaratura, 2003)
——, *Tamu, chto znojdzie ... Kachańnie dy inšyja kazki: Vieršy, proza, p'esy* (Minsk,
    Lohvinaŭ, 2008)
ŚCIEBURAKA, USIEVALAD, *Krušnia* (Miensk: Viktar Chursik, 2007)
——, *Bieh pa samaadčuvańni* (Minsk: Halijafy, 2013)
ŠAJBAK, MIRASLAŬ and ADAM HLOBUS (comps), *Choku bielaruskich paetaŭ* (Miensk:
    Litaratura, 1996)

ŠAŬKIAKOVA, IRYNA, *Sapraŭdnyja chroniki Poŭni: artykuly i recenzii* (Minsk: Litaratura i mastactva, 2011)

——, '(Vy)tvorčyja bitvy ŭ kumirni', *Teksty*, 4 (2014), 116–28

ŠOSTAK, ADAM, *Spatkańnie Nie* (Minsk: BielSaES 'Čarnobyľ', 2006)

——, *4.33* (Minsk: Bielaruski Dom druku, 2012)

TRENAS, VIKA, *Cud kanfiskavanaha dziacinstva* (Minsk: Lohvinaŭ) 2005

UPALA, ANKA, *Dreva Entalipt* (Minsk: Lohvinaŭ, 2012)

Vieliet, Ciemryk, *Most* (Minsk: Lohvinaŭ, 2007)

VIŠNIOŬ, ŽMICIER, 'Halasy hubliajucca ŭ šorhacie liesu', *Maladość*, 2014, 2, 25–26

YVANOŬ, VIKTAR, *Asarci* (Minsk: Halijafy, 2009)

INDEX OF NAMES